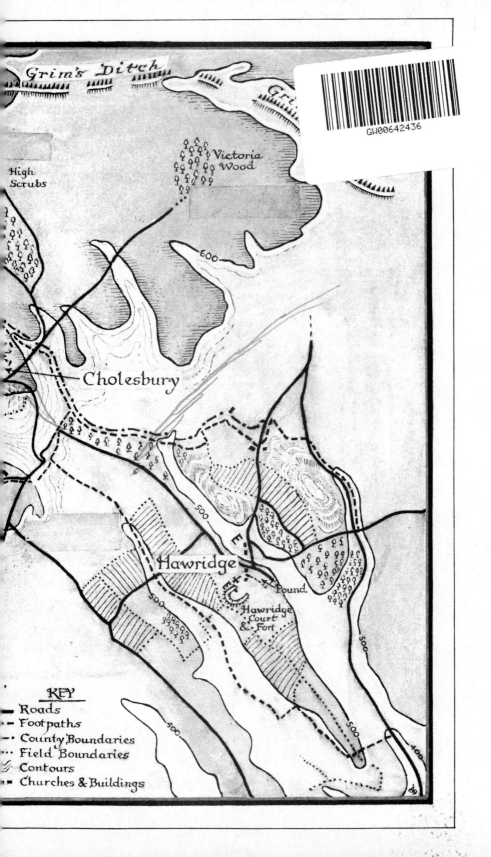

Grim's Ditch

Grim

Victoria
Wood

High
Scrubs

600

Cholesbury

500

Hawridge

Pound

Hawridge
Court
& Fort

500

500

500

400

400

KEY

— Roads
- - Footpaths
- · County Boundaries
··· Field Boundaries
ⅅ Contours
- ■ Churches & Buildings

HILLTOP VILLAGES
OF THE CHILTERNS

Hawridge Court, the seat of the Lord of the Manor. The 4,000-year-old Bronze Age moat encircles a medieval building and the old church

HILLTOP VILLAGES
OF THE CHILTERNS

Cholesbury, Hawridge, St. Leonards, Buckland Common

by

DAVID and JOAN HAY

Illustrated by

*Violet Saunders, David Hay
and Douglas Atkins*

*Frontispiece by
Denis Mallet*

PHILLIMORE
London and Chichester

First published 1971 by
PHILLIMORE & CO. LTD.
Shopwyke Hall, Chichester, Sussex, England

REPRINTED 1983

ISBN 0 85033 505 1

Printed and bound in Great Britain by
BILLINGS BOOK PLAN
Worcester, England

CONTENTS

List of Illustrations and Maps   vii

Acknowledgements   viii

Preface   x

I   No Famous Names
The people of four small villages and their part in English history   1

II   The Hills Take Shape
The geological background   7

III   Man Settles in the Chilterns
From Prehistoric times up to about 1500 BC   14

IV   Cholesbury Takes Shape
Our history starts in the Bronze Age   19

V   The Forts Are Built
Life in Bronze Age Cholesbury—from about 1500 BC   27

VI   Iron Implements Bring Prosperity to The Villages
700 BC–AD 43   45

VII   The Lamps Go Out in the Land beyond the Hills
Our villages between the Roman and the Norman Conquests   60

VIII   'One Sore Sparrow Hawk'
The villages reappear after the Norman Conquest   67

IX   'A Chapel of Ease and Noe Free Chappell'
St. Leonards has its worries in the 16th century   82

X   'He Played Football in his Shirt'
Hawbridge and its people as the village develops – 1520–1640   100

XI   'Four Closes Called Halfacres'
Cholesbury spreads across the common in the late 16th and early 17th centuries   112

XII   'Four Brasse Potts'
       The Civil War and its impact in our villages   124

XIII   'The House wherein Edward Avis Formerly
       Dwelt'
       Village life in the latter half of the 17th century   133

XIV   'Having Not Wherewith to Cloathe Them
       Decently'
       Peter Hill: a country parson in the 18th century   146

XV   'Our Officers Being Confused'
       From yeoman to squire in the 18th century   155

XVI   'The Health Is Doubtless Much Affected'
       Sidelights on village life about 1750–1820   166

XVII   'This Rate Could Not Be Collected'
       The village that went bankrupt, 1820–1833   181

XVIII   'A Small Organ Would Remedy this Evil'
       Village life from 1832 to 1900   194

XIX   The Child Is 'Sown in for the Winter' and
       'Lord Rothschild Has Made an Encroachment
       and Is Amerced 6d'
       Village life in the early 20th century   212

Appendices

A   List of Sources and Bibliography   228

B   Property of Hawridge Church in 1552   234

C   The House wherein Edward Avis Formerly Dwelt   234

D   The Cholesbury Jubilee Celebrations, 1887   238

Index   239

LIST OF ILLUSTRATIONS

1	Hawridge Court: Bronze Age moat, medieval cottage and church	*Frontispiece*
2	Middle Bronze Age urns and pygmy cup	21
3	Bronze Age sword, knife and dagger found in or near our villages	22
4	The entrance of Cholesbury fort as it would have looked in the late Bronze or early Iron Ages	28
5	Bronze Age huts	30
6	A two ox wooden plough from Somerset	32
7	A similar plough still being used in Kurdistan	33
8	Bronze Age cauldron and bucket	35
9	Bronze Age costumes	38
10	Iron Age pots found at Dundridge Manor and within Cholesbury Fort	49
11	The house of a wealthy farmer in the Late Iron Age	56
12	The Moat, Dundridge Manor	70
13	Chapel Farm, St. Leonards	86
14	Twentieth-century Cholesbury	96
15	'The Full Moon', Cholesbury Common	106
16	The impressive roof of the Manor House at Cholesbury	116
17	Typical 'Brass Pots' taken as distraints—skillet, warming pan and kettle	129
18	Folly Farm, Buckland Common	138
19	Jugs from the Buckland Common Potteries	139
20	'The House wherein Edward Avis formerly dwelt'	141
21	Home Farm and barn, Cholesbury	152
22	St. Leonards Chapel	167
23	One of the old Inns—the Black Horse, below Hawridge	173
24	A Straw Plaiter at work and her implements	175
25	Old Bassoon from Hawridge Church	196
26	Cholesbury Church after reconstruction	209
27	The Manor House, Cholesbury	220

LIST OF MAPS

1	Location map	3
2	Geological map	9
3	St. Leonards at the time of the Field Survey, 1581	93
4	Hawridge about 1550–1650	102
5	Cholesbury, 17th century	119
	Relief Map	End papers

ACKNOWLEDGEMENTS

We are indebted to so many friends for extensive and willing help over four years of the research necessary for this sort of book that it is not easy to know just where to begin. The work has meant lengthy sessions in dusty corners of Archives and transcriptions of Wills and records written in Latin and old English in many different places as far apart as Lincoln, Aylesbury and London. The book was undertaken at the request of our own Cholesbury-cum-St. Leonards Local History Group, so no one will be offended if we start there.

We are grateful to everyone who has given us such warm encouragement, but in particular we are indebted to our old friend Major General Robin Money, who was Chairman four years ago and had already done a lot of work on the village records including photographic records of the older houses. Next, we must mention Audrey Ellis, who has not only spent many days discovering and looking at *every* Will relating to our villages at the County Record Office, but has also undertaken the greater part of the indexing. Margaret Phillips, who succeeded General Money as Chairman, has always been ready with practical advice, help and criticism of early drafts and has herself spent much time on research as well as helping with the proof reading. The local knowledge of Horace Brackley, whose family have for so long been pillars of the village, has been invaluable and so freely and helpfully given. We are also indebted to Myfanwy Phillips, Susie Benda and Kenneth King, who did the pubs for us, for their indefatigable probing into old piles of paper, to Mr. Arnold Baines of Chesham for advice, information on field names and material from articles and to Teresa Matthews for passing on the results of family researches as well as for the loan of books.

Many other members of the four villages have contributed ideas and information, but we are particularly grateful to those who have so willingly allowed us to look inside and make drawings of their houses, and to the older inhabitants, who have beguiled us with their recollections extending over the last 70—80 years, which have provided much of the material for the last chapter.

From the Buckinghamshire Archaeological Society we have had constant help and encouragement and particularly from the Librarian, Mrs G. Elvey and her husband, who have not only helped us to discover the material available in the archives, but have always been so willing to give up their own time to assist in deciphering and translating the most difficult manuscripts. We are also grateful to Mr Elliot Viney, on behalf of the Society, for permission to use both published and unpublished material from their records.

We are most grateful to John Randall, the present Lord of the Manor, for allowing us to work on the Manorial records at home—thus saving many lost hours—and to the Rev. C. H. C. Edwards, vicar of Cholesbury, for access to the Parish chest; to Mr D. W. Plaistowe for his family history; Mr M. Fletcher for information collected by the late Miss J. Fletcher; the Vicar of Wigginton for his records; the Trustees for the Neale Trust and their solicitors, Messrs. Halsey, Lightly and Hemsley; and Messrs. Vaisey and Turner, solicitors for the St. Leonards Chapel Trust.

As will be seen from the text, we have leaned heavily on the kindly help of Mr J. F. Head, who has given us permission to quote from his *Early Man in South Buckinghamshire,* and our background reading has owed much to the guidance of my cousin, Denys Hay, the Professor of Medieval History at Edinburgh University. Without the willing help of Mrs Sadie Murdoch we would have been in grave difficulties with the typing and clerical work.

Official Sources

Thanks are due to the Buckinghamshire County Record Office and the Museum for their understanding assistance, to the Lincoln Archives Committee, the British Museum, the House of Lords and lastly to the Henry E. Huntington Library, San Marino, California.

———————

Our villages have been lucky in their Lords of the Manor. In the first printing we set down our thanks to John Randall for his understanding help. Joan and I now wish on everybody's behalf to thank Dennis and Pat Smith for their generosity in making it possible to reissue our village history.

PREFACE

L iving in the shadow of two early British forts tends to make one curious about the past, a curiosity which has led us to the fascinating job of disentangling village history. The main families quickly become friends as one begins to discover where they lived, how they made a living, the houses and land they bought and sold, their relationships with each other through marriage and the family wrangles which now and again are all too clearly revealed in their Wills.

It is even more exciting, however, when by luck we find ourselves sitting on the sidelines while important events in national history come vividly to life in their effect on our friends of the past. We use the word 'luck' deliberately because in the past the preservation of records and their location has been fortuitous. We have had our share of this sort of luck. Events such as the dissolution of the Chantry Chapels and Chapels of Ease and the imposition of Ship Money, and social problems such as the effects of the old Poor Law in the early 19th century, to take three examples, appear as arid facts in some history books. But the inner story of their actual effect on the people of England is anything but arid and it is this inner story, as seen through the eyes of a small but very real village community, that we have tried to set down.

NO FAMOUS NAMES

The people of four small villages
and their part in English history

The problems of writing our history; the significance of the village; the location of
our four hilltop villages overlooking the Icknield Way.

The significance of the Village

This is not a history of a famous family and the village that grew up round their doings. It is merely the continuous story of four little villages that now lie peacefully among the Chiltern beechwoods behind the escarpment that looks over the Oxfordshire plains and along which ran the old Celtic highway from east to west—the Icknield Way that carried the life blood of pre-Roman Britain.

For this reason it is has been more difficult to piece together the scattered evidence of the continuity of life in these human settlements. But the result is perhaps even more rewarding, because, at the end, you have the life and history of the common people of England, without whom there would have been no history and famous names would be mere ghosts in a formless vacuum without background or natural frame. Even the historian concerned with the famous has difficulty in distinguishing a man from his acts. From his acts, John Hampden was a graduate of Magdalen College, Oxford, a Member of Parliament and country landowner who became famous as the leader of resistance to the imposition of ship money, was impeached in 1642 and escaped to be killed in a skirmish at Chalgrove Field; but he was also that unique animal, a human being who became a boy, a boy who became a man, carrying with him a sense of continuous identity, aware that his acts were mysteriously independent of him and that whoever judged him by them, irrespective of his environment, was basing that judgement upon an irrelevance. It is difficult for the historian, even with personal letters and a record of conversations, to get at his thoughts between sleeping and waking, his small

follies of hope and disappointment and the thousand little
personal happenings that are necessary parts of the whole truth of
man and the basis of his acts.

How much greater are the difficulties of the historian of John
the carter, of Tom the cowherd and Edward the smith who had no
biographer but who lived just as surely, who knew the smell of wet
earth between primroses in the spring, the scent of wood fires, felt
the sting of the north-easter across the flat lands and saw the love
light in another's eyes and were, as certainly as John Hampden,
part of the history of England. Their history must be pieced
together laboriously from massive Court Rolls that tell of their
misdeeds, from Parish Registers of their baptism, marriage and
burial and a host of Terriers and Wills that each contribute a
separate glimpse of that complicated and exciting being—man,
who is fast becoming mere fodder for the statistician to feed to his
insatiable computer from which come the vast, deceptive general-
izations of today.

This, as far as we have been able to piece it together, is the
history of four little Chiltern villages—Cholesbury, St. Leonards,
Buckland Common and Hawridge. It is of special interest to us
because we live here but, because their records reflect so much of
the history of the England that passed through them, their
fortunes concern equally all who wish to catch a glimpse of the
English village while there is yet time—while it is still recognisable
in that happy sense that English villages have of growing out of the
ground. In a way, the history of the village is indeed the history of
England itself. Our own story has been enriched and enlarged as
much or more than any other group of villages by our actual site.
For nearly 4,000 years we have enjoyed a sort of grandstand view
of history in the making. When you have a look at the local map
(page 3) you might think that we were nowhere in particular, and
be right. But if you take instead the map of England, you will see
that the world and his wife, the Kings and counsellors, merchants
and wandering minstrels, have most of them had to pass by our
front door in order to get from the metropolis to the large areas of
England that lie to the north and west. And before there were any
maps—before the Romans established London as the hub of their
radial road system—we were still at the window, this time on the
first great prehistoric trackway between the two most densely

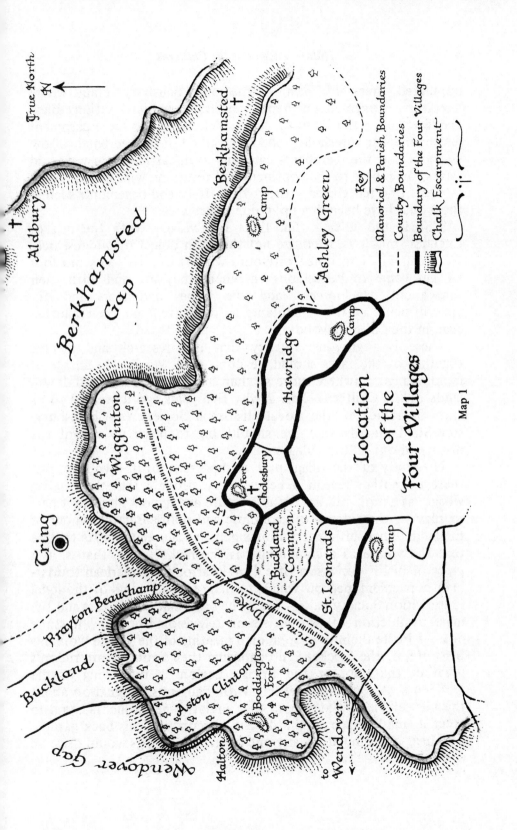

True North

N

Aldbury

Berkhamsted Gap

Berkhamsted

Camp

Ashley Green

Key

Manorial & Parish Boundaries

County Boundaries

Boundary of the Four Villages

Chalk Escarpment

Wigginton

Tring

Hawridge

Camp

Fort

Cholesbury

Frayton Beauchamp

Buckland

Aston Clinton

Dyke

Grim's

Buckland Common

St. Leonards

Camp

Boddington Fort

Halton

Wendover Gap

to Wendover

Location of the Four Villages

Map 1

populated areas of East Anglia and Salisbury Plain where Neolithic, Bronze and Iron man developed their civilisations. Back and fore along the Icknield Way which ran along the escarpment just below our threshold, rode and walked the armed bands of the warriors and the merchants carrying corn, cattle, metal ware and slaves for export to the continent and returning with luxuries such as glass, fine red glazed pottery from Italy and ornaments such as those that have been dug up in our village area.

This is the setting that links our villages with the rest of England, but it is of course not the main object of our research. We are mainly concerned with our own history; with why our four villages came to be established where they are and with their subsequent development and the hopes and fears and disappointments of the inhabitants as they lived out their allotted span in the Chiltern woods.

There is a growing urgency that this research and piecing together of the facts should be done now. We live in an age of rapid change, nowhere more so than in the woodlands and downlands of the Chilterns. This is why five years ago it seemed to us and to friends in the Local Historical Society of Cholesbury-cum-St. Leonards that we should try to place on record the history of our hilltop villages.

The study of 'the village past' is important for its own sake. But there is another reason. I believe very strongly that the English village, as a unit, still has a viable future and a most important part to play in the balance of economic and political development of England. When efficient businessmen or sage economists tell me that the village as a community is finished, except, that is, as a piece of history or a sort of cultural carrot for American tourists or a convenient peg on which to hang the fur coats of the local Preservation Society ladies—when they say that motor cars and the mass production of pop artists on television has killed it stone dead—I invite them to drop in on a meeting of the village Women's Institute, or the Cricket Club choosing their Saturday afternoon's team in the pub, or the British Legion in full swing or the Residents' Association seething with righteous indignation about the bus service or the rumour that a relative newcomer is about to erect a small garage in the decent obscurity of his back garden. The heat engendered by any one of these meetings would drive an entire fleet of atomic submarines for the next year. No, the corpse is still breathing very healthily and politicians will ignore it at their peril. The trouble is that the setting is changing so rapidly and, as usual, time is getting short. That is why we have tried to place on record, before fact becomes folklore and memory merges with imagination, some account of what manner of men and women passed across the common before we came on the scene: how they fashioned their working lives in the fields and woods that we look out over; how they came to build the houses we can still see— houses of local timber and brick or wattle and daub—and set up potteries and forges for the domestic furnishings.

We must rediscover how they—the Seares, Gearys, Putnams, Batchelors, Wrights and Puddiphats, the Gomms, Birches, Eyres and Dells, and a hundred others that wander in and out of our early Court Rolls, amused themselves and fitted willingly—or unwillingly—into the pattern of the human community that is, after all, the real village.

I have a feeling that we must record their story before the planners arrive and tidy up the countryside and its villages in a way that may be sanitary and efficient but may also destroy the affinity of the village with its surroundings and even with its history. We are in the era of plastic gnomes and municipal gardens with their ordered double pink cherries. These are no proper substitutes for the Chiltern woods, nor will man appreciate the symmetry of the model villas and desirable residences as a substitute for the little village he grew up in. Though plastic gnomes thank goodness cannot yet breed or sing, once established, they are semi-indestructible. I am sure modern man, when he bursts out of his industrial cage, will still want to take his Sunday pint on the bench outside the *Pig and Whistle* and not in the synthetic comfort of a Letchworth model motel. He will need the contact with the past for a renewal of the simple sense of the eternal things that children are born with, that we can sometimes retain to illuminate middle age and perhaps to bind the years pleasantly together when we are put out to grass. Transport has caused the whole world to huddle together, and we must ensure that we rediscover and recognise our village heritage before the evidence is obliterated and we are reconstructing what no longer exists.

The wider significance

I cannot help feeling that this and other local histories have a much wider significance. The history of an English village, more truly than any other institution reflects the ebb and flow of invasion and battle, of prosperity and plague, agricultural toil and industrial revolution and the enclosure of common lands that have passed into the melting pot of the English story. It is our oldest institution; older than the Mother of Parliaments and almost as old as man.

When the first seasick Roman soldier stumbled up the beach at Dover, cursing the climate and his unlucky posting, he found villages that had been in existence for three thousand years or more, and a coinage and craftsmanship second to none throughout the continent.

Location of Villages (see Map 1)

Now you may like to know just where you can find these villages in relation to London and the rest of England. The statistician would give you the grid reference on the one inch Ordnance Survey map as SP 928.072. But that is a prosaic way of going about it. I would rather advise you to take the old Roman road from St. Albans (Verulamium) through Berkhamsted to Tring and then turn southwards up into the wooded hill country; you will find Cholesbury still huddled round the old Celtic fort (now called the Danish camp). To the south-east on the road to Chesham you will find Hawridge, and to the west lie both Buckland Common and St. Leonards.

II

THE HILLS TAKE SHAPE

The geological background

The chalk escarpment; the clay topsoil; the effects of the Great Ice Age; the formation of our clay-with-flint soil.

T he early geological origins of the area are as fascinating as the later use made of it by man (see Map 2). For a full and authentic account I would commend to you S. W. Wooldridge and D. L. Linton *Structure, Surface and Drainage in South East England*[1] as well as a transect of the area by R. Bourne to be found in *Regional Survey,*[2] together with sundry articles and local accounts listed in the Appendix A.

For those who do not wish to indulge in the complications of our geological origins, let me try and tell you very simply how the basic landscape was formed and then we can trace, in the pages that follow, how man gradually altered its surface appearance to suit his needs for food, shelter and protection from his enemies.

I am well aware that the purist will snort when he reads this over-simplification of what can only be adequately covered in several technical volumes, but this is not a book about geo-morphology; it is about the human beings that came after the land was formed.

The main feature conditioning the landscape of our villages is, of course, the Chiltern chalk escarpment which lies two miles to the north and runs roughly from south-west to north-east. This falls steeply about 400 feet through a narrow lower chalk platform to the clays of the Oxfordshire plain and is indented by many a dry coomb between the Wendover and Berkhamsted gaps. The plateau to the south-east is mainly clay with flints, interspersed with gravels and sandstones in depressions. How did this state of affairs come about?

The Chalk Escarpment is formed

We can conveniently forget nearly 400 million years of exciting movements before what is called the Jurassic period, about 125 million years ago, except to say that while our land lay under the sea, layers of sedimentary rocks such as the various clays and limestones mixed with ironstone and marlstone were being laid down by water action mixed in places with sandy clays in estuary deposits. The whole sort of sandwich cake was then subjected to pressures which resulted, not only in periodic raising and lowering of the land above and below sea level, but in sideways compression which folded the layers into wave-like formations. At times when the land was high and dry, the tops of these waves were weathered away by frost, wind and river action until the harder rocks stuck out of the denuded and tilted plains in between. It is what is called the 'dip-slope' from one of these tiltings which gives us the London Basin. But several other things began to happen, of which we must take a little more notice.

About 100 million years ago, in what is called the Cretacious period (*creta* = chalk), our village area lay between a northern and southern sea and this shallow area was invaded by sea water and the great bands of chalk were laid down. It used to be thought that chalk was a deep sea deposit because of its similarity to the globigerma oozes but it is now agreed it must have been formed about this time in very clear but comparatively shallow water. It was formed right across Europe from what is now Ireland to Russia and is very consistent in character. Then there came another general retreat of the sea partly due to an uplift line to the north-east of our part of the Chilterns. The important thing is that this was accompanied by a gradual uplift movement to the north and west of our villages which accentuated the dip and slope, already mentioned, down towards what is now London and along the bottom of which a river (the Thames) was later to form between us and another weathered ledge, the North Downs.

The Topsoil is formed

But I'm afraid we can't quite leave it at that because two more important things happened. First, the top of the rounded fold above our area was subjected to weathering, that is it was ground away by water, wind and frost action. As soon as the hard crust

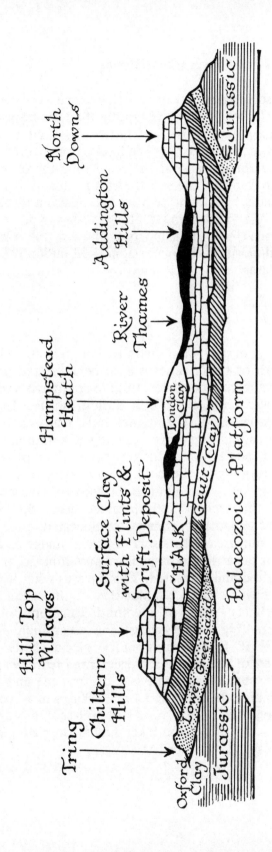

Hill Top Villages

Tring

Chiltern Hills

Surface Clay with Flints & Drift Deposit

Hampstead Heath

River Thames

Addington Hills

North Downs

Oxford Clay

Jurassic

Lower Greensand

CHALK

London Clay

Gault (Clay)

Jurassic

Palaeozoic Platform

The London Basin

Section Through Chalk Escarpment by the four Hill Top Villages

Map 2

was penetrated, the softer clays to the north became exposed and were worn away much more easily and rapidly than the projecting end of the chalk escarpment which was left as the Chiltern edge we have today. Then incursions of the sea levelled the plain to the north-west of our escarpment and at the same time the elements got busy on our hinterland to the south-east and dissolved much of the calcareous (chalky) material, leaving behind as an insoluble residue the mess of clay-with-flints that we suffer from in our fields and gardens today. At the same time the sea was washing away the edges and depositing the material in the London basin as a sort of top clay, later to be reinforced by river-born sediment from the west.

Glaciers of the Great Ice Age finish the job
1. The Escarpment

Lastly, as if the poor old land hadn't been mucked about enough, the area north of the Thames was to be subjected to the grinding process of a great ice sheet from Scandinavia, which ebbed and flowed over most of Britain during the last 18,000 years BC. It is interesting to remember that early man was about by this time in our area and was driven to struggle with bears and the larger mammals for possession of the few caves which provided some sort of protection from the cold. There were, of course, warmer periods in between: although it is difficult to separate out the actual work of the second and third ice ages (the latter actually generated in the southern uplands of Scotland) they did, between them, cover our area with a sort of glacial sludge scraped up by the grinding rocks carried in suspension and dumped on our plateau as the ice melted and retreated. This gave us what we call the 'drift soils'—the lower chalky boulder clay of the second Ice Age and the upper chalky 'drift' of the third. Furthermore, by damming back the melting water against the escarpment as it retreated northwards, it formed temporary glacial lakes and probably gave us many of the coombs and indented features, now of course dry, in the northern side of our escarpment and thus necessitated many winding turns in the Icknield Way which wound along above the heavy scrub that had accumulated in warmer times across the plain. In places the lakes spilled over altogether and cut the Tring and Wendover gaps.

Two features are worth noticing. The second Ice Age, which gave us our so-called brick-earth, also gives us evidence of early Mousterian man—a short, broad fellow with very prominent eyebrow ledges, generally known as Neanderthal man, a fine workman in stone tools. He left his implements in the lower beds of this deposit along with the skeletons of his great enemy, the mammoth. Indeed, it is possible, though the pundits argue about this, that the damming back of the Rhine and its tributary, the young Thames, by the great solid ice sheet over the whole North Sea, forced the first breakthrough of water along the south-west gap to form the English Channel, thus achieving the first break between the continent and Britain, only about seven thousand years ago.

2. The Hinterland Soil

Now we must also have a word about the clay-with-flints soil of the hinterland on which our villages are situated. I have explained earlier how this was formed. It is, you remember, a brown clay absolutely riddled with flints and left behind, because of its insolubility, after the easily soluble calcium carbonate had been removed. It also contains certain rocks which formerly lay above the chalk and it made a soil quite different not only from the lowland clays but from the chalk itself. Whereas the chalk is naturally rich in lime, the clay-with-flints forms a heavier soil which is difficult to work except under certain conditions and at just the right time each year, dependent on the season. Another noticeable feature is the number of dry valleys. These are accounted for by the porosity of the chalk subsoil which ensures that the water table has long since gone underground. Some were, and still are, occupied by temporary streams after wet seasons. In our area they are called 'bournes' and only occur when the water table is exceptionally high when the 'bourne' is said to be 'up'. It is this peculiarity of the chalk plateaux, according to a consensus of experts, that partially accounts for the number of steep sided valleys that we have when there is no evidence of actual water having cut them. The chalk, a relatively soft rock, being so porous, allows the moisture to pass through unimpeded. Hence it is not subject to most of the agencies of river erosion and the tops of the ridges are not worn away to anything like the same extent as the clays of the lower main plains.

I am not, of course, speaking of the much larger gaps to the east (Berkhamsted) and west (Wendover) of the chunk of escarpment on which our four villages stand. These had their origin in the overspill of pent up glacial waters, as explained earlier, and are now dry because the containing glacier on the plains has long ago melted away.

Perhaps I should explain that chalk is really a soft white lime-stone, often of great purity so that all but a hundredth part will dissolve in dilute acid. In addition to the valleys, this accounts for most of the pits which are so common a feature of our hinterland. About ten per cent of it is made up of small shells from micro-scopic organisms called *foraminfera*. Most of the rest is made up of a fine calcium carbonate probably derived from the disintegration of larger shells and similar matter. Some is hard and some marly and soft. Nodules of flint are frequent in the upper layers, black or brown in the centre and white where they merge into the chalk. They are formed of silica, a hard insoluble substance, derived generally from the skeletons of sponges which lived in the shallow seas when the chalk was deposited. Often we find them enclosing whole shells and fossils of sea urchins, looking perfect and com-plete because the silica has replaced, exactly, their original structure.

Vegetation then creeps back to dress the landscape
eventually found by Early Man

I hope I have been able to give you enough of the formative earth movements for you to appreciate how the scenery, in which our villages are set, gradually developed over four or five million years. As we see, three distinct types of scenery evolved, as a result, in the vicinity of our villages:

1. The general rounded hills and steep wooded valleys of the peneplain or dip slope, at the north end of which our villages stand.
2. The Chiltern scarp just to the north and along the lower slopes of which runs the Icknield Way.
3. The Icknield loam belt and Oxfordshire clay plain beyond, because much of our history has to do with the adjacent low

land and most of our ecclesiastical and secular boundaries run up from it in narrow strips over the escarpment.

Notes and References

[1] S. W. Wooldridge and D. L. Linton, *Structure, Surface and Drainage In South East England* (London, 1955).

[2] R. Bourne *Regional Survey* (Oxford 1931).

III

MAN SETTLES IN THE CHILTERNS

From Prehistoric times up to about 1500 BC

The first settlements; the flints in our soil are valuable; ancient trackways linking the hilltop camps; the year 1500 BC in relation to world history.

As the last of the ice retreated gradually northwards and woods and foliage once again covered the bare deserts of rock and soil left behind by the glaciers, the little animals and the great mammoths crept back gradually and furtively explored the oak, ash, thorn and juniper and bramble thickets for food and shelter. After them came man to hunt them, now with better weapons of polished stone and ingenious traps for the bear, fox, wolves, lynx and rabbits. He had also learned in the south how to make better houses and to domesticate wild animals for food and transport.

Then, still in the mists of pre-history, the great revolution happened. Man began to dig in the ground and grow things for himself from the wild oats and seeds he improved. In fact he had become an agriculturalist and settled down to farm and hunt from one spot. He had ceased to be a nomad—the village had been born. His tools were still primitive—stone axes and sickles, which could only cope with thin scrub and light soil, but up on the Chiltern escarpment the elements, in the last few thousands of years before modern agricultural man arrived about 3000 BC, had worn and washed away the heavier soils from the exposed top of the ridge leaving, on the thin soil, only the short turf of Ivinghoe Beacon and the Wendover Hills which barely covers the white rock. The fields, where they exist, are a pale cream with white gashes of chalk pits along the hillside. Rough flinty tracks wind up through the woods from the flat land and about the whole landscape there is that delicate colouring and filmy effect as the cloud shadows chase each other across the rounded slopes, found in no other type of landscape. Beech now grows in clumps in the more sheltered hill-

14

sides but the main escarpment is still scrubland suitable only for sheep. Professor Trueman[1] quotes Huxley as referring to these chalk areas as 'suggestive of mutton and pleasantness' and this is not a bad description of the wide expanses of grassy downland and the smooth rounded curves of the hills along the escarpment.

Here, early man could establish himself in scattered settlements, as well as in a few clearings in the thick woods of the tableland. His settlements were mainly along the line of springs and it must be remembered that the water table was considerably higher in the Bronze Age, about 2000 to 700 BC and the weather warmer and wetter than it is now. Where there was no spring, or insufficient water for sheep, dew ponds were used to augment the water supply. These were depressions filled with alternate layers of clay to hold water, straw to insulate it from ground heat at night and stones to facilitate precipitation from moist air.

By about 2000 BC Neolithic and Bronze age man had cleared the light scrub around these early settlements and had learnt to grow not only food but also flax, so that his lady wife was able to dress herself in gaily coloured clothes instead of making that old bearskin do another winter. He domesticated wild animals, learned how to make and use fire and left behind many implements and traces of his occupation of the Chilterns in general, including a flint mine not far from our villages.

But in spite of all this he changed the landscape very little. His meagre clearings were but drops in the ocean of upland scrub and he was still unable to tackle the heavier forest of the clay lands in the plain or even the clay-with-flints soil of the dip slope running down towards the London basin. The valleys were still swamps, which had to wait until the last century BC for the heavy iron shod Belgic plough and its even more efficient Saxon successor before the great waterlogged jungle of the plains beyond the escarpment could be opened up.

For all his progress our early man couldn't control the landscape and was still mainly dependent upon what nature dropped into his lap, while supplementing the meat he hunted with the wild berries, domestic animals and scanty crops. He didn't learn to extract metal from rocks and forge it into implements and weapons until about 2000 BC, so he continued to use the only locally abundant raw material—the flints that we nowadays curse when we dig our gardens or plough our fields. We must remember that the beastly things were a boon to these ancestors of ours and indeed they have had a greater influence on our history than any other ready-to-hand material. The Romans surfaced roads by splitting the flints and bedding them in with the flat face upwards and houses were faced with them until very recently. But far more important, they provided these early men with their cutting tools.

Being rich in flint, our chalk escarpment area attracted relatively large prehistoric populations and mining became a wide-spread industry. There were two great areas of chalky outcrops, Salisbury Plain and East Anglia. Between them stretched our own escarpment and so along it naturally ran the great linking pre-Roman road, the Icknield Way, which must have brought immediate and permanent prosperity to our hilltop settlements. They not only mined flints but probably grew surplus crops and made more woven garments than they themselves needed because they had an easy and handy communication system along this route to dispose of their wares to east and west. In any case the flints in the Cholesbury area are especially good for arrow heads—second only to those of the Grimes Graves area of Norfolk. Indeed, I suspect, they also made a good living by carrying on a sort of protection racket, by charging tolls to all users of the route so that they might be allowed to pass by the ravines and wooded slopes in security.

Because of the relatively impenetrable lowlands, travel would be confined to the ancient hillside trackways with the hilltop camps like our villages and the shrines and tumuli and occasional white horse sign that we still preserve today. Below and on the plateau, paths would wind between patches of damp oak scrub, hornbeam and gorse which bordered the hill pastures. This explains why most flinty subsidiary trackways in our area are found running up into the hills from the main road, because the settlements were there. Later, village and manorial boundaries were to run in narrow strips up and down in the same direction, because when the rich farms developed on the better soil of the plains, the clearings round the old settlements were still kept on as valuable hill pastures for summer grazing and probably as holiday living quarters for the well-to-do farmers of the plain.

In the last few pages we have conveniently disposed of about

500,000 years, give or take a few thousand, of pre-history, during which time man or sub-man was existing by hunting and gathering the wild fruits in season and also the subsequent 7,000 years when he was getting domesticated and learning how to settle in comfort in his chosen area. We do not know when during this period Man first came to our villages. We know of his existence nearby but in the absence of any real evidence it would be quite improper to include Neolithic and Early Stone Age man in any factual village history. So, we have skipped quickly over these thousands of years in this introductory chapter to reach the time, about 1500 BC when some strange foreigners, stocky little German farmers from the lower Danube would have been seen in increasing numbers pushing warily up the Icknield Way. The evening sun would glint on their copper coloured shields and body armour and the ox carts were full of metal pots and implements. I am sure there would have been hurried gatherings in the thatched halls of the hill settlements as the animals were gathered in for safety. The Bronze Age had crossed the Channel and the traceable origins of our villages are about to take shape.

Where was 1500 BC in relation to what you know?

Before we start the real history of our villages however let me try and fix the so-called Bronze Age for you, both in time scale and in relation to events you will be familiar with. If we look across the known world, with of course a bit of foresight and convenient hindsight, we find a number of things going on which I am sure you will remember when I mention them. In Egypt, for instance, Karnak and Luxor were being built. Indeed, someone was cutting out 'Cleopatra's needle' for us. The Exodus of the Israelites was still 200 years away in the future and so was Tutankhamen. In passing, we must not forget that the Bronze Age really started about 3000 BC on the banks of the Nile when an economically minded and revolutionary society converted some riverside villages into cities and compelled surrounding farmers to produce a surplus of foodstuffs, over and above their own requirements, and used it to support an urban population of specialised craftsmen who developed the use of bronze for the wealthy burgers. It took, of course, as you will see, another 1,000 years for the news to filter into the insular brains of the average Briton.

In Crete the Late Minoans were busy rebuilding the great palace of Knossus, first built some 500 years earlier. In Greece the first Olympiad was still 700 years away and 1,000 years were to pass before Herodotus was born or the Parthenon built. Babylon and Assyria would have to wait 200 years for Nebuchadnezzar, and in about 500 years David and then his son Solomon would be combining the states of Israel and Judea into one of the most powerful kingdoms of the Near East. The date when, as you will remember, David knocked six bells out of Goliath was not until 1064 BC. Another name which you will remember, Moses, the Law Giver, had been born 71 years before and Noah had finally died about 500 years earlier.

To come into home waters again, the English Channel had been opened for about three and a half thousand years, and the Phoenicians, the little dark seamen from the Eastern Mediterranean, were very busy trading with Cornish tin miners and south coast pottery merchants. I don't mean to imply in any way that the high state of mathematical genius of the Sumerians or the solar researches of the Egyptians or indeed any of the social or cultural graces of the Near East were in any way reflected in the simple pastoral life of our Chiltern villages, but, as we shall see, they had by 1500 BC achieved a certain standard of living which was considerably removed from the barbaric discomfort of the Stone Age.

Notes and References

[1]A. E. Trueman, *Geology and Scenery in England and Wales* (Penguin Books 1952).

IV

CHOLESBURY TAKES SHAPE

Our history starts in the Bronze Age

Bronze Age invaders; local evidence in the area; reasons for the choice of the village site.

The Bronze Age covers a period of 1300 years from 2000 to 700 BC. In England it was marked by waves of invaders, many groups settling in a relatively small area, and is divided by the experts into four periods. You will be relieved to read that I intend to ignore the details of these different nationalities. It doesn't really concern us in Cholesbury, you can read about them in hundreds of books by competent authors and the authorities are still arguing with each other about their exact origins anyway.

The group that concern us in Cholesbury are the south German farmers from the lower Danube plains, popularly known as the Beaker People because of their distinctive domestic pottery. They are important because for the first time we have actual evidence of their permanent occupation of the escarpment area, including our own village sites, both from implements found on the surface and from the results of investigation of 'Round Barrows' of Bronze age origin a number of these being found in the neighbourhood of the Chiltern escarpment.[1]

The Beaker people may not have founded our villages but they lived and had their being in the shadow of our woods[2] and by importing their improved methods of agriculture and hunting, certainly must have set the scene for the generations to come. They imposed themselves and their culture upon the resident small dark Iberian population who had originally come up the west coast from the Mediterranean and, because of their stone monuments were later known as the Megalithic people. We have so far found no trace of their occupation and so must begin with their conquerors—the Beaker folk.

It is impossible to say exactly when the Beaker folk actually

reached our villages—it could have been any time between about
1800 and 1500 BC. The difficulty with all those early civilisations
in our area is that there has been so little excavation. We have
numerous forts, tumuli and settlement areas because of the high
density of population in both the Bronze and Iron ages but the
Cholesbury fort is the only earth work within the confines of our
four villages that has so far been partially excavated and the
findings assessed by Professor Hawkes.[3] Even Grim's Ditch, that
great earth work running across between the villages and the
Icknield Way has not yet been excavated and one can only hope
that the younger generation will find the energy and the time to
do what we have so signally failed to achieve ourselves. Indeed if
this book succeeds in stimulating further interest in these matters
it will have been worthwhile in itself.

For evidence of the origins of our villages we must therefore
rely primarily on surface finds and the careful piecing together of
authenticated evidence of local occupation. The main interest, I
think, of the diggings within the fortification itself seems to be
that though some of the pottery assessed by Professor Hawkes was
of a later origin—Belgic or general Iron Age—much of it was pre
Belgic in design, surface texture and construction. Furthermore,
the discovery of pygmy cups in the vicinity certainly suggests a
period about 1500 BC, as these didn't make their appearance in
Britain until about this time with the arrival of a new group of
invaders from Brittany who, better armed and organised, began to
supplant the Beaker folk as the most influential settlers. They had
extensive trading connections with the Baltic as well as the
Mediterranean and brought a large number of skilled smiths with
them—indeed you can really call this 'the age of specialists' with
society demanding more and complicated luxuries. Some of the
dead were still buried in long barrows but the popular craze for
cremation was sweeping the country and boosting the sale of
pygmy cups and funeral furnishings as a whole, similar to those
found in nearby round barrows near the escarpment.

Taken as a whole, this weight of evidence would seem to
confirm permanent occupation of the settlements at this time and
it is the reason that we have taken 1500 BC as the start of our
history.

In the absence of further evidence from excavation it is

Fig.2 Middle Bronze Age urns and pygmy cup, dug up nearby in the Chilterns.

impossible to say how far Cholesbury had been a thriving community before this time, but there is little doubt that such a desirable site would have been occupied, probably permanently, by several preceding waves of settlers.

While on the subject of these Bronze age pottery finds, I must mention one very interesting point made by Professor Hawkes. He records that some of the 200 sherds recovered were of a distinctive native local design, not found elsewhere. As you will read later (see Chapter XII) we had our own potteries at Buckland Common in the 18th century and are rather proud to have preserved samples of the work. This automatically sets one thinking and I wonder whether this early evidence of a very distinctive local pottery isn't also evidence of the earliest use of our own kilns and the particularly suitable earth that is found in our villages. Furthermore, as a local industry would have taken some time to evolve, I wonder if we have not got in this discovery further indications of the Bronze age occupation of our villages.

Bronze Age finds of this period include an early knife or sickle, at Aston Hill just to the west of St. Leonards, a much ground

down knife or dagger at Lee Common council school and other
sherds of Bronze Age pygmy cups, axes and food vessels which
have been found along the Icknield Way and near the ridge. Mr J.
F. Head has an interesting comment,

> 'The newcomers were a numerous, skilled and well organised
> people . . . they seem to have made no attempt to penetrate into
> the interior'.[4]

The most exciting event was the accidental finding in 1851,[5] of
a Bronze Age sword; interesting because of the local bronze
industry which was characterised by a form of axe known as a
'palstave'.[6] There were also, I believe, local variations on the
rapiers and looped spearheads. As the rapier had developed from
the dagger, so the sword came as a more efficient weapon. This
particular sword was of a design known as the 'leaf sword' and at
that period was a popular innovation. This one was found (where a
careless chap had dropped it in a hurry or when he was being
chased), in Geary's Wood in Hawridge just opposite my study
window where I am writing now. Perhaps I should add that in this

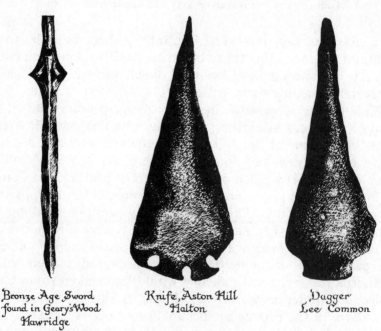

Bronze Age Sword
found in Geary's Wood
Hawridge

Knife, Aston Hill
Halton

Dagger
Lee Common

Fig. 3

type of sword the tang for the handle was cast on the blade and the edges slightly flanged up. In between these edges and on either side, pieces of horn or wood were riveted to form handle grips and a round pommel was clipped on to the end. The scabbard, which has long since rotted away, would be made of leather with a chape, or tip, of bronze, the beginning of an armaments race!

As we have already seen these finds also indicate that the inhabitants, basically a mixture of older Iberian and later Beaker people, were by now coming under the influences of the newest group of invaders from the Breton areas of the western continental peninsula.[7]

Reasons for choice of Village Site

Whether the village or the fort came first, it is impossible to say; I don't know, nor do the experts. We shall never know whether some wandering warrior said 'Let's build a bit of a fort on that pleasant hill top over there' and then invited his friends to join him and form a village, or whether, as I rather suspect, things got a bit too exciting for the herdsmen in their collections of thatched huts and they combined to raise a small fence around the area for the protection of themselves and their herds. It does not really matter. Whatever the date and the motives of these first settlers, the reasons for its development would have been the same, a good defensive site, a good water supply and a strategic position astride the main lines of communcations at the time. Before we look more closely at the village it is worth going into these three factors in a little more detail.

A Good Defensive Site

The importance of this needs no stressing. There must be an eminence from which you can see your enemies a long way off and prepare for them. It was important, especially in those days of short range weapons—slingers and bows and arrows—not to be overlooked from another eminence. You also chose a place where the natural contours of the land could easily be accentuated by running a deep ditch round the site and piling up the earth on the inside of this ditch. This is made even higher by a wooden palisade of the kind illustrated. (Fig. 4, p. 28.)

It is also important to be able to communicate easily with your neighbours in time of trouble, by means of beacons or other visual signals when help was needed. Cholesbury had the large fortress of Boddington (above what is now Wendover) to the west and Hawridge to the south and one probably somewhere in the area of what is now Marlin Chapel Farm on the east. They would also be in direct communication with the powerful urban populations along the Pitstone and Ivinghoe ridges, as well as the fortified camp in Brays Wood, just beyond the St. Leonards boundary by Three Gates Bottom. Indeed, if you look at a pre-Roman map of the Chiltern Edge you will see a veritable line of forts all along above the road. Later, they had to dip further and further down the gaps as the land was cleared and communication was possible through to the busy areas of the Thames valley.

A good water supply—safe from interference

Water is the key problem in any hill fort. Though the water table in our area was higher than it is now, it was only in freak formations, like a clay saucer under the porous top soil, that a permanent pond or spring was possible right on top of a hill. Most of the springs were lower down where the chalk rested on the gault subsoil which forced the water out into the open.

Here at Cholesbury we must have that lucky formation, as we know from Saxon times there has always been an everlasting well or pond right inside the fort; in fact the fort was perhaps built round it after it had been discovered. This would have been supplemented by dew ponds for the cattle out in the fields as the population grew. There may have been other sources; we know at least there was another pond within the confines of the fort area because it is shown on the old tithe map of 1838 and later in the 19th century another pond was dug at the edge of the common. I only mention these to show that there was an unusually good supply of water for a site so near the edge of the plateau.

The strategic position

Because of Cholesbury's situation dominating one of the main bastions of the thickly populated escarpment above the Icknield Way. it is quite inconceivable that the local chiefs would have omitted to fortify the obvious central eminence, especially as the paramount chieftains of the middle Bronze Age had for many years been established on Salisbury plain to the south west of our area and in what came to be known later as East Anglia to the north east. Connecting the two, was the great highway running just below our villages over the escarpment and the power and prosperity of these chieftains is shown by the traffic which was building up along this highway in fashionable amber from the Baltic, gold plates, jet and beads from Egypt—particularly the pretty blue beads which their careless women folk fortunately scattered all over the place for us to dig up—together with necklaces and general ornaments. These, the first actual foreign imports known to have reached this country, were being exchanged for surplus foodstuffs, dogs which were being bred in the Chilterns for export, and to a lesser extent, riding horses. No draught horses had yet been produced of sufficient calibre and weight to compete with the oxen. Convoys would of course need heavily armed guards as they passed through the denser woodland and paid tribute at the staging posts along the escarpment and by this time a fully clad warrior must have been rather a splendid sight especially if he were tall and stalwart like the fellow buried in the Bush Barrow at Normanton. He had a very efficient looking axe, two massive daggers one of which had a hilt sparkling with gold inlay and gems and was hooked on to his belt by a finely chased gold plate. In fact his dress was spattered with gold plates and he carried as a badge of rank a curious sceptre with a stone head and elaborately cut bone mount.

To defend this highway, the earlier inhabitants must have been set to work building a chain of rudimentary forts and, whatever the course of events was that determined that a fortified settlement was to be established at Cholesbury, a glance at the map will show you that it is a magnificently central spot from which to control the whole of our little peninsula of Chiltern hills and hence the stretch of the Icknield Way beyond it. And when the powers that be found a water supply without even the necessity for digging a well and hauling it up—who can wonder at the choice? In their key positions our escarpment villages would be enjoying a reasonably high state of civilization at a time when all the present large towns like High Wycombe, Chesham, Aylesbury and others were, at most, small clearings in the hinterland forests, probably visited by the good people of Cholesbury in their longer hunting expeditions. Indeed, though the Thames Valley becomes an even denser area of early civilization there were relatively few settlements at this time in the hinterland between the Thames and our own ridge.

Notes and References

[1] J. F. Head, *Early Man in South Buckinghamshire* (Bristol 1955), Ch.VII.

[2] J. F. Head, op. cit. p.42.

[3] The Cholesbury excavation took place from 16 May to 17 June 1932. It was run by Mr. G. Day Kimball, advised by Sir James Berry, the mineralogic finds being sent to Dr. H. H. Thomas of the Geological Survey for examination and the ceramics to Professor C. Hawkes. In the short time available six trenches were dug in the 'Triangle' between the outer and middle ditches, and inside the fort an exploratory trench right across the middle with several shorter trenches in other parts of the interior. In addition several hearths were uncovered. The depth reached was 20 inches where 'the undisturbed reddish "brick" clay which underlies all the neighbourhood was reached'. In the opinion of the Excavators this was an 'unmistakable natural clay floor'. The total area uncovered was only 2,275 sq. ft in an area of over 9 acres — about 0.5%, clearly an inadequate sample. Professor Hawkes analysed the finds as:

Pre-Belgic	15
Belgic (Native)	8
Early Romano-British	6
Imported Roman, late Romano-British or Saxon	0
Mediaeval	14

The high proportion of pre-Belgic finds points towards a flourishing Bronze Age community. Notes are from an article by G. Day Kimball, 'Cholesbury Camp' *The Journal of the British Arch. Assn., Vol. 39, 1933, pp187-212. Quotations of Professor Hawkes' opinions are from the same source.*

[4] J. F. Head, op. cit. p.51.

[5] V.C.H. Vol.I, p.181.

[6] J. F. Head, op. cit. p.60.

[7] J. F. Head op. cit. and C. and J. Hawkes, *Prehistoric Britain* (Penguin Books 1952) Ch. 3.

V   .

THE FORTS ARE BUILT

Life in Bronze Age Cholesbury—from about 1500 BC

A Bronze Age fort; domestic life evolves; agriculture; local craftsmen; the huts; dress; farmhouses.

The Cholesbury Fort

Though some of the hill forts are of Stone Age origin and others as late as Iron Age, there is reasonable unanimity among the experts that the vast majority of them were built in the Bronze Age, the second millennium BC. The earliest forts would have been no more than a small fence around the huts. This would be followed, as time and labour allowed, by a deep ditch and vallum (or rampart) on top of which they could put their fence of sharpened stakes cut from resistant oak or elm if they were good workmen—or local pine which was resinous and plentiful in those days, if they were in a hurry. The latter would be softer and easier to fell and shape.

You can still take a walk round and see just what it looks like because it hasn't changed very much since it was built—earth ramparts are pretty solid though, of course, the wooden fencing long ago disappeared. On the more important sites like Berkhamsted it was replaced by stone and brick walls—the Normans saw to that; but as soon as the Icknield Way ceased to have any great significance Cholesbury subsided into obscurity and later inhabitants cut through one of the entrances to make a path to the church that was set up inside the fort in Saxon days. At a later date medieval 'gentlemen' like John Baldwin were to level the southern part of the vallum to build the Manor House. But the whole of the remainder is still there for you to see any time you are passing through this way to London. The ramparts are now, of course, covered with beech trees and the interior is fields, except for the churchyard. Lipscombe, the 19th century county historian has a long piece about it[1] but I think we can skip that because one earth rampart is just like another basically.

27

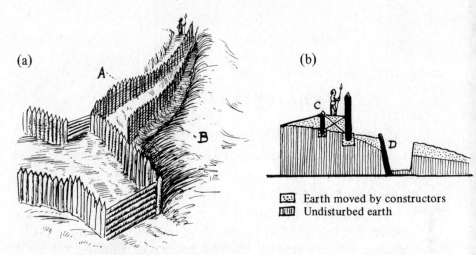

Fig. 4 (a) Cholesbury Fort main entrance – double gate – as it probably was during the later Bronze or early Iron Ages.
(b) Section through A to B on Fig. 4 (a)

Notice: C. Main palisade posts tied by cross members to subsidiary row of posts beneath the fighting platform.
D. Inner wall of ditch lined with stout trunks to prevent subsidence.

The important thing is that there were two entrances (see Fig.4, above) which would be heavily defended by flanking walls making the entrants weave to left and right before getting to the main gate of great tree trunks slotted between double posts on either side. I am fascinated by the defensive theories of the Bronze Age engineers—Vauban himself was hardly able to improve on them—it was the summit of pre-Roman engineering from which the Italian sappers learned a good deal. But we are writing about the village so I must contain myself. I had better say that the fort covers about ten acres and lies north-east—south-west, in the form of a rectangle with rounded corners. It follows the contours of the eminence and so is classified by the Archaeological Conference as a B class hill fort—or contour fort. That is, one which is not entirely dependent upon the slope of the hill for defensive effect. These forts are sited where the natural position has been strengthened by artificial earthworks and stone or wooden fences and buildings. The ditches are very deep. They are still about 20 feet and would obviously have been much deeper before the frost and weather got to work several thousand years ago to fill them in. Before you read the full descriptions in the county histories, two things should be said. Firstly, Lipscombe ascribes its origin to the Danes—over two thousand years later.[2] We can forget this mental aberration on the part of an otherwise very useful historian writing well before any excavation had established beyond any doubt its pre-Roman origin and obviously not knowing much about Danish military engineering. Secondly the Rev. Hastings Kelke[3] in the first half of the 19th century claims to have found traces of four entrances. I think by this time it is anybody's guess and it doesn't really matter.

What I find much more exciting is the vicissitudes of its subsequent history. During the time from about 700 BC until the final Roman conquest, the Iron Age people from Hallstatt and La Tène would have improved and added to the fortifications but it would probably be difficult to see much difference from the outside. Then during the *Pax Romana* it would have been allowed to fall into disrepair and the rampart and fences would have been replaced by flimsier ones to keep cattle in and wolves out. The wheel would have come full circle. However, the old fort would have another lease of life and usefulness when the Romans left. With the policeman gone the villagers had to re-learn how to defend themselves. There was no King Arthur in the Chilterns and the Saxons were creeping up the estuaries and beginning to filter down the Icknield Way. Our villagers together with their neighbours along the ridgeway kept the English at bay for a further two hundred years, with forts like Cholesbury—in fact, until the great and last defeat at Aylesbury in 571, not bad going! After that it would have been dismantled again by the Saxon conquerors and has probably remained as a nice cosy enclosure for the fields that are still there today and for the churchyard and little church that the Saxons eventually built. But to return to the Bronze Age origins.

One can't help feeling that this age must have been one of great community effort in the building of these forts. A family can build a home or hunt or develop a farm; but it takes a very sustained and well organised community effort to build a series of walls and ditches round a ten acre encampment and to accommodate its complicated bits of military engineering.

From the time the first defences were put up, most of the villagers would probably have their huts inside the fortified area

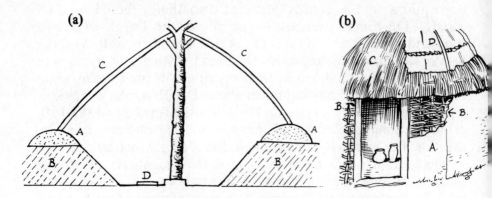

Fig. 5 (a) Section of Neolithic or Early Bronze Age Pit Dwelling
              A. Built up Earth
              B. Original ground
              C. Withies supporting thatch or turf
         (b) Middle and Later Bronze Age House, showing construction
              A. Mud covering of walls
              B. Wattle Walls
              C. Thatch
              D. Withies supporting thatch

but close proximity has its problems, especially when there are large numbers of cattle and sheep, as well as pigs, to fence off at night. So, gradually in the long spells when peaceful conditions prevailed the small holdings and larger farms would have left the shelter of the walls and spread as far away as the present Parrott's farm to the north; in the south they would be grouped round what is now the piece of common land. The layout can be seen from the 17th century map (p. 119). The bothies of the craftsmen, wheelwrights, turners, blacksmiths and carpenters tended to group round the entrance to the fort for the convenience of customers. The potter and the flint knapper would, of course, be away where their raw material was handy. All would be within easy reach of the fort in case it was necessary to take precautions on news of unfriendly comers or when called out by the local chief. 'Home Guard' practices would be the order of the day now and then.

Under these circumstances, the main part of the interior of the fort would have been cleared of domestic buildings so as to allow room for the increased herds of valuable cattle which had to be preserved very carefully during any military emergency.

Hawridge Fort

To turn for a moment to another of our four villages; this British encampment authenticated by Ditchfield and[4] mentioned later under the Iron Age civilization may well have been in existence during the Bronze Age like its neighbour above. But lacking any excavation or other evidence we are at present unable to express an opinion. From an examination of the site I would be surprised if excavation did not reveal some settlement at this time.

Domestic village life evolves

Let us leave the military part of this establishment. We can perhaps envisage in passing, the wretched slaves clearing up all the rubbish after the weekly market and junketing. I will try to re-construct for you what the village would probably have looked like in the Bronze Age, with its ordinary round houses, the farm buildings and the craftmen's huts, and we can refresh our memories as to how the villagers of that time were living and enjoying themselves.

Cholesbury, at this period, would be basically a self sufficient agricultural community, enlivened and made more gracious by the growing efficiency of trade made possible by the local industries and by organised hunting.

You remember the general plan, as might have been seen from the ramparts of the fort, the area of small rectangular fields to the north where Parrott's farm now is; another similar area to the south west from where Home Farm now is, over to what used to be Ray's Common and the piece of open land fringed by deep woods, much where the present day Common lies. The latter part of the age may have seen one or two more prosperous farms just over the brow of the hill or in the woodland clearing to the north east of the present common where more good land might have been fenced in after the coming of the new wooden ploughs that were beginning to make their appearance from the continent. In fact, I think you will agree that the introduction of oxen instead of women, to draw the plough was one of the most important domestic revolutions of the Bronze Age. This two-ox, man steered wooden plough—the first ever seen in the Chilterns—transformed crop raising from pick and shovel horticulture in the back garden into a great industry that absorbed as many acres as were available,

Fig. 6 A two ox wooden plough used in Somerset until 150 years ago

seeing how long it would take to fell the trees and dig out the roots. Once the ground had been prepared, the new methods together with an improved kind of corn soon produced considerably heavier yields per acre. If you could have visited one of the larger farms you would have seen new storage pits being built about this time to keep the corn safe from rats and mice after it had been dried. A new pit had to be dug each year because the onset of mould had not yet been diagnosed and conquered. Until the coming of the Belgae with their powerful eight-ox ploughs at the end of the last century BC, the fields remained rectangular and very small, rather like the Cornish ones in our own century. This has become known as the Celtic field system to distinguish it from the strip system of long narrow fields favoured by the Belgae and the Anglo-Saxon farmers because of the difficulty of turning their larger ploughs.

There was no need to mark the boundaries by fences because the plough tends, over the years, to work the soil towards the lower side of each field until there is a high ridge and ditch between each. Similarly at the headland ends, the mere process of turning the plough casts up the earth into standing balks.

I have seen one of these Bronze Age type ploughs many times in Kurdistan, where the ground is stony and the likelihood of disturbance by raiding tribesmen so great that deep cultivation is hardly wise. (See fig. 7.) you notice it can't turn a sod as it has no coulter or disc—only a long straight share like a scuffle which two oxen can pull through heavier ground than a man's wife used to be able to cope with.

Fig. 7 Light two ox wooden plough, similar to the Bronze Age plough, still being used on stony soil in Kurdistan in 1935

However, taking the village as a whole, the primary interest was still in stock breeding. The curious thing is that now communities were anchored to one spot by the permanency of the ploughed lands and could not wander on to a new pasturage area when the old one got used up, the pressure on permanent village pastures multiplied alarmingly. In most places, and I imagine this would have been done in our own village, the inhabitants solved the problem by opening up what we would call 'ranches'—I envisage ours on the north-east side of the fort. A plough would probably have been run round the perimeter to form a marker ditch. This is cold land and not much use for cropping, and anyone with a little stock would be allowed to use it provided he took his turn patrolling the ditch and dealing with the scrub growth.

Once a year the custom gradually grew up of a gathering of nearby villagers for the sheep shearing. It was found to be quicker and more efficient to organise a co-operative effort but in due course the attendant jollifications were probably the prime motive for its continuance. Later would come a great salting down for the winter when the breeding animals had been selected for corralling in the thorn kraals round the larger houses. Short horns were the most popular breed, but towards the end of the period long haired mountain cattle from the north were being bred and doing rather well.

Sheep were the great standby, for obvious reasons, and not the least, a couple of boys could look after a large herd with a dog and small sling shot. It looked much easier than the business of agriculture, which demanded a relatively large labour force to deal with a small number of fields even though the new idea from Harlshof in the Shetlands of ploughing cattle droppings into the soil had improved the output and made use of waste products.

By 900 or 800 BC, before the first of the Celtic peoples began to arrive, our villages in concert with others along the southern chalk hills would have begun to breed their own shaggy little ponies. They were very sure-footed and could carry a sixteen-stone man all day, though they only stood some thirteen hands. Very soon these 'Shetland' type animals were being exported to the continent as being different from the breeds available there. Their size, of course, still precluded their use as draught animals either for the plough or the great heavy clumsy carts then used. Later they were crossed with some of the continental breeds and developed into a more powerful animal.

Even the dogs were being sorted out again in the larger farms. Originally, selection for breeding had centred on those animals best suited for retrieving game or standing up to wolves in winter attacks. About this time one notices a tendency to develop a herding animal who could save a great deal of time, when trained, in the open pasturages where pigs were kept, especially in the new clearings on the south-west of the fort, where the woods in the little valley have almost been eliminated over the years. This meant that a couple of boys could keep an eye on everybody's pigs during the summer and in the winter each pig lived with its owner in the hut—all very cosy! Only the very wealthy farmers would have thatched pig houses.

The bothies of the craftsmen would, as already mentioned in the preceding chapter, be grouped mostly round the entrance way into the fort, but some such as the turner who was just beginning to use a pole lathe (as he still does in the woods round High

Wycombe today), would be well away in the woods.

It is interesting to speculate at what period nests of sycamore bowls would be made. Sycamore, thorn and holly wood is especially suitable for kitchenware as the more you scrub it the whiter it gets. Whether or not he was turning out domestic plates and bowls by that time the turner would certainly be working with a wooden chuck and a plank treadle which revolved the post or bowl while he used chisel and gouge. The long weighted ash pole hinged near the thin end above the stock would revolve the pole backwards again ready for the next stroke. His trouble would have been that the bronze chisels and gouges would have required constant sharpening, as the metal does not keep its edge. He would build himself an open shelter for the summer and probably revert to other work during the winter. There also, we would find the charcoal burner turfing up his pyramid of saplings ready for a slow burn. The potter, if the village was lucky enough to retain one, worked on a fixed bench with no wheel and by this time he was indeed beginning to feel the competition of the new fangled sheet metal cooking pots and buckets that the bronze founder was beginning to turn out on continental models for the more wealthy.

Fig. 8 Typical late Bronze Age cauldron and bucket as used in Cholesbury during the period.

But the potter would be kept pretty busy, as it was all too easy in the dark recesses of an unlit mud hut for the housewife to stumble over the earthenware pots and break them. This would mean she would have to find a domestic hen or piece of salted meat to pay for another.

The carpenter had by now made himself socketed gouges and chisels to add to his age old hammers, tracers and punches. He would still be cutting large logs by burning them through and chopping the charred ends square. He lacked an efficient saw, and the soft bronze ones didn't keep their cutting edge anything like as well as the flint ones.

There would probably be a copper smelting courtyard, and the craftsman might have come down the road on a winter's night with a flint arrow head in his back and perhaps one of the women got it out and cauterised the wound so that he recovered. By that time he would have become part of the furniture and taken a local woman, so that he didn't feel like packing up his tools and copper pigs again. That would be lucky, because this fellow might have come up the Danube with a new process in his head called 'the lost wax'. He made a model of a pot or figure or ornament in beeswax from the hives, and then coated it with a thick layer of clay. This was put in the oven and baked hard, by that time, of course, the wax ran out and when the mould was cool the molten bronze could be poured in to set hard in a perfect image. He sometimes trained assistants to mass produce sickles, axeheads, spears and farm implements—especially wheel naves and fastenings. In his spare time he would make a supply of double-edged razors and mirror backs for the young men when they got back from hunting.

It must be remembered, that a great deal of his time was still spent on the less spectacular chores such as sheets of metal to be riveted together to make cooking pots and large wood buckets, for which there was a good sale in the Low Countries where there was a shortage of ore; most of ours would come from Ireland and the west, as well as the tin to mix with it. You would also see some of his work on the walls of the larger farms in the shape of ornamental shields which could now be made larger and stronger than the wooden round bossed ones of the ordinary fighting men. These could be made to look rather good in the home where the women slaves would keep them polished.

The two-post loom was beginning to come into use towards the end of the Bronze Age, probably only in the larger farmhouses, and plots of flax were being grown to supplement the spun wool fibres. This could be grown in the more exposed sites and we have, indeed, found a number of spindle whorls in the area.

Back in the village the ordinary round huts remained virtually unchanged, with their earth floors, central firestones, wattle and daub walls and thatched or turfed roofs. One of the larger farms would probably have stood where Home Farm is now, on the edge of the steep little valley. This would be near enough the fort to be able to dispense with palisades and so could be sited on the sunny side among its own series of quarter-acre fields. There would be a rectangular farmyard round the outside, with a ditch on the down side and a strong thorn fence round the remainder. Inside, rather like a small edition of the fort, would stand the round huts of the labourers and the slaves—there wasn't really much difference except that the slaves were better cared for, being valuable property—and circular barns for the sick cattle and implements. The sheep and a small herd of short horns would be squattering about in the yard mud as they had to be brought in at night. In the two round barns we would find the querns for grinding the barley and corn, and the thrashing floor for continued spells of wet weather. There would be a dairy in the far corner where some of the milk would be turned into butter and some into cheese, and another hut where the hides were skinned and prepared roughly and where the fleeces could be stored until they were woven by the farm women or sent in the one precious ox cart to the Ivinghoe merchants for export or local sale—foreign pottery, ore and ornaments being brought back in exchange.

You will see from the illustrations that the farmer and his wife are both by now wearing quite colourful dresses. He is wearing a rather jaunty knitted woollen cap and a long woven cloak with a knee length kirtle held up by a woollen or leather belt. The wife has an outdoor cloak and underneath, a short-sleeved and rather fashionable jacket in blue cloth which she has made herself. In winter she wears one or two long woollen dresses tied up at the waist and opening at the neck when indoors sitting over the hot hearth, cooking. A goatskin overjacket would be hung up inside the porch against the really bad weather when she had to see to

Fig. 9 Some Bronze Age costumes

the proper milking of the goats or help with the lambing. In
summer she would wear a simple corded fringed skirt and leggings
against the brambles. Shoes were still nothing more than tough
hide with an inner lining, and long leather thongs round the edges
would be gathered up and tied round the ankles. I hate to think
what they would be like in wet weather! As to jewellery, if there
was some sort of fiesta in the air after the day's work was done, it
might be difficult to diagnose for certain just what she would be
wearing. If there was wealth somewhere in the family, she might
have those lovely great gold twirls or torques in glistening spirals
of four flanged rods and, maybe, inset with precious stones that
were coming up the caravan trackways from the Near East. Not
this farmer's wife I think, but you might well be completely
fooled because, as we have mentioned, some Sumerian and
Egyptian citizens had been playing about with their chemistry sets
about 1,000 years earlier and discovered that alkaline silicates
could be fused very much like metals.[5] Also they knew how to
make ornaments by heating silica (sand) and mixing it with potash
(burnt wood) or natron which is a metal found in the desert. They
could make glass which could be melted and cast or spun and they

introduced the art of colouring it in the process. The imitation jewellery industry had been launched.

By the end of the Bronze Age we would also find in the larger houses imitation glass beads and 'faience' which were being imported, probably via the Phoenicians from Spain, in exchange for native tin, hides and wool; obviously traditional things to flog to natives of undeveloped countries as a couple of thousand years later, you will remember, those same 'natives' were happily using the same sort of baubles to get what they wanted from similarly placed inhabitants of the East Indies and other undeveloped colonies. But in our Bronze Age villages these decorative colourful bits of jewellery must have brought immense satisfaction to the womenfolk on festive occasions. Even their gold bangles were not always what they appeared to be, because, as we know from diggings, the bronze founder had early discovered that he could beat out a thin sheet of gold and work this round a heavy bronze ring so that to the neighbours it would appear as heavy solid gold.

The farmhouses of this time would be oval and larger than the round huts by 10 feet or more, say about 28 feet by 20 feet. The interesting thing is that the floor might by this time be above ground level by about six inches, which saved having to dig a ditch round the outside for wet weather. Nineteen posts would have been sunk two feet in the ground round the edge and linked together with cross branches bound on for a wall plate. It was really rather ingenious, because as there were obviously not enough posts with forked tops at the time of building, many were often turned upside down and the roots used as crutches for the cross members. There were generally four main king posts down the middle to hold the ridge pole. This was duplicated just above head height and strongly strutted out to the wall plate all round to hold the strain of the weight of the roof, and incidentally these poles made very useful rafters to hang skins or cloth on to curtain off various parts of the room as necessary.

On top there would be nice warm straw thatching, weighted down with flints and bound on with withies. It was only five foot to the eaves inside—but that was generally enough as they were very short folk in those days. Virtually all the wall space was taken up anyway by the shelves and beds. The walls were what we would call wattle, that is, split nut twigs woven across between a number

of subsidiary posts just driven lightly into the ground and taking
no wall weight. Then both sides would have been plastered with
good old Chiltern mud—which sticks like a limpet and only needs
patching once a year with any luck—warm but a bit buggy. The
floors of these wealthier farmhouses were interesting. They were
mud, of course, but unusually hard and even. They could be swept
and even in some places, polished. I think they achieved it by
mixing the mud with ox blood with makes a surface almost like
marble. It was still being done on the west coast when I was a boy.

There were two fire hearths, one towards each end. I expect
they cooked on one, and there would be shelves in the alcove for
the earthenware and copper pots, while the buckets and scoops
would be hung up beside them. Sometimes the great bronze
cauldron, a sign of real wealth, was hung on the pot hook for a
stew, while vegetables were cooked in the ashes as the laddies do
round the bonfire on festival nights. The stones would be swept
clear after a hot fire and the bread baked on them—a sort of
unleavened chapati made in flat rounds and well beaten out
between the hands first.

The oats being used by now had developed considerably in both
quality and yield from the original wild oat that had been
collected, resown and developed by the Early Stone Age men.
There would still be a stone slab with a wooden plank on it for all
the domestic butchery and the preparation of food that would be
back breaking if done on the floor. Along shelves on the wall
would stand jars for the mead, a favourite drink made from honey,
and sometimes home-made wine from the wild berries that the
children would bring in. This would drive away the cold and damp
of winter evenings.

The second fire hearth at the other end would be for general
warmth and the family and guests would all sit round on the floor.
There was virtually no furniture yet, that is no tables or chairs as
we know them; everything would be done sitting flat on the floor
just as in India or parts of Africa today. In fact if you want to see
what Cholesbury and the other villages would be like in the
Bronze Age you have only to look at a Yoraba village or a Kurdish
hill khan in the mountains of Luristan. The chimneys are still just
holes in the roof with a flat stone to keep the rain out, and the
sleeping bunks are ledges along the walls like a ship. These would

be lined with a layer of springy birch twigs with soft dried grass
and skins as a mattress—very cosy on a cold night when the pig
skins are tied closely over the window openings and the fat dips
gutter in the sheltered alcoves as the east wind whistles up under
the thatch with a feel of snow in its teeth. But that won't be often
because there wasn't much night life. Everybody went to bed
when it got dark most nights to save burning the fat dips; now and
then the youngsters would play dice or pitch and toss for a short
time and, of course, when there were guests, or it was a feast day
for the local gods, there were torches of resin that looked
picturesque but made more smoke than light and needed slaves
standing by with some copper buckets of water near the thatch,
just in case. However, it must have looked quite cosy with the
light flashing from the polished surfaces of the copper shields and
other gear hung up on the beams.

There might be an alcove for spinning and for the big two-post
loom with its turned whorls and stone weights, but I think in this
establishment, the goodwife might have put her foot down and
relegated them to one of the round barns where there was also a
fireplace for winter nights. There would probably be game hanging
up in the black depths of the smoky rafters and a lot of mutton
getting partially cured and being given a taste. It would have to be
well out of the way of the dogs. They were as large as wolves, and
woe betide the stranger approaching the farm during the night
unannounced; they had been taught to hunt in complete silence
and he would know nothing until a great shape dropped on him
out of the blackness of the night, with teeth bared.

There was often a fascinating little shelf above the double bed,
which would be the wife's make-up shelf. It was much simpler
than her sisters' of the Mediterranean lands but she had an iron-
handled copper mirror, bronze tweezers for plucking eyebrows
and, of course, the pots of rouge, in widespread use all over the
southern part of the country and a black substance like stibium
for darkening the eyebrows and eyelids—all a little wasted, one
would imagine, on the hairy types peering into the smoky murk of
the home fires and might look a little overdone in the glare of the
noonday sun when it condescended to shine in that wet climate.
She had a wardrobe too, of soft leather clothes as well as her
brightly coloured woven flax garments, mostly longer than the

kilts of the men, with goat and bearskins handy for outdoor wear in really bad weather—you can just imagine her pushing her little pink, rouged cheeks through the head hole and pottering out into a quagmire of a thunderstorm cursing, while it all washed off.

She also kept the fire-making equipment there; the wooden tray with the flint and the piece of iron pyrites to make the spark which could then be dropped on to dry leaves and blown up—a sort of Bronze Age tinder box and forerunner of steel and flint. Indeed, there is not much new under the moon; women often used woven pads to form the basis of a 'bird's nest' or elevated hair style. The hair was brought over the top and worked into a pyramid; I expect it made a change from the usual plaits hanging down or done in a bun or the simple but popular 'windswept' style with a woven band to keep at least some of the hair in place.

I think this part of the Bronze Age development is perhaps the most exciting and fascinating aspect of our own village history because it concerns so directly the human story and that is the thing we are really interested in. We are still in the infancy of our ultimate knowledge of how people lived, but the few facts we have do tell us what they looked like, what their amusements were and what life might have been like for us if we had by chance been born and raised in our own villages 3,000 years ago. Perhaps before leaving the farm life, I should mention that archaeologists have come to the conclusion that the cropping from an acre at this time was of the order of ten bushels, that is about a third of the modern yield, but still very considerably more than the yield achieved under the early Bronze Age 'man-push-woman-pull' system. The fascinating fact is that the Bronze Age boffins had discovered that wet grain gives off a kind of gas (carbon dioxide we call it in the 20th century) which effectively kills all kinds of things that rot the grain if it is left wet, i.e. what we now call bacteria. So they came to divide the grain into two portions. All the main crop required for grinding into flour during the winter was dried in the sun or in ovens, but the portion needed for next year's crop was left a little wet ready for germination. They knew that dry grain would not germinate and so would keep well but they also discovered that about 75% of wet grain stored in these underground chambers, already referred to, would germinate quite happily at the next year's sowing.

I have said nothing about burial grounds. I don't know where they were in our villages as we haven't found them yet. There were plenty in the surrounding countryside, both inhumation and the popular modern cremation which accounts for the pygmy cups dug up. They provide us with much of our information about the life of our Bronze Age ancestors because their belief in some sort of life after death had not only taken a lot of the sting out of death itself but has left us with a grand store of domestic items, ornaments, weapons and food. These were put in the graves to assist the departed on the journey to the happy hunting grounds but they tell us a great deal about the life and the craft development. As it doesn't really affect the local picture of our village, I will not go into the methods of disposing of the dead, except that I must mention one rather charming detail that gives a very human insight into the very close relationships that had certainly developed by this time.

In graves, not too far from Cholesbury, a man and wife were buried together. Now even if this means an early Bronze Age version of suttee or wife sacrifice, it certainly points to a very real belief in the continuance of marriage after death. And there are some quite touching examples of burials where the couple were laid face to face, in the attitude of affectionate embrace. When there was the death of a tiny child at the same time, it was, as often as not, placed just at its mother's back so that she could carry it best on the last long journey, in a net, as she had been used to carrying her children in her days at home in the Chiltern Hill villages. This is the first exciting and human evidence of the intimate life and thinking of our village ancestors—a mental bridge across 3,000 years of man's coming and going.

I am afraid we must tear ourselves away from Bronze Age Cholesbury and its neighbours or we shall never have time to investigate the other periods of history that tread lightly across this land of ours. I hope the village has at least become something tangible, with a soul and a promise of the future. The villager has, at last, become a man of property and his family is already part of a clan with some of the attributes of gracious living, if only for the well-to-do. But the day of the 'common man' is dawning; the coming of the 'wizard smiths' and the smelting of the universal, easily obtained iron was to give him the comforts and power that copper and tin ore from distant parts had given to his masters. But for all that, we shall not be far wrong if we envisage our Bronze Age villagers living a life very similar to that of the Homeric Greeks, with more than the breath of a new culture.

Notes and References

[1]G. Lipscomb, *The History and Antiquities of the County of Buckinghamshire* (hereafter referred to as Lipscomb) (1847) Vol.III, p.314.

[2]Lipscomb, Vol.III, p.315.

[3]V.C.H., Vol.II, p.24.

[4]P. H. Ditchfield, *The Counties of England (Buckinghamshire)* (George Allen & Co. 1912) p.369.

[5]G. Child, *What Happened in History,* (Penguin Books 1952) p.180.

VI

IRON IMPLEMENTS BRING PROSPERITY
TO THE VILLAGES 700 BC–AD 43

The Iron Age invaders–the Celts; Hawridge fort; Iron Age finds in Cholesbury;
evidence from other nearby settlements; coins; Iron Age life.

We have seen the Bronze Age set the pattern for what later became known as the 'English countryside', a land of enclosed fields and little hamlets. At that time they lay uncertainly along the chalk ridges and in scattered clearings in the shadow of the great forests that threatened to reach out and re-absorb them at the slightest provocation. The quickest way of getting the picture is to think of Britain at that time as an impenetrable mass of uninhabitable boggy woodland, with the few inhabitable areas linked by well worn but unsurfaced trackways. These could almost be counted on the fingers of one hand; the mountainous areas where trees wouldn't grow, the marsh and fen lands where movement was possible only by water and the chalk ridges of the North and South Downs, the Cotswolds and our own Chiltern hills along which ran the Icknield way linking east and west.

The most important thing about the changes induced by the arrival of various groups of people from the continent was that these were very gradual. Indeed, at the time it would have been difficult to pinpoint any specific date at which anything on a national scale happened. There was no invasion as such; little groups of continentals came across from time to time and settled peacefully or by force of arms in a few villages at a time, and the tribal loyalties and ownership of properties changed piecemeal over a great many years from about 700 BC until some time after the eventual Roman occupation of AD 43. The interest to us is that we have found, by excavation or chance, sufficient material evidence of all periods of the Iron Age to be able to say for certain that there was continuous occupation of our villages during the whole of this period.

General Population Movements from the Continent

Before setting down the Iron Age finds in our village area it would be as well to recall the chief events in the country as whole, and the chronological sequence, relative length, and approximate dates of the cultural periods to which reference will be made.

The Iron Age is really the story of the Celts, the tall, light-haired warriors and 'wizard smiths' who, like the Saxons a thousand years later, overran much of the continent and Britain, imposing themselves as an aristocracy on the resident mixed inhabitants of the preceding period. In the end the races mixed so completely that it is quite impossible to tell in what proportions they arrived. They were obviously very thin on the ground in Wales, Cornwall and the Highlands of Scotland, where the colouring is still mainly Iberian. The proportion was probably higher in the richer south and east of Britain, which includes our villages, and we still know very little about their economic and cultural relations with the natives. Their great contribution was their knowledge of mining and the working of iron ore which had a revolutionary effect upon the social life. Ore was cheap and easy to obtain locally in most districts and so brought effective weapons and agricultural implements within the range of the average villager. No longer were these things the province of the wealthy as when the copper had to be brought all the way from the remote mines of Wales and Cornwall or Ireland. Later, the Roman way of life with its luxury and sophisticated architecture and domestic comfort was to seep across the channel with merchants and returned soldiers serving as auxiliaries in the Roman army long before Caesar made his first abortive raid 55 years before the end of the last century BC.

The main groups of invaders in this last Celtic era are generally distinguished in history books under three headings:-

The Goidels (or Gaels), who are still found in Ireland and Scotland. They arrived in about the 6th or 7th centuries BC.

The Brythons (later referred to as Britains) who predominated from then down to about 100 or 50 years BC.

The Belgae (related to the Gauls) who continued to arrive after the Roman invasion. They really made things hum and revolutionised agriculture with their massive eight oxen ploughs.

However, at the risk of sounding like *'1066 and All That'* I had better say that these gentlemen are now more often referred to by the places they came from, the first as Hallstatt people and the later groups as La Tène I, II, and III civilisations.

The first group seems to have left little trace in our villages, and it may be a fair assumption that our predecessors heard many rumours and perhaps watched warily as strange tall men of a new Alpine physique passed down the Icknield Way in carefully contained armed bands intent on peaceful penetration if possible. They spoke a strange Celtic language and probably looked askance at the wild tangle of Chiltern hill country and disappeared beyond the woods to the west. The Brythons and their cousins the Belgae certainly took over the fort and the villages and left their stamp on the surrounding countryside as their tools and domestic crockery have been found in the fort and its environs. It is probable that our Bronze Age villagers were left in peace, or kept in suspense, for a long time because we must remember that we are about in the centre of Britain and would have been one of the last areas to be absorbed by any newcomers.

Local Evidence

As I have said, we still need much more detailed excavation not only of the forts but of the village areas and local earthworks like Grim's Ditch which runs through the woods just north of our villages and has never, to my knowledge, been cut into. We know it was not of Roman origin and that it was there when the Saxons arrived, because they looked at it in awe and promptly named it the work of the Devil (Grim); apart from that it was not the sort of thing they favoured either as a fortification or á boundary, especially in a heavily wooded tract. It looks to me much more like a Belgic construction to strengthen the line of forts behind the escarpment above the main traffic way along which any invader would arrive. Only knowledgeable excavation will tell us when it was actually constructed.

There is another curiosity I might mention in passing—the earthworks at Hawridge Court. They are generally written off by those to whom I have talked, as relatively modern, i.e. medieval moat works round the earlier house. They have not yet been excavated and, indeed, Mr Head could not help me to date them. I still cannot believe they were merely a ditch surrounding a house.

Where they have not been levelled to provide ingress, they are still about 15 feet deep and would have been much deeper before the weather and leaves partially filled them up. Furthermore, they do not look medieval in construction. There is a high revetment or retaining wall on the inside of the ditch which would have been only an incubus to domestic living and defence but is typically Belgic in conception and would have had a wooden palisade and sentry walk along the top. I would have kept my feelings modestly to myself had I not by chance recently found that the Rev. Ditchfield F.S.A. an eminent historian in the early parts of this century, when he was Rector of Barkham in Berkshire, lists earthwork in his History of Buckinghamshire firmly as a British Camp along with Cholesbury.[1] I have been unable to trace his notes so I do not know upon what grounds he came to this conclusion.

Knowing that at this time the interior of the Buckinghamshire plateau was in all probability still fairly heavily wooded, it is easy to think of this fortification as an outlier of Cholesbury, for it is a relatively small affair, but I feel fairly sure there was little or no communication in a direct north west and south east line between the two forts. I would suggest, even at this time that the settlement of Hawridge, such as it was, ran north east to the other fort established near the present Marlin Chapel Farm. As you will see in later chapters, my wife has found evidence to suggest that the medieval village ran in this direction to what is now Heath End where the old parsonage still is. There is indeed no house on the present road to Cholesbury older than early Tudor. This is about the time that the main areas of scrub and woodland were finally cleared, though much remained well into the 18th century, to the great relief of outlaws and hunted men.

Turning to our actual evidence, the most important source is the excavation by G. Day Kimball of the earthworks and enclosure of our Cholesbury Fort, and the assessment of findings by Professor Hawkes. The pottery and domestic implements found established evidence of Pre-Belgic occupation of the central area because a 'coarse degenerate ware of the Early Iron Age' was mixed with the pottery of the Belgic period in that area. Professor Hawkes equates the Belgic occupation with the period of the rule of Cassivellaunus, of whom we shall hear more in the Roman period.[2]

These potteries (Fig. 10) were, according to Mr Head, part of a later Wessex culture known from the situation in Wiltshire as 'All Cannings Cross' and indicating that the potters arrived in the Icknield Way villages about 300 BC. Adjacent sites have been dealt with in papers by Miss K. M. Richardson and Mrs Allison Young[3] and by Mr Head and Mrs C. M. Piggot[4]. Numerous surface finds have been made in or adjacent to our villages, including contemporary Iron Age hooks, spindle whorls, and fragments of farm and domestic implements.

A Middle Iron Age urn was unearthed in a badger's set above a spinney 450 yards north of Sir Alan Barlow's residence in the Wendover valley. On the north side of the villages, Belgic pedestal urns were found at Aston Clinton, as well as a number of contemporary finds near Dundridge Farm in St. Leonards. Also at this site, which is about 600 feet up, an empty iron pot was found in the face of a quarry about 18 inches below the present ground level. More interesting still, this find was on the edge of a 'stepped smelting pit' about three feet in depth. There were traces of iron in the surrounding soil (iron-stone and sand indurated with iron

(a) (b)

Fig. 10   (a) Iron Age pot found at Dundridge Manor
(b) Iron Age pot found during excavation of the Cholesbury Fort
(Reconstructed from fragments – now in Aylesbury Museum)

oxide). Unfortunately for us, the owner, Mr Matthews, was apparently unable to prevent the whole invaluable site and contents from being destroyed by quarrying and it is now not possible to say whether the smelting pit and the Iron Age pot were contemporary or, indeed, connected with each other. We do know, again from Mr Matthews, that many other similar pots were found in previous years in similar circumstances.

In the later years of the period, coins were becoming quite numerous and almost entirely supplanted the awkward iron bar money or tokens of exchange. The original ones were copies of Greek coins and from the 2nd century BC their use on the continent and in Britain became general.

It is tempting to associate many existing names such as Cindery Wood and Cindery Bottom with iron workings, but this would be quite misleading as these local names grew up much later, and indeed, Mr Horace Brackley of St. Leonards has recently sent samples of the soil up for analysis. This has proved beyond doubt that the residual material is all of much later origin.[5] In any case, the word means originally 'remote situation' or 'assunder' and has nothing whatever to do with the modern word 'cinders.'

We have at present no further Iron Age finds from within the actual village boundaries, but fortunately the next of the adjacent forts along the escarpment to the north east on Ivinghoe Beacon has recently (1963—5) been excavated by Messrs. M. A. Cotton and D. S. Frere.[6] This fort has been established beyond all reasonable doubt as belonging to the same periods as our own Cholesbury fort. The finds may thus be safely used as typical of what we may expect to discover when it is possible to mount more extensive and thorough excavation of our own earthworks. Apart from similar Bronze and Iron Age implements which included fragments of pins, rivets, studs, tweezers, bars, armlets and a damaged razor, numerous chalk weights or spindle whorls were unearthed together with loom weights and part of a sandstone quern. Although, like the finds in the Cholesbury fort these are not closely dateable objects, they do bear out the evidence of Cholesbury in so far as they prove conclusively the continuing occupation of the site during the Bronze and Iron Age periods.

The earlier pottery was stated by Mrs Helen Waugh to have been of a period before the wheel came into use and the later Iron Age pottery, both fine and coarse wares, appears to have been wheel-made. The only complete vessel found in pit No.24 is referred to as a differentially fired haematite slip which she states is 'apart from the normal range of pottery of the period in the Chilterns.'

Much more interesting to us, because of the lack of sufficient evidence in the Cholesbury Fort excavations, is the analysis of bones from Ivinghoe Beacon by Mrs Betty Westley. This does give us a very useful indication of the type of farm animals being reared during this period and the main animals in the wild still available for hunting. Apart from human fragments, the domestic animals represented include dogs and cats. The horse remains indicate a small type of animal such as we have mentioned previously when dealing with the Bronze Age in our own villages. The pig remains are of typically domestic and rather small animals and appear to have been slaughtered before complete maturity. Mrs Westley notes that domestic pigs may have been left to fend for themselves in the woods and may, according to Zeuner, well have crossed with the wild boar, *sus crofa*. (*A History of Domesticated Animals*). Only one very large tusk, possibly of a wild boar was found. Remains of wild animals hunted locally include those of the red deer, the roe deer, foxes, hare, and vole and a few bears. Bones of frogs or toads were also discovered as one would expect.

The majority of the bone fragments were accounted for by cattle, 59% of total, and sheep/goat, 31% of total. The cattle remains are those typical of the Celtic ox already mentioned, with small, sturdy limbs. The sheep are typical of the small pre-historic horned breed resembling the present day Soay sheep. They were small-boned slender animals, and, as Mrs Westley points out, it was not possible in the rest of the material available to distinguish sheep from goat, though she adds that 'if goat is present it is likely to be sparsely represented.'

Many of the bones were gnawed, and the interesting thing is that the carcasses were apparently butchered much as at present. Again, about a quarter of the bones show evidence of immaturity and slaughter apparently took place about the second year. According to Mrs Westley, there were no 'baby' bones and so no evidence of autumn killing. This she ascribes to the fact that such delicate bones did not survive well.

Identification of Tribes in the Cholesbury Area

Future work on local sites will undoubtedly reveal a more accurate picture of tribal boundaries during this period. But for the moment we must rely mainly on the incidence and location of coins found in the vicinity.

We have already referred to the disappearance of the 'Iron Bar' tokens and in the later years of the Iron Age the coins which replaced them were becoming quite numerous. As might be expected, many have been found—a few within our boundaries and many more along the Icknield way. The early ones were copies of Greek coins of the 2nd century BC but the wealthier chieftains, though continuing to use barter for internal dealings, were beginning to mint their own coins on the spot with very rough designs, using the horse or wheatsheaf or merely crude versions of the herring bone and wreath, according to their respective tribal badges.

The distribution of these coin finds is a guide to the extent and influence of the various chiefs, though in our own village area the picture is blurred by the number of coins not only of adjacent tribes like the Icene but of other southern people trading along the Icknield way. These would be dropped in passage or lost in brushes with robbers and ambushes by local village bands. Our own four villages were in the territory dominated by the powerful Catuvellauni, whose headquarters were first at Wheathamstead, until their chief Cassivellaunus was defeated by Caesar with the help of a non Belgic tribe based on Colchester, after which the headquarters was moved to St Albans. You remember, (page 48) Professor Hawkes has equated some of the pottery found in the Cholesbury fort with the period of his occupation. There was an interim period, however, when the villages were taken over by the Trinovantes because by 15 BC we find coins of Tasciovanus (who finally drove them out of our area) minted at St Albans and marked VER (for Verulamium—the Roman name for the town.) So we know that the villages had a most unsettled period until Cassivellaunus' son Cunobelin (the authentic Cymbeline of Shakespeare) consolidated once again the kingdom of the Catuvellauni and so increased their hegemony in the south and over the fens sufficiently to style himself on his gold coinage 'Rex Brittonum' and to be so referred to by the Roman chroniclers.

Village Life in the Iron Age

It is now time to take a back look at the villages themselves and see what changes the Celts would have been likely to have made in their appearance and way of life. We might first consider the fort itself. We do not know whether it was permanently garrisoned or merely used as a refuge in emergency and a cattle corral in times of relative peace. We can assume that there was little change in its general shape and extent for we find no obvious signs in the earth-works except a possible elaboration of the defences at the part round the main gateway. Like the others in the chain, it would have been refortified after the long period of Bronze Age peace. It would, for instance, have been very busy during the tribal battles mentioned above.

The interesting thought is that this would have entailed quite a considerable change to the surrounding landscape because, after deepening the moat and repairing the ravages of the wind and weather, the first job would have been to replace the wooden palisades round the top of the revetments. The normal method was to cut and drive in a row of sharpened stakes, and by stakes we mean good medium sized tree trunks, all round the outer edge of the high bank. Then another row was mounted right round the inner edge of the high bank. They were finally braced together by cross members and the whole of the gap between both rows was filled with clay and rubble. In the larger forts a defender's platform was then run round the inside to form a fighting platform. The gateway was at right angles to the main earthworks and, as you can still see, was further strengthened by arms of inturned barbicans and claw like mounds and palisades so that the attacker was made to approach by weaving from left to right between high walls before arriving at the actual gate with its double rows of horizontal logs dropped between stout uprights. During this process he was open to a wide field of fire from the defenders.

The consensus of opinion among the experts is that a medium fort the size of Cholesbury would need between 10 and 15,000 trees felled to achieve this and that is what I mean when I say that the area of woodland felled and, presumably cleared for agriculture in the process would be quite intensive.

Outside the fort itself we would expect to find certain changes in the appearance of the fields and perhaps the wealthier farm buildings but not a lot in the general layout of the village. The Celts still tended to group themselves in family communities scattered over the escarpment within easy reach of the nearest fort or fortified village. So, while the majority of the huts would show no change, the larger farms would reflect the increasing use of the rectangular shape favoured by their Romanised cousins on the continent. Professor Childe[7] sums up the La Tène phase of the Iron Age as 'still being dominated by subsistence farming supplemented by a minimal development of specialised industry and by trade in metals, salt and a few luxuries, not very different in kind from that which had been conducted ever since the beginning of the Bronze Age.' This economy was well adapted to a wooded area such as ours and was still more pastoral in nature than agricultural. But we have, by the end of the Iron Age, the beginnings of a feudal society because the better, or luckier, farmers were doing so well that they could afford to take on labour and so become first small employers and often petty chieftains. Fighting and plunder were rife and it soon became wise to attach yourself to a powerful community.

Indeed, although there is still a conflict of opinion between authorities such as Vinogradoff and Seebohm as to the extent of the Celtic revolution in agricultural methods[8] I think we can safely say that the greatest change was brought about by the introduction of the powerful Belgic eight-oxen plough. This could not possibly have been worked in the small rectangular fields of the Bronze Age or earlier Iron Age villagers. A team of eight oxen could not possibly be turned in a small headland, and so the seeds were laid for the familiar pattern of the later Saxon and medieval long strips—the 'Open Field' system in which each villager had his long strip. These Open Fields as they developed later were vast areas of several hundred acres and on our hilltop sites there is no area of relatively flat land large enough to have been developed in this way and be worked by the 8 ox plough. Despite this, the agricultural revolution may have had some effect, resulting in the enlargement of the old small fields and their combination to form the two field system in Cholesbury which we shall refer to later in the book. Some of the flint and earth walls of the little Celtic fields may have been removed to make way for the longer run of the heavier plough but, probably, we would find that the bulk of the small original enclosures would have remained.

Another factor in the village life, curiously enough, was a marked change in the general pattern of the weather over the last 1,000 years under consideration. The Chilterns, along with the rest of· Britain, had become cooler and wetter. It had by this time, passed out of the sub-boreal warm dry spell and from about 700 BC onwards was enjoying a sub-Atlantic phase of moist, cool climate. This had meant that although the former had helped the inadequate tools of the early Bronze Age to clear the lighter soils of the escarpment, the near dust bowl conditions of cleared land had militated against any consistent cultivation. The greater moisture was an asset to the deeper cultivation and increasing use of wheat in the Chilterns. This was gradually ousting the small patches of oats that continued to be the main crop further north.

The plough itself was a powerful instrument made partly of iron bedded in oak, with a coulter, or knife, to cut the turf, a share to undercut the sod and even a wooden mould board to turn it over. The old breast plough and the two-oxen light wooden plough would still be in full use in the small ordinary fields. We would be unlikely to see much change in the farm animals. The cattle would still be of the small shaggy, horned type, like the present day highland cattle in Scotland; their bones have already been mentioned as found locally, together with those of the 'Celtic Ox'.

The only real innovation was in the breed of horse. Most were still the little shaggy 'Shetland' type, but by now the strain had been improved by the import of continental types that were better riding animals and some that were trained for the chariots of the wealthier landowners. No plough horses would be seen because no one had yet bred anything large enough to replace the slow oxen. They were riding horses, and it is still quite incomprehensible to me that in the tribal wars or to repel invasions such as that of Julius Caesar, no one seems to have thought of developing the cavalry arm instead of sticking to the outmoded chariots. Cavalry might well have turned the day against the less mobile legions and would have had immense advantages in re-grouping small bands of mobile guerrilla forces. Chariots could, at best, be used only on the few reasonably smooth trackways and for getting to a battle-field. It takes little imagination to envisage the result of an

attempt to use these unwieldy, unsprung boxes over the normal
rough open ground strewn with large stones and branches; the
occupants would have been thrown smartly out on the first bad
bump. They could have been used on the Icknield Way because
the surface had by that time been reinforced with flints.

Fish ponds were being introduced in sophisticated areas but I
am sure they would not have been seen at Cholesbury. Remains of
dogs and cats, as you remember had been found and these would
have been a feature of our villages by now.

The round huts of the original Iberian peasantry would still be
there and only at the end of our present period would we have
been likely to see change in the structure of the larger and more
isolated farmhouses. The villages would have spread considerably
because, as the authorities have said, this was about their heyday.
At no other time were they so relatively thickly populated as in
the Iron Age and, long before any Roman army set foot in Britain,
Roman ideas of comfort and architectural sophistication had
spread across the Channel. It must be remembered that there were
many links. Merchants were trading freely, exporting wool, metals,
hides and domestic animals. In return they were importing luxury
goods such as perfumes, Samian ware, glass vessels, beads and
other ornaments. Wealthy chieftains like Cunobelin were aping
Roman luxury with tessellated pavements and central heating
(hypocausts) and living rather like the British Raj in India during
the 19th century.

Nothing of this sort would have been likely in our villages nor
has there been time for excavation of possible sites to prove or

Fig. 11 House of a wealthy farmer, Late Iron Age

disprove the shape of the larger farmhouses. These may have been of the 'corridor' type, in which a row of rooms is connected by a long passage into which they open. The other is known as the 'courtyard' type in which three similar rows enclose a court or quadrangle. Around these would be grouped the huts of the farm weaver, the maker of bone needles and pins, the carpenter and the blacksmith. The last, as at Dundridge, already mentioned, would be well away from the house because of the obvious risk of fire. In several adjacent sites, the crucibles, remains of smelting furnaces and the nozzle of a bellows have been found obviously mingled with the ash and charred fragments of the walls and roof—evidence of the destruction of the whole edifice by fire. In spite of the prevalence of 'brick-earth' in the area, it is probable that wood was still used for the framework of the houses, the walls being of wattle and the roof thatched, with lofts for drying corn and for sleeping.

The interiors of the round huts would show little change, with their sleeping shelves round the walls, mattresses stuffed with bracken and straw, and the same earth floors. But the larger farms now had more and better household utensils including iron pots, crockery, pottery cullenders, basins, plates, dishes, jars, wooden spoons made on the pole lathe which was now in common use, trenchers, bowls, cups and bottles with wooden stoppers. Long pothooks and iron tripods stood permanently over the central fire for the stockpots and stews and there would still be the bronze cauldrons and stone hand mills for grinding corn. There was no furniture as we know it, space was too valuable. Housewives and craftsmen would work squatting on the floor as in India today. The practice of exacting tolls along the highway, mentioned earlier, might have produced some items of luxury such as glass and ornaments.

Away from the buildings, nothing much would have changed since we looked at the Bronze Age village. The flint knapper would still be at work, the charcoal burner in the clearings, any surplus of milk, cheese, hides, wool and wooden implements would have been sent under escort in ox carts to the nearest towns in exchange for goods from the continent or reeds for thatching, as these were becoming popular because of their long-lasting properties.

We cannot leave our appreciation of the Iron Age village without a reference to the work of the women themselves. Not only were they beginning to dress in a much more colourful and varied selection of costumes but they were paying much more attention to the latest continental 'hair do', as the contemporary drawings show. Their make-up for formal occasions was complicated and extensive. Kohl was imported to darken the eyelids, and even Caesar records being struck by 'the ladies with the pink cheeks and dark eyebrows'. Their finger rings, mirrors, torcs, brooches and beads were ornamented with brilliantly coloured enamels and they affected long plaited tresses sometimes worn hanging down and sometimes wound round on top of their heads. After all, they had to keep pace with the dressy clean-shaven men who were only allowed moustaches and, when not busy on the farm were addicted to colourful woven cloaks and baggy trousers. The kilt, beloved of the Goidels or earliest Celts, was fast going out of fashion.

But perhaps the women's greatest contribution was their inventions. It seems that the wealthier ones had more time than the men, who were kept very busy hunting, farming and trading. The women seem to have been responsible for the developments in weaving, speeding up the process with faster shuttles. As a result, drapes and tapestries began to appear on the mud walls because of the discovery of the natural dyes to be made from lichen and birch bark with which to enliven the patterns. These were still being used for the tartans in the Highlands until a very short time ago. They are said to have improved the design of oil lamps working on animal and vegetable fat and, above all, we probably owe to them the first rudimentary surgery. This was natural because the care of the wounded in any scrap would undoubtedly be left to them and the temptation to try to relieve pressures from skull wounds by attempts at trepanning would be irresistable and would follow naturally from trying to plug the holes in the skull. We have evidence from skeletons that some of their patients actually survived the treatment and lived for some months after they were operated on. They certainly knew how to set limbs and a number of these seem to have been quite successful. Our village ladies may even have got their tinsmith to copy one of the water clocks now in use in town houses to supplement the ordinary sundial, but we shall probably never know. We do know they were addicted to playing at dice; in fact this seems to have been the most popular winter game.

Nor do I think there is any point in mentioning the religious life because we have no evidence of its practice in our particular villages. Living as they did on the great religious highway from the east to the temples and centres of Avebury and Stonehenge, there must have been wayside shrines at which the more devout could worship if they had a mind to do so.

By AD 43 the Romans arrived in force though they appear to have had little noticeable impact on the hilltop villages. The consensus of opinion is that these were left more or less in peace, as there are no remains so far found and the new conquerors preferred the more comfortable gaps and valley bottoms for the construction of their villas and encampments.

Notes and References

[1] See note (4) Ch. V.

[2] See note (3) Ch. IV.

[3] K. M. Richardson and Alison Young 'An Iron Age A Site on the Chilterns' *Antiq. Journ.* Vol.XXXI, (1951) p.132.

[4] J. F. Head and C. M. Piggott 'An Iron Age Site at Bledlow, Bucks', *Records of Bucks.* Vol.XIV (1944) p.189.

[5] The Iron and Steel Institute after analysis place the sample from Cindery Bottom as 'finery slag'—i.e. 'sixteenth century or later.' (Letter dated 1 July, 1969).

[6] These excavations were reported in a special number of *Records of Bucks.* (Vol.XVIII, Part 3, 1968). The articles in this number are:
M. A. Cotton and S. S. Frere 'The Excavations'
D. Britton 'The Bronzes'
Helen Waugh 'The Pottery' and 'Pottery from Pitstone Hill.'
G. W. Dimbledy 'Interim Report on Environmental Investigation' (App.I)
Betty Westley 'Bones from Ivinghoe Beacon' App.II)

[7] G. Childe, op. cit. p.243.

[8] G. M. Trevelyan, *History of England* (Longmans 1926) p.14.

VII

THE LAMPS GO OUT IN THE LAND
BEYOND THE HILLS

Our villages between the Roman and the
Norman Conquests

The Romans come and go; the Saxons arrive and the first Chiltern civilization
sinks into obscurity; the last battle against the Saxons, 571 AD.

The Romans come—and go.

As we have suggested, at the end of the last chapter, the
Roman invasion probably had little direct effect upon the
continued occupation of our villages except to delay
permanent settlement by the Saxons for about 400 years. The
thousand years from AD 43 to the Norman settlement was
probably a period of slow rundown for the hilltop sites. Further
excavation of the sites may reveal evidence of occupation and the
nature and speed of the change from relatively thickly populated
settlements to something so near extinction that they were not
deemed worthy even of a mention in *Domesday Book.*

On the other hand, it is almost inconceivable, as most
authorities maintain, that valuable grazing sites and thriving settlements round a large fort would have been discarded altogether,
especially as the good agricultural land on the plains was fast being
absorbed by a rising population. It would not have been
economically sound to use such land for the rough grazing of
sheep and pigs, so it was probably the fate of the hill sites by the
end of the period to be maintained as summer residences and all
the year round as grazing sites with accommodation for herdsmen
and shepherds.

However, this process took 1,000 years to accomplish, and we
have enough knowledge of the events in the vicinity of the villages
to make a shrewd guess as to how far they would be affected.

Hence these years are worth a brief mention, first because there
would be some hundreds of years of useful life in the Celtic

villages and secondly, because we both feel sure that occupation was continuous in some form or other, even if it was, in the end, subordinated to the wealthier and more comfortable towns and villages of the lowlands.

The turbulent period of tribal warfare that affected the villages during the invasions of Julius Caesar has been mentioned in the preceding chapter when dealing with coins. Once the Romans had swept northwards and established the *Pax Romana* that was to last for nearly 400 years, it is probable that Hawridge and Cholesbury would be left to carry on agriculture and trade much as before.

The forts of both villages, (if indeed that at Hawridge existed in those days, as Ditchfield I think rightly suggests)[1] would have been left to fall into decay as they were on no Roman through way and of no use even as staging forts. The fertile gaps in the escarpment and the main valleys were cleared of scrub, along with much of the low land, and were policed and settled. Villas began to appear below the hills and down the Risborough Vale. These were not always Roman, as many were built by the wealthier Britons and were self-contained economic units.

Most of the British village communities such as Hawridge and Cholesbury were left in peace, being poor land and not worth consideration for possible 'take-over'. Taxes would be collected and as the population in the plains grew, arrangements would probably be made for their partial use as summer grazings.

Communications

I think the chief change came about because of better communications. The Romans drove a network of roads across the newly opened-up country, mostly radiating from the trading centre of London. One to the east of us, now known as Watling Street ran, via St. Albans, to the north-west and nearer still, a subsidiary road, subsequently called Akeman Street, branched off from St. Albans and ran under the Cholesbury Downs through Tring and Aylesbury to Alchester. These soon took much of the traffic from the old British Icknield trackway, which declined proportionally in use. It must have been still used for geographical reasons as the link between east and west, but by this time the Thames Valley had come more into favour. Later, many stretches were taken over by the Roman civil engineers and surfaced with *pavimentum* in the usual way.

Indeed, a chain of villas grew up along the old Icknield way route where the springs flowed from the foot of our escarpment. Mr Head points to a curious feature, in that these seem to terminate at the Cattle Brook and run down the Risborough High Wycombe gap without spreading into Oxfordshire. Apart from these, the British village system seems to have continued un-interrupted.

As he says, 'The Icknield Way settlements suggest an undisturbed continuity of occupation. The hills—and the winds of freedom have ever blown about the Chilterns—stood close at hand in case of need, and we may picture these inhabitants in a simple pastoral setting peacefully rearing their sheep in the shadow of the downs.'[2]

Mr Head also notices an old track way leading from Sarratt in the direction of St. Albans and suggests that this may, with more field work, perhaps be traced through eventually to High Wycombe. This would increase if anything the isolation of our villages, especially as between London and the rest of what later became Buckinghamshire there stretched the swampy, undrained clay plain of north-west Middlesex covered with thick oak forest and scrub. This gave way to the black peaty marshland of the Coln Valley often heavily waterlogged even today.

During the Roman period, therefore, we can fairly certainly envisage our hilltop villages continuing relatively undisturbed as a self-supporting native British population, still centred for commercial and administrative purposes upon Verulamium (St. Albans).

The Saxons Arrive—and the first Chiltern civilization
sinks into Obscurity

When, at last, the Saxon warrior farmers reached the Chilterns in force, they probably regarded our hill villages as 'mysterious settlements beyond the woods where strange natives lived on, worshipping dark Gods.' Early Saxon farmers in the plain must have looked askance at the little dark men of the hill tops and fenced in their new fields all the more securely.

As the old Roman colonial society finally disintegrated the villages behind the escarpment would feel very isolated and could have taken little heart from the temporary successes of British chieftains such as Arthur in the west. This state of affairs was allowed to continue partly because the newcomers, from habit, avoided all centres of habitation, partly from superstition and partly because there was, in the Chiltern Area, no need or point in penetrating the inaccessible hill country. There was unlimited rich land waiting to be cleared in the valleys and across the Oxfordshire plains as far as the Cotswolds. Probably for these reasons we find practically no traces of Saxon occupation in the villages themselves until later on. A Saxon church was built during the 9th century inside the ramparts of the old fort, which, by now must have been used as a convenient corral for cattle and little else. Lipscombe[3] and one or two other sources have suggested that the fort was taken over by the Danes when they conquered the Chilterns in the five terrible years between 866 and 871 when the whole Mercian kingdom fell apart, but I can find no satisfactory evidence to support this theory. In any case, Edward the Elder soon drove them back at the battle of the bloody hill and cut the crosses on the chalk sides to mark his victory. After that, the boundaries of the Danelaw were established to the north of a line along Watling Street.

But before that happened certain evidence and local events allow us to fill in some of the gap with reasonable certainty. First it must be remembered that there was no organised Saxon invasion as such. The warrior-farmers had been arriving in isolated boatloads long before the Romans gave up control. They had had to set up a defensive network commanded by 'The Count of the Saxon Shore' who covered the coast from The Wash to Portsmouth. This did not prove very effective and the Saxons continued to arrive in both large and small bands. The pattern was generally that every now and then they would combine into a 'Host' which drove rapidly north and west and when it had uncovered sufficient new territory would dissolve into small groups again to settle and open up the new land for farming and the construction of wooden hamlets as a nucleus in each area. They engulfed the Chilterns by penetrating along both sides, up the Thames and down along the Icknield Way. There is abundant evidence of their presence in the plain below the Ivinghoe, Pitstone and Cholesbury British villages. Burial grounds at Pitstone to the east and Bishopstone to the west, together with lynchets and other evidences of farms and houses are to be discerned from the remains of the postholes.

But the most significant evidence of the virility of the British inhabitants of the hill villages is that they are known to have held their own against the English for nearly two hundred years after the virtual collapse of the Roman colonial empire. As late as 571 the local British fought what was probably their last great battle against the Saxon invaders near Aylesbury. They lost, and Aylesbury and three other towns were occupied, but the interesting fact is that they were still strong enough to engage in combined, organised warfare as opposed to more local defensive actions round individual forts. From then on, they were a subject race living in suspicious isolation in the fastnesses of their wooded hill country. This situation is summed up by Dr J. N. Myres in *Roman Britain and the English Settlements* quoted by Mr Head, in that the physiographical disadvantages and difficulties of the district 'did prevent much Saxon settlement in central and north Buckinghamshire before the formation of Ceawlin's empire in the third quarter of the sixth century.' When they did settle in force along the lower slopes and in the plain they seem to have avoided direct contact with, and certainly occupation of, the hill country for some hundreds of years. This reluctance to face the spirits of the hills shows up in their naming of the places as they came across them. Our own village, Chelwoldesbur in the Valuation of Norwich (1254), or Chelewoldesbyr, Assize Rolls (1266) comes, I feel, from the Saxon origin of the second and third syllable *Weoh* (as in Weedon to the north) meaning an 'idol' or 'secret place' in a fortified camp (Bury). They were pagans at that time and this would mean a place to be left severely alone. The great Celtic fortification that they found right across the woods between the villages and the edge of the Downs, they promptly named the work of the Devil, or 'Grim.' We do know from excavation that the nearby Saxon settlements were not only facing outwards into the plain but their burials indicate that they were small settlements of a backward and primitive people who would lack cohesion, battle power and leadership even if they had wished to interfere seriously with the Celtic settlements deep in the protection of the woods. This situation changed when the wealthier thanes from the east took over the development of the area in later days.

There is considerable evidence of Scandinavian trade flowing along the old line of the Icknield Way, as witnessed by the incidence of cowrie shells. We know that Cuthwulf, the victor of the battle of Aylesbury, was buried in the vicinity, but it was probably as late as the 9th century that the Christian Church was built in the Cholesbury fort. There is, unfortunately, no direct evidence of what the church looked like. The very features that deterred possible Saxon settlement in the early centuries would have made the area attractive to political exiles and refugees such as the exiled Prince Caedwalla who took refuge here in the 7th century. The area, especially St. Leonards, remained a hide-out for highwaymen and London escapees as late as the 19th century.

I omit any reference to the coming of Christianity itself, as there is no evidence of its effect on our settlements. Indeed, there is little more to be said. We do know that Edmer Attille held a Berewicke in nearby Berkhamsted in King Edward's time and this was usurped by one Hunfrid after the Conquest and that by the 8th century a powerful tribe, the Cilternsaetan, had occupied 4,000 huts in the area below the villages on the plain along the Icknield Way. Again, they would probably be using the hill settlements and what remained of their occupants as rough pasturage and hired or enslaved shepherds. The whole area was by then in the Kingdom of Mercia and, indeed, remained in the diocese of Lincoln until the 19th century. The lamps had gone out and children no longer played at the edge of the woods on summer nights. Except for the shepherds' bothies and little fires, snug in the shelter of the old earthworks, the village huts once bustling with life, had again become part of the landscape of their origin and it was to be a long time before any comparable sort of community would once more bring life and laughter to this part of what the English and later *Domesday Book* called *Cilterne*—the Celtic name for the land beyond the hills.[5]

Notes and References

[1]See note (4) Ch. V.
[2]J. F. Head Op.cit. p.83.
[3]Lipscomb, Vol.III, p.315.

[4]R. G. Collingwood and J. N. Myers, *Roman Britain and the English Settlements* (O.U.P. 1937).

[5]Mr. Head tells us (op. cit. p.104) that Cilternsaetan, a tribal name, occurs in the Tridal Hidage, a 7th or 8th century record of assessments for a Mercian ruler.

VIII

'ONE SORE SPARROW HAWK'

The villages reappear after the Norman Conquest

The long narrow Parishes of the Chilterns; connection between the Hilltop hamlets and their parent villages in the plains; absence from Domesday Book; early inhabitants at St. Leonards, the Hermit of the Woods; Cholesbury and Hawridge and their positions round the forts; evidence for open fields; Buckland Common; summary of the two types of village development.

T he hilltop villages had lost their separate identity with the shift of centre of population to the Vale of Aylesbury. On the flat ground there was space for the large open fields of Saxon times and a more tractable soil for the eight ox plough, but this fertile land was too valuable to use for feeding 'the beestes'. It would provide pasture for the plough oxen which could not go too far away to graze at nights, while the cattle, the sheep and the swine were driven up into the hills. All along the northern slopes of the Chilterns the parishes developed as long narrow strips often no more than half a mile wide but penetrating some six or seven miles up into the hills. The peculiar shape of these parishes is no accident. It reflects the economy of the 10th and 11th centuries, its need for extensive land for grazing as well as arable and the competition for the flat lands which prevented any village from acquiring an unreasonable share.

In our area these long villages run roughly north-west to south-east and, as the map on page 3 shows, Aston Clinton extends to St. Leonards, Buckland includes Buckland Common and Drayton Beauchamp owns Cholesbury. There is a link, too, between Marsworth and Hawridge, though as these villages are not, like the others, contiguous this connection is a more complex question which is discussed more fully on page 77.

When *Domesday Book* was compiled in 1088 none of our villages were mentioned; it must be assumed that they were regarded as an integral part of their parent villages down in the plains and described as the 'Woodland for 300 swine'[1] which Aston Clinton and Buckland possessed, or for the 200 for which there was room in Magno le Breton's 6 hides in Drayton or the 800 for Marsworth.

We should perhaps add here that these connections between our own and other villages complicate the task of the local historian and at times deprive us of records which should be available because it becomes impossible to disentangle two sections of a composite record. For example, taxation returns of 1525 for Drayton Beauchamp may well include Cholesbury names which we cannot pick out with any certainty.

The tracks which the herdsmen used are still obvious enough from the steep, high banked roads which we drive up today. Their names are suggestive both of their antiquity and of the long, tedious climb—Aston Hill, Dancers End and the Crong, Shire Lane and the Twist, roads which only 40 years ago were remembered for the painful flints which littered the surface, flints hidden by slippery clay in wet weather with little streams trickling down the gulleys. Today we can revel in the glorious colours of the beech woods through which the roads run, but our ancestors, ten centuries ago would have little time to enjoy any natural beauties. The woods would have been thicker and scrubbier; when a beast strayed from the track they would have had to battle with the undergrowth to drive it back and all the time they would be keeping a wary eye open for enemies, whether outlaws or wild beasts.

The important point in the history of our villages, however, is that these tracks *were* kept open. If they had been disused for any considerable period they would have been overgrown so quickly that the chances of their rediscovery would have been remote. Even more important is the obvious fact that these tracks must have led somewhere. The herdsmen were not just wandering off into the unknown, they were making for some traditional clearing where they could find shelter, some protection from their enemies and, above all, water for their thirsty beasts. From Aston Clinton the herdsmen wandered across the Icknield Way and Grim's Dyke until they reached Black Mere behind St. Leonards Chapel, a popular watering place for centuries; from Buckland they would have found that the shallow depression in the hills which is now the village of Buckland Common offered the best shelter. The Drayton Beauchamp herdsmen were the luckiest of all, the old fort providing a cosy haven with its sheltering embankments and its perpetual spring. The route between Marsworth and Hawridge is again left for later discussion.

The absence of our villages from *Domesday Book* is not in itself conclusive evidence that at this time their only use was as summer pastures, which might be called the Chiltern Alps. The Domesday Commissioners were not infallible, their record was compiled too quickly to permit a visit to every remote hamlet and the local witnesses from the larger villages may have been hazy about the exact situation up in the hills, or even have felt that they could get away with a little mild deception. Within 100–150 years of *Domesday* there is evidence of permanent settlement in three of the villages. The question is whether these were new settlements carved out of the waste as the demand for land led to the extension of the cultivated area or whether the facts point to the development of hamlets which had never quite disappeared. There is no single answer to this fascinating question; each of the villages must be examined separately.

St. Leonards

The founder of St. Leonards is traditionally thought to be a quaint character known as 'the Hermit of the Woods'. It is an enchanting theory conjuring up a picture of an old man wrapped in a coarse hairy cloak, picking his way through the undergrowth until he chances on a spot where he chooses to remain and bring comfort to the outlaws roaming about in these hills. The hermit himself is no mythical character for in the Pipe Rolls for 1196 we find the entry:[2]

		Due	Paid
Escheats:			
Eston' of Will, de Clinton, farm		20. 9. 3	17.14. 1
a. in stocking this manor, for 100 sheep	2.10. 0		
b. to the Hermit of the Wood of Eston, what he used to have of the gift of Jordan de Clinton, in one acre of corn, and in hay and money by roy. writ	7. 0		
	2.17. 0		
Less surplus credited	1.10		
xiii H/1a.	2.15. 2		

It is not known whether our Hermit came from Missenden Abbey or the old hospital of St. Leonards at Aylesbury. It doesn't really matter. What is important is that he was certainly there. He may have built some sort of tiny chapel and must have lived a spartan existence on his acre of corn and grass.

With some reluctance, however, we must discard the picturesque theory that our Hermit was the founder of St. Leonards. It will be remembered (p. 49) that part at least of the present village, Dundridge, has produced evidence of Iron Age occupation, and though we have no definite evidence for continuous habitation, the house was certainly built in an age when the surrounding country was still so wild that a moat was needed to protect the cattle from marauders, wolves or human. Moated farmsteads of this type are not uncommon in Buckinghamshire and many of them are of 9th century origin, though it is rare to find them above the 400 foot contour line and Dundridge stands more than 100 feet above that. How far this early settle-

Fig. 12 The Moat, Dundridge Manor

ment extended we cannot tell, but the site of the present village is
a likely one, standing as it does not only at a watering spot, the
Black Mere, but at a crossroads between the track up from Aston
Clinton, which continues across the Dundridge fields to Chartridge
and the road connecting The Hale and The Lee with Cholesbury.

Leaving speculation aside, we have definite evidence that in the
second half of the 12th century, and probably before our Hermit's
arrival, there was both a Manor and a Chapel in the area. The
Manor, Dundridge, had been alienated by William de Clinton, Lord
of the Manor of Aston Clinton to Henry de Crokesley before 1187
when the latter granted to Missenden Abbey

> 13 shillingsworth of rent arising from his tenement in Dundridge
> and a third part of his demesne except 13 acres which he has
> given to St. Leonards Chapel.' [3]

It can be assumed therefore that there was a small community
living at St. Leonards by about 1150, a community large enough
to justify the foundation of a Chapel, though formal permission
for this is not recorded until the 13th century when we hear of the
first Chantry Priest–'Thomas'[4].

By itself, Henry de Crokesley's grant to Missenden Abbey tells
us little about 12th century Dundridge, but this grant was confirmed in the next century by two of his successors in exactly the
same terms and it seems safe to assume that a fuller description
contained in an extent and rental of about 1300 would have been
equally applicable in 1187.[5] This document tells us that the
Abbot's lands in Dundridge consisted of:-

In mansione ibidem	v acr. et di. et valet per ann.	
In Fennymerefeld	xv acr. iij rod. "	"
In Hamondesfeld et Blakemerefeld	. . xxvij acr. i rod. "	"
In Buttesfeld.	x acr. "	"
In Waggeskyn	ix acr. et di. rod."	"
In Feldputfeld.	xvij acr. et di. "	"
In Welyfeld	ix acr. iij rod. "	"
In ij campis ibidem	xij acr. et di. "	"
In bosco de Dunrugge.	iiij acr. "	"
In Brokgrove et Foure acres	. . . xvii acr. et di. "	"

The field names in this list cannot be related to any which appear in later centuries, but the name Blakemerefeld indicates that the original Dundridge Manor extended to a point near the Chapel, while Hamondsfeld and Brokgrove suggest that Hamo of Stagsden and the del Broc family, whom we shall meet again shortly, were early landowners in the area.

The wording of this survey suggests that the Abbey held a portion, or perhaps a number of strips, in each of seven fields, the total area of about 300 acres (Missenden Abbey it will be remembered held a third of the demesne lands) being subdivided into at least these seven fairly small fields. The reason is clear from the geography of the district, cut by a fairly steep sided valley which limited the area of flat land. The effect of this can only have been that the ploughed fields were fragmented, each of them too small for the eight ox plough. We get nearer here than any-where else to discovering the pattern of agriculture which was almost certainly common throughout our area. The great common fields of the flat land could not exist in these hills. They were replaced by a series of small, distinct and possibly enclosed fields, each divided between a number of owners and ploughed by the smaller, lighter two or four ox plough which could do little more than scratch the surface of this heavy soil. It was a pattern which could slip much more easily and quietly into an enclosed pattern 300 years later than the large open fields which demanded sub-stantial redistribution before enclosure was possible.

The tenants of this land are named in the Rental which follows the Extent, and tells us of the rentals due:

> De Willelmo Sagar per annum pro terra Petri ijs. et j hominem ad precariam Abathie.
> De eodem Willelmo pro terris quondam Ricardi de Tours xiijs.
> De eodem Willelmo pro terra dominica quam tenet ad terminum vite . . . xxxiijs iiijd.
> De Emma le Spenser pro tenemento Rogeri Gerueys per annum iijs. et j hominem ad precariam Abathie.
> De Willelmo Strut pro tenemento Thome de Balyngere per annum iijs. et j hominem ad precarian Abathie.
> De Willelmo Z enlonde pro tenemento Walteri de Z enlonde per annum et eciam pro tenemento quondam Willelmi Snow vijs. viijd. et precariam (blank in M.S.)

There were, therefore four families farming on this land. Willelmo Sagar must have been a descendant of Sagar son of Norman who held land in 1187. His predecessor in one holding, Richard de Tours had Vaches Farm. Of the other owners we know nothing, but the one interesting name is that of a Rogeri Gerueys, sounding remarkably like the Geary family who are prominent in our history three and four centuries later.

We are left, therefore, with a picture of the Manor of Dundridge in the early 14th century extending over most, if not all, of the land south of the Chapel, a land of small fields interspersed, as it still is today, with belts of woodland, and housing at least four families.

Between St. Leonards and Aston Clinton there is one other small Manor on the edge of our area, Chivery, which came into existence at the end of the 12th century, when William de Clinton had to provide a dowry for his daughter, a typical example of 12th and 13th century development. Neither Dundridge nor Chivery, however, included the hamlet of St. Leonards and its Common, which remained part of Aston Clinton for several more centuries.

Cholesbury

In Aston Clinton the separation of the three manors surrounding St. Leonards from their parent Manor can be dated within a relatively short period of time. The Manor of Cholesbury, however, seems to creep into existence unnoticed. At the time of the Domesday Survey its owner was Magno le Breton, but Lipscombe cannot be right in assuming that

> "Cholesbury was intended to be described in the six hides and
> three virgates, there called a Manor,"[6]

in the tenure of one of his tenants, Helgot. With its 165 acres, including the Common, Cholesbury can hardly have been assessed as 1 hide, let alone 6, nor could it have supported 4 teams. It would have been much more like or could even have been included in another holding of Magno le Breton's in Deneslai (Dunsley in Tring), a third part of a hide where

> "There is land for one ox".[7]

Small as it was, however, there must have been some sort of a hamlet at Cholesbury early in the 12th century as the Church was already in existence, the advowson being given to the Knights

Templars about that time. 100 years later the Church was being built or rebuilt as architectural experts date the south porch from the time of Henry III and in 1230 there was clearly a large enough population to justify a resident parson as one Abel was instituted with the firm instruction that 'he is to serve personally'. The presentation reads:-[8]

> "Ad eandum admissus est, et in ea canonice persona institutus,
> cum onera ministrandi personaliter in eadem".

Two of Abel's Parishioners are known—Roger, son of Roger and Alice and Robert, son of Will. The latter owned 5 acres of land in 'Chelewoldesbyrie', the former 4 acres previously held by Richard de Hodenhale. They agreed to exchange holdings, Roger paying 21d. a year for the extra acre.[9] The Calendar of Feet of Fines does not record the reasons for this transaction but it may well have been an early attempt to exchange strips in order to build up larger holdings of continuous strips.

Abel's Parishioners almost certainly included also some members of the le Breton family and it is possible that Magno le Breton or his heirs separated the Manor of Cholesbury from Drayton Beauchamp in order to provide an estate for one of his sons. At all events, we hear in the Calendar of Feet of Fines for 1248 of a transfer from Will le Breton to Hugh le Breton of the

> 'Manor of Chelwerderbir & 1 caruc. land in Aston; W. acks. right
> of H., as in demesnes, homages, services of free men, wardships,
> reliefs, escheats, villeinage, woods, meadows, pastures, waters,
> ponds, mills etc. as of his gift; to hold for ever paying yearly 1
> den. & doing to the chief lords etc.; H. gave W. 1 sore sparrow-
> hawk.'[10]

This is important as the first firm evidence of Cholesbury as a separate Manor with all the normal Manorial rights.

There is one significant difference between this Manor and those of Dundridge and Chivery—Cholesbury is smaller than either of these two farms and like them suffers from the same intractable clay-with-flints soil, but whereas they remain as isolated farms, Cholesbury develops into a village or hamlet, a village clustered round the fort just as the old Iron Age village had been (see Chapter XI for fuller explanation of later developments), a typical 'round village'. The old name has not been forgotten either, a name which may have worried the inhabitants for several centuries after the Norman Conquest, judging from the variety of their attempts to spell it.

One further fact is important here. The newer farms carved out of the waste in the 12th and 13th centuries were usually free enough to break away from the traditional open field system of cultivation and to develop from the outset as modern looking enclosed farms. One of these newer type farms, situated across the Cholesbury/Drayton Beauchamp boundary was Parrott's which dates from at least 1330 when the Escheat Rolls[11] tell us of a Thomas Perot who was seized of lands and tenements in Chilwaldesburye. We believe however, that the rest of the Manor had some form of common fields cultivated in severalty. The only evidence for this is of a late date, coming from the first of our existent Court Rolls in 1599 and by that date we are pretty sure that enclosure had taken place (see Chapter XI). This Roll refers to a holding of Henry Putnam's described as,

"4 closes in the fields of Cholesbury called Halfacres amounting to 15 acres."

There are two important points in this entry. The term 'Halfacres' was so commonly applied to denote the size of strips in the common fields that it is difficult to believe that it can denote anything else here, while the 15 acres which comprised the total holding was the traditional half virgate which dates from Saxon times. As at Dundridge, the fields would have been tiny by standards of medieval times and though we feel we have just enough evidence to suggest that they were shared between and cultivated jointly by a number of small farmers we have deliberately used the term 'common' and not 'open' fields to emphasise the difference between our sort of fields and the great 'Open Fields', usually spelt with capital letters, of the plains.

These facts, the site and shape of the village, the continuity of the name and the evidence, flimsy as it is, of common field cultivation all lead to the conclusion that Cholesbury as a village has had a continuous or nearly continuous existence since it was originally founded in the Bronze Age. If it was ever deserted, it was only for very short periods, never long enough for it to have disappeared in the invading scrub.

Hawridge

The omission of Hawridge from the *Domesday Survey* is more surprising than that of our other villages. Assuming that we are right in dating its fort as Iron Age, it must have been the site of an ancient settlement and a settlement which, like Cholesbury, can never have disappeared completely. Like Cholesbury, too, it appears by the 13th century as a separate Manor, and Hawridge was large enough with its 696 acres to be rated as a Knight's fee.

Some of our difficulty may come from a misunderstanding of this village and its geography. Today, lying between Chesham and Cholesbury on a good metalled road, its connections with these two places seem natural. But, drive up from Chesham after 24 hours' rain when every passing car forces one into a miniature river on the west side of the road and remembering that the water table even fifty years ago before the Pumping Station was built was considerably higher, the Chesham connection in the days when roads were unmade begins to look a little tenuous. A thousand years ago this would have been marshland and the high level route across the hills on the west side of the vale shows no signs that it was ever more than a footpath or pony track. Towards Cholesbury, as we shall show later (see Chapter X) the Common may have extended from about Tudor Cottage in Hawridge to Tall Chimneys in Cholesbury—and common in the 11th century could have meant impenetrable scrub.

The present road, therefore, a modern construction, makes the Chesham/Cholesbury connection look unpromising. To find out how Hawridge linked with the rest of the world we must turn to the footpaths and signs of old steep banked tracks. To the south west, there is one coming down from Bellingdon, dipping down to the valley bottom on the parish boundary and up again to emerge just above the *Rose and Crown*. Going north again, the Ordnance Survey map shows footpaths down to Bottom Farm, perhaps before the present road was built. From there, two old tracks appear—one goes up past Heath End and then west to Wigginton; it is not insigificant that the blacksmith's shop was, later at least, situated at this important road junction. The other track turns east for a short distance before climbing up to Hill Farm, down to the Wigginton Road where another short detour to the east takes one to Hog Lane and thence up to Berkhamsted or Ashley Green. By the 17th century the former of these two lanes from Bottom Farm was known as Parsonage Lane, the latter as Berkhamsted Lane.

All this suggests that Hawridge's original connections were not with Cholesbury and Chesham but with Berkhamsted and Bellingdon.

As we have mentioned on page 67 the position of Hawridge is complicated by its connection with Marsworth, a parish some six miles away as the crow flies across the Tring salient, a part of Hertfordshire which here puts out a long finger into Buckinghamshire. Parishes with detached outposts are by no means uncommon, though the reason for these curiosities is often difficult to discover. This link could have dated from a time, well before the Norman conquest, when parish boundaries were first established and Marsworth, short of grazing grounds, obtained its share at Hawridge. It is equally possible that in the disturbed times of the tenth century the owner of Hawridge, a small landowner, decided to commend himself to a more powerful lord for protection. One of the most powerful nearby was Brichtric who, besides being Lord of the Manor at Marsworth, owned 3½ hides in Wiggington, a portion of the land which the Count of Mortain took from Tring.[12] At Marsworth, Brichtric's Manor was given to Robert d'Ouilly and held of him by Ralf Basset. He did not acquire Wiggington, but may well have managed to annexe Hawridge and claim it as part of Marsworth. It is certain, at least, that Hawridge got into the hands of the Bassett family and that, like Marsworth, thus became part of the Honour of Wallingford eventually coming into the ownership of the Black Prince.

Marsworth and Hawridge remained linked for administative purposes; as we shall see later in Chapter XII, for example, they appear in the Ship Money assessments as 'Marsworth cum Harridge'. Apart from this, however, the connection seems to have little effect on the history of Hawridge. The two are mentioned as separate Manors in a list of the Black Prince's Manors in Bucks in 1375 and Church records, so far as we have them, show Hawridge as a separate Rectory and not a Chapel of Ease serving an isolated hamlet but retaining its link with the Parish Church of Marsworth.

The few references to Hawridge in official records are uninteresting and uninformative. The Church is first mentioned in

1227 when William Mauduit is the Patron and there is one reference to a transfer of land in 1253 when,[13]

'Laur. del Brok quer. and Ralf de Berleg, and Emma his w. imped; 1 mess. and 30 ac. land and 2 ac. wood in Haruge; R. and E. ackn. right of L. as of their gift, to hold of R. & E. and the heirs of E. for ever; paying yearly 1 pair of white gloves and doing to the chief lords of the fee all other services; warranty; L. gave R. and E. 27 mks of silver.'

The del Broc family at the time owned land extensively round about in Chesham and Wigginton; they also owned the neighbouring Manor of Mandelyns, now Marlin Chapel Farm. The question is whether Mandelyns comes into our history more closely. In 1513 Robert Morton, then Lord of that Manor,[14]

'Demised to Nicholas Loote all his partable land called Hertruge lying in fields called Hertruge field, Byregrove field and Wynch's field parcelled in common between the foresaid Robert Morton and Martin Brutwell of Stoke.'

For some time we thought that this Charter might refer to Hawridge and give some evidence of open fields in that village. We have recently learnt, however, that there are other fields between Mandelyns and Chesham with a similar name—a name moreover to which the variation Hertruge is more likely to apply than it is to Hawridge, and reluctantly we must discard this evidence.[15]

The modern Hawridge appears to be unusually shapeless (see Map p. 93). Geographically, it consists of a long flat ridge rarely more than a quarter of a mile wide enclosed by the 500-foot contour line extending from the Cholesbury border southeastwards towards Chesham Vale. On the southern side this ridge drops sharply into a dry valley separating Hawridge and Bellingdon; on the north it falls away gradually at first but with increasing steepness into Chesham Vale which would have been swamp or river according to the season. The modern road from Cholesbury runs just below the top of this ridge with the houses along one side and overlooking the common for about three-quarters of a mile; a quarter of a mile beyond the last house is a pub, the *Rose and Crown*, and another quarter of a mile on towards Chesham the old fort with Hawridge Court within the moated area and the Church and an old tithe barn just outside. Opposite Hawridge Court and to the north another road at right angles drops steeply down the valley across the common to climb up again to the hamlet of Heath End and another area of relatively flat land before it falls away again into another valley coming down from Wigginton and joining the first to form Chesham Vale. Hawridge today, therefore, is a sort of L-shaped village with the fort standing at the junction of the two arms.

The original village is unlikely to have been as far away from its obvious centre as either of these two groups of houses. It would have been clustered round the fort and the Church, and Hawridge seems to be an example of a deserted or, to be more accurate, a dispersed village. An aerial photograph has shown signs of at least one more house within the moated area. Church Meadow behind the Church may mark the smallholding originally belonging to the Rectory and Pound Field beyond it must surely mark the site of that essential enclosure, the village pound.

Despite the lack of written evidence, we are still inclined to think on geographical evidence that Hawridge once had common fields. Along the ridge on both sides of the fort there is space on relatively flat land for two such fields, of about 160 acres each. These fields may have been divided by a central ridge at the watershed with the strips running up to it with the gradient. Towards Chesham, indeed, the footpath runs for some way along a raised bank which could be the remains of this ridge.

Two-field systems of cultivation were not unusual in this part of the Chilterns, but Hawridge may have had three. A 16th century will refers to East Field, a typical name for a common field and a name which could have applied to Heath End area on the side where the Parsonage lands were found later. This is where an understanding of Hawridge's communications is vital. Once the importance of the tracks up to Heath End is accepted, it is easy enough to envisage a third field in this area. Measurements there show that there would have been just enough space and at least one significant S-shaped boundary hedge. It would have been an awkward shaped field, extending on both sides of the existing road and full of odd corners and gores and short strips. But it would have been cultivatable, and provides a third area of nearly 160 acres.

Hawridge, therefore, in its early days faced roughly north and south. Heath End is not just a detached hamlet; it was an integral

part of the original village, the Cholesbury road being scrub from
Tudor Cottage onwards and not opened up until about the 14th or
15th century.

The evidence for Hawridge is much weaker than that for
Cholesbury, but it may not be unreasonable to suggest that this,
too, was the continuation of a very old village, hidden away in the
woods and living its own life undisturbed by any illustrious owners
except for periodic visits from the Steward to collect rents. Here,
too, it is significant that the village keeps its old name, a name
which cannot be later than Saxon in origin.

Buckland Common

With neither a separate Manor, nor a separate Church, it is
impossible to disentangle any early information of value about this
village. It seems likely that it is an example of one of the newer
villages carved out of the waste, but the owners of Buckland, the
Church of Lincoln, never found it necessary to alienate their lands
and even the larger farms like Leylands remained part of the
Manor.

Summary

To sum up, therefore, it looks as if our four villages illustrate
two different types of village development. On the one hand we
have two very old villages, Cholesbury and Hawridge, continu-
ations of Early Bronze or Iron Age settlements. However flimsy
the evidence, their location on the site of the old forts and their
ancient names must make this the most likely reason for their
existence on their present sites. Buckland Common is a typical
example of a 'new' village carved out of the waste as cultivation
extended. In the absence of any evidence for the Roman period,
this development should probably be dated at any time from the
8th to the 11th century. The Dundridge Manor part of St.
Leonards has not only produced Iron Age finds but was occupied
in Saxon Times, so once again we are assuming continuity, though
this early origin does not necessarily apply to the main part of the
modern village.

Notes and References

[1]References to Domesday Survey for Bucks. from *V. C. H. Bucks* Vol.1 Astone (Aston Clinton) p.263 – Bocheland (Buckland) p.233-4 Draitone (Drayton Beauchamp – Magno le Breton's holding) p.270 Missevorde (Marsworth) p.258.

[2]*Pipe Rolls, Bucks and Beds.* ed. by G. Herbert Fowler and Michael Hughes (B.A.S. 1923) – Roll 42 xiii H. p.119.

[3]*The Cartulary of Missenden Abbey* Vol. 1 ed. by J. G. Jenkins (B.A.S. 1938) p.225-6.

[4]Lipscomb states that 'Thomas', the first Chantry Priest died 1273 - Vol.II, p.94.

[5]B. M. Harley M. S. 3688 folio 203.

[6]Lipscomb, Vol.III, p.315.

[7]V. C. H. *Herts.* Vol.1, p.341. We are grateful to Mr. G. Elvey of the B.A.S. for the suggestion that this entry may refer to Cholesbury.

[8]*Rotuli, Hugo de Welles,* Vol.II, ed. by W. P. W. Phillimore (Lincs. Rec. Soc. 1913) p.80.

[9]2 Hen.III – *A Calendar of the Feet of Fines for Bucks. 7 Ric.I to 44 Hen.III*, ed. by M. W. Hughes (B.A.S. 1940) p.55.

[10]12 Hen.III – op. cit. Note (9) p.88.

[11]Lipscomb Vol.III, p.316.

[12]V. C. H. Vol.1 – Domesday Survey.

[13]37/38 Hen.III – Op. cit. Note (9) p.100.

[14]B. M. – Harley Charter 53 f.14.

[15]We are grateful to Mr. Arnold Baines for this information resulting from his researches into Chesham field names.

IX

'A CHAPEL OF EASE AND NOE FREE CHAPELL'

St. Leonards has its worries in the 16th century

The village, its population and agriculture in the 16th century; Muster Roll of 1522; the Baldwins and the Batchelors; a public enquiry 1547; the Field Plan of 1582.

In 1522 St. Leonards was a hamlet with 30–40 residents. The Muster Roll of that year gives eleven names of adult males, three of them probably still living in the family home at Dundridge; in 1547 there were nine households (see page 88) and at a census in 1563 eight families.[1]

The Manor of Aston Clinton had for the last three centuries belonged to the Earls of Salisbury and Warwick, except for a short period when the political activities of Warwick the King-Maker had been terminated by his attainder and execution and the seizure of his lands by the Crown. It was restored to Warwick's sister Margaret, who was created Countess of Salisbury in 1513. The sub-tenancies of Dundridge and Chivery had long ago lapsed and the ownership of Aston Clinton therefore involved that of St. Leonards, with two exceptions. Missenden Abbey still held part of the original Manor of Dundridge and there must have been a freehold plot in the village itself owned by William Bukenall who in 1509 granted to Thomas Playstowe[2]

> 'All those lands called Jenkyns londdes with close called Ryddyngs and also another close with wood called Archard Ffyld and another croft called Cherchelands lying in the Parish of Aston Clinton aforesaid. Also one close with wood called Kyrkelade and also another croft called Stonicrofte with 2 small closes and wood lying in the Parish of Wendover.'

Two days later Playstowe transferred it again to a group of Trustees consisting of:[3]

> 'Sir Ralph Verney, Sir Thomas Brian, Ralph Verney Esq., John Cheyne Esq., Thomas Greenway Gent., John Blakehed, William Bukenall, Robert Bawdewyn and Thomas Tolevyle.'

This deed marks the foundation of the Chapel Trust, though, curiously, there is in the original deed no statement of the purpose for which the Trust was founded.

The official owners of the Manor are interesting, but their history is only incidental to that of the village and our real concern is with the inhabitants listed in the Muster Roll of 1522[4] with their property as:

	Land Value	Goods
Robert Baldwyn (Dundridge)		£20
Robert Baldwyn Jr.		40/-
Richard Baldwyn		20/-
John Ginger		£20
Thomas Playstowe	3/4	10/-
John Chamber	10/-	40/-
Andrew Bacheler	4/-	£20
William Bacheler	-	-
Robert White		£4
Thomas Cooke		£4
Thomas Russell		26/8
The Churchwardens have in box		20/-

This roll also listed the weapons available, but the inhabitants of St. Leonards seem to have been a peaceful group who had none; among the 45 listed for Aston Clinton the available armaments consisted of 5 bills and 2 bows.

Thomas Playstowe, whom we have already mentioned, may have been a gentleman, though his connection with the family which later owned the Lee is obscure. The others are probably all yeoman farmers. Of the three wealthiest, John Ginger may have been a tenant of Missenden Abbey, his descendants buying one of these farms Brune's about the end of the 16th century, but though this remains a prominent St. Leonards family, they have left us little information about themselves and we must turn to the other two, the Baldwins and the Batchelors, for knowledge of the village. Both families are too complicated for the family trees to be sorted out in detail, but it is clear that they were both typical of the wealthier yeomen farmers of this part of Bucks who had acquired land wherever they could in any of the surrounding parishes. They may, too, both have come from Chesham, where in 1468 John Baldwyn and William Bachelor were the two 'most aged and best' in Belenden and as such were required to certify the survey of the glebes and tithes in that hamlet belonging to Leicester Abbey.[5] We do not know when they came to St. Leonards, but they must have been settled there by 1522.

The Baldwins, as shown in the Muster Roll, were at Dundridge, where the family were to remain for two and a half centuries, first as tenant farmers and from 1578 as owners. They were a family with marked physical characteristics whose bright blue eyes still make them immediately recognisable when, as is the habit of Americans, descendants of the branch which emigrated in 1642, return to visit their old family home. In 1525 Robert Baldwin managed to get his assessment reduced from £20 to £13 because, according to an explanatory footnote, he was,

'Decaeid by corn and maryage of his son £8.' [6]

The son concerned may have been Richard, who eventually inherited the lease of Dundridge. The Robert junior of the Muster Roll disappears, but another son, Thomas of Wendover, married one of John Ginger's daughters, and the eldest, John of the Hale, we shall meet again shortly. Robert Baldwin's 'decay' seems to have been only temporary, for when he died in 1536 he had lands and tenements at Bellendon and at Dungrove in Botley and his three sons, whether from inheritance or by their own efforts are found with lands at Great Missenden, The Lee, Wendover, The Hale, Aston Clinton and Cholesbury.[5]

Fifty years later the Baldwins dominated St. Leonards, but at this stage early in the century they shared the village with the Batchelors, the first of whom, Andrew, has left us a Will dated 1527 of absorbing interest. It not only demonstrates the process by which the yeoman farmer built up his lands but it also throws much light on the agricultural patterns of the village at the time.[7] He seems to have started out owning jointly with his wife 'Jone' lands and tenements in Nettledon and further lands and tenements 'within the parishes of Aston Clinton, Wendover and Buckland'. To these he had added

(1) Lands and tenements bought of Richard Edmunds lying in Hawridge

(2) Lands and tenements bought of William Bennyng and Thomas Bennyng in the Parishes of Cholesbury, Chesham and Hawridge.

(3) A house, garden and appurtenances in Berkhamsted with an
acre of land and wood called Clayacre in the Parish of
Hawridge.

He owned two oxen, presumably plough beasts, but he was
mainly a sheep and cattle farmer, leaving to his five sons 140
sheep, 80 beasts and one cow to which must be added an un-
specified number of beasts and sheep which he said were already
in the keeping of William, his eldest son. In the Muster Roll of
1522 Andrew's lands were valued at only 4s, but his goods,
including his stock, had the high value of £20.

William was left the lands in Berkhamsted and Nettleden and
does not come into our story. John had the Richard Edmunds
holding in Hawridge; Thomas the land and tenements in the
parishes of Cholesbury, Chesham and Hawridge. Andrew received
Clay Acre in Hawridge with lands in Berkhamsted; Richard the
lands and tenements in Aston Clinton, Wendover and Buckland
after the death of Andrew's wife. We shall come back to John and
Thomas shortly.

Andrew Batchelor describes himself as of Aston Clinton. His
Will, however, suggests that he actually came from St. Leonards, as
he left 40s to the Chapel there as compared with 6/8d to the
parish churches of Aston Clinton, Cholesbury and Hawridge and
3/4d to four other churches. From later information we discover
that he was the tenant of part, at least, of Chapel Farm, so his
lands 'within the Parishes of Aston Clinton, Wendover and
Buckland' could have been a connected farm. He did not,
however, have undisputed possession of the Plaistowe Trust lands.
As already mentioned, the Trust deed omits to mention a purpose
and the Chaplain of St. Leonards may have felt justified in
assuming that its intention was to supplement a poor living valued
at only £6. 0. 0.[8] Authority felt differently, and in 1530 John
Laughton, the King's Escheator, was commanded to hold an
enquiry at Cholesbury which pronounced that,[9]

'A certain William Preston, Chaplain of St. Leonards has
appropriated 4 closes of land and a Grove of Woodland, 40 acres
without the King's permission and orders how the Estate is to be
administered.'

The outcome of this enquiry seems to be a little vague but new
Trustees were appointed including Sir John Hampden, who by

Fig. 13 Chapel Farm, St Leonards (now called Buckland Grange)

1541 finding himself the sole surviving Trustee, appointed four members of the Baldwyn family, with John and Henry Gynger and James Birch.[10]

The St. Leonards farmers might carry on their own lives oblivious to national events and affairs of state, but their owners were too distinguished to disengage themselves. Missenden Abbey disappeared in 1539 when the major religious houses were dissolved and in the same year the old Countess of Salisbury, accused of complicity in one of the many plots of Henry VIII's reign, was imprisoned in the Tower. Two years later at the ripe age of 80 she was beheaded. There is no evidence that she even saw Dundridge, let alone lived in this remote upland farm, so the local tradition that as 'Silky' she still haunts the house with a soft, silky swishing sound on hot summer evenings may not bear much examination.

The lands all came into the hands of the King until he needed to raise money by selling them. Dundridge was bought by Sir John

Baldwin, Chief Justice of the Common Pleas,[11] but the identity of name with that of the tenants may be accidental as extensive research has failed to find any connection between the eminent branch of the family and the humbler yeoman of our villages, who remained in possession.

Ten years later, however, the general attack on the Chantries and Chapels of Ease was much nearer home and there must have been general unease when the village learned that St. Leonards Chapel was to be the subject of an enquiry. This enquiry into the need for their own local Church touched every individual in the parish. With churchgoing compulsory, few can have relished the prospect of a long wet walk in both directions and with Sunday the only day of freedom, the thought of wasting two hours on this walk—two hours that could have been spent in more entertaining activities such as archery or maypole dancing or even bull or bear baiting—must have been distasteful.

Henry VIII's and Wolsey's attack on the religious houses is generally represented as a high-handed and dictatorial affair with enquiries so rigged or biased that they can only have produced one answer. But at St. Leonards the 'Interrogateryes and Deposicons' have every appearance of being as fair and impartial as any public enquiry would be today. The Commissioners Robert Dormer, Robert Drury and George Wright, had summoned to give evidence the following group of distinguished old men from the surrounding neighbourhood:[12]

John Wyer of Wendover	aged	60
Stephen Rowbird of Chesham	"	58
John Baldwyn of The Hale	"	59
John Naisshe of Weston Turvey	"	60
William Grange of Aston Clinton	"	50
Richard Playstowe of Missenden Magna	"	60
William Marvie of Aston Clinton	"	55
John Moncke of Chesham	"	50

How the 'Jury' was selected is unknown. None of them actually lived at St. Leonards though John Baldwin, one of Robert's sons, must have known the Chapel well enough and from Dundridge would have attended it regularly as a boy. Even from The Hale he may himself have been one of those who found it easier to go to St. Leonards than to his own parish church.

John Wyer was the first spokesman and the enquiry started off with the question,

> 'Ffyrst whether there is and hathe bene in tyme owte of memorye of any mane one Chapell in the sayd parryshe of Ashton Clynton comenlye called the Chapell of Seynte Leonardes ye or no?'

and his answer,

> 'There is and hathe been sythens his remembrances and by fore tyme out of mynde as he hath herd a Chapel within the parishe of Aston Clynton in the said county of Buck. called St. Leonards Chapell.'

There was no disagreement to this answer. John Baldwin added,

> 'He hath knowne the sayd Chapell called St. Leonards to be a Chapell fiftye yeres.'

Next John Wyer was asked,

> 'Howghe fare distante the sayd Chapell stondythe and is seytuate from the Paryshe Churche of the sayd parishe of Aston Clynton?'

to which he replied,

> 'The said Chapell stondeth and is distante from the parishe Church of Aston Clynton aforesaid iii mylls or thereabouts.'

The Commissioners decided to pursue this important point a little further and continued,

> 'Howghe fare the Inhabytans which have used to repare to the seyd Chapell to here there dyvyne service shoulde goe and travell yf they shalde be compelled to goe and repare to there sayd paryshe Churche of Aston Clynton there to heare there dyvyne service?'

The answer which was agreed by all the other elders was,

> 'IX households beinge the Inhabitants of the hamlett of St. Leonards aforesaid are distante eny of them iij miles and some of them iiij miles from the said parishe Churche of Aston Clynton and also he affirmeth that diuse other Inhabitants whereof some bene of the parishe of Cheshme and some of other parishes are likewise distant from there parishe Churches iij miles or more and that by reason thereof the same Inhabitants have for theire easement likewise repared to the said Chapell to here theire divine service.'

The Chesham parishioners presumably came from the edge of

Bellingdon. The other parishes may well have included a few inhabitants of Buckland Common who would no doubt have been delighted to avoid, if they could, the five-mile tramp to their own parish church.

These first three questions were practical ones, the fourth was probably the crucial point of the enquiry. The question went:

> 'Whether the said Chapell of Seynt Leonards hathe been knowen and taken as a Chapell of Ease for the Inhabytants dwellinge within the seyd paryche of Aston Clynton and nygh to the seyd Chapell or as a Free Chapell?'

A Free Chapel was one which had endowment separate from its parish church. Thomas Plaistowe may have been more far-sighted than he knew in failing to specify the purpose of his Trust, for whereas the Free Chapels disappeared some at least of the Chapels of Ease were allowed to remain. In this case Stephen Wyer could answer,

> 'The said Chapell hathe bene sythens his knowledge and remembraunce and as even he hath herde a Chapel of Ease and noe Free Chapell and that noe preiste there hath had any certen lyvinge or Stjpend but that suche prieste as hath served & Saide Divine Service there hath bene from Sonday to Sonday and from tyme to tyme hired by the said inhituts of the said hamlett of St. Leonards at there owne proper costes and charges.'

Again the Commissioners pursued this point and asked,

> 'Whether those lands and tents whiche be in the tenure and occupation of Johane Bacheler widowe and of Thoms, Tracher were fyrst geven for the fyndynge of a prest to mynyster and serve in the sayd Chapell of St. Leonards or to what other use the said lands and tenements were fyrst given?'

The reply went,

> 'He never herde no knewe that the lands and tents were given for the fyndynge of any preist theire but saith that suche men as hathe been thereof seised to theire owne uses have imployed part of the Revenewe of the same lands as well towardes the hyringe of a preist to say divine service at the said Chapell and for the reparacons of the same with the tents thereunto belonginge as also for and towardes the amendinge of the highe wayes there-aboughts. And furder the said deponent saith that for the bettre accomplishmente of the same they the said owners of the said

landes have not onely burdened themselves at their owne charges but also have procured the ayde and charitable helpe of the inhitunts of the parishes thereaboughts.'

Again John Baldwin added to this,

'He hath knowen that parte of the proffytts of the same landes hathe ben used and employed to the relieffe of the poore inhabitants of the said hamlett.'

The Commissioners were probably suspicious and perhaps disappointed by these answers, so they continued,

'To what use the same lands and tenements have bene imployed and bestowed by the space of XX or XXX yeares nowe last past?'

Stephen Wyer was not to be caught in this obvious trap and the reply reads,

'The pryffetts of the said landes and tents have ben employed by the space of XLti yeares and above to such entente as are abovesaid.'

This is supplemented by William Marvie, who added,

'The proffiths of the said landes hathe ben employed at the pleasure of the ffeafies as they have thought good.'

Finally the question was asked,

'Of what yerelie value the seyd lands and tents be nowe of?'

John Wyer replied,

'The said landes and tents being in the tenure of the said Johan Bacheler and Thomas Tracher over and besides the rentes reasolute goinge out of the same are of the clere yerelie value of XXiijs and furdre the said owners are and doe stonde chargeable to the grettre parte of the reparacons of the premisses out of the same value and not the said tenaunts.'

Stephen Rowbird and one or two others were unable to answer this question. John Baldwyn again was able to add details and told the commissioners,

'The said landes and tents are of the clere yerelie value of xiij over and above the resolute rentes which amounteth to the some of 24/8d. Ob vidz to the Mannor of A.C. XViij—to the Mannor of Myssenden Vs—to the Mercers of London as to there Manor of the Vaches Xiiijd—to the Certente vid ob.' (halfpenny)

The Chapel was allowed to remain, St. Leonards obviously being luckier or the local witnesses more effective than in some other villages such as Edlesborough, where the Chapel disappeared though it was just as far from the parish church as St. Leonards was from Aston Clinton.

The 'Johane Bacheler widowe' mentioned in this enquiry is Andrew's widow. It will be remembered (page 84) that he left his lands in St. Leonards to his son Richard after his wife's death. When Richard made his Will in 1548 he obviously thought it would be a near thing whether he or his mother died first as[13] he left to his son William,

> 'Such houses and lands being and living in the Parishes of Aston Clinton and Buckland and Wendover whereof I shuld or might be heyre after the disease of my mother if I were the longest lived.'

As it turned out, she outlived him by ten years. Richard could still leave his stock, 2 oxen, 17 cattle and 32 sheep to his children and one son, Richard, received a cottage and three half acres in Tring, while another, John, was bequeathed the messuage in Hawridge in the occupation of Richard's brother John but the lands in St. Leonards were not his for disposal.

Another Batcheler, William[14] turns up about this time at Chivery, possibly as a tenant. His Will in 1555[15] contains no bequests of land, but he had a part share of a plough and plough gear, 30 or 40 sheep, a cow called Nowte and another called Lily. Most of his property went to his brother-in-law, Thomas Gewat, and this branch of the family disappears.

From these Batchelor Wills, St. Leonards emerges as an area mainly devoted to cattle and sheep, a likely enough situation in view of the very small population for a village of about 970 acres. Soon after Mary came to the throne, the parent Manor of Aston Clinton was restored to the Countess of Salisbury's descendants, Sir Thomas Hastings and his wife Winifred who, after being widowed, married Sir Thomas Barrington[16], and it was these new owners who must have initiated a Field Survey of their property in 1582.[17] Dundridge was excluded as it had by now been bought by 'our' Baldwins, but with this exception the Survey probably covered the whole village and shows that the land was occupied as follows:-

		Rent
Henry Baldwin	Copyhold	2 closes of pasture called Grovers — 6 roods 7 poles

		Rent
Silvester Baldwin	Freehold	1 cottage, 2 acres of pasture called Fledells
Silvester Baldwin	Copyhold	2 little closes of pasture one called Black Mere Close containing 1 acre, 2 roods and the other Grove Orchard (This is repeated in a later entry and attributed to Silvester and John on a life tenancy) 12d
Silvester and John Baldwin	Life tenancy	3 parcels of land called Chivery Hiding, Smylcroft and Chivery Wike containing 18 acres 2 roods 5/-
Feoffees of St. Leonards	Freehold	One messuage now in the tenure of Silvester Baldwin with 60 acres of lands, pastures and meadows, lying in diverse parcels
Feoffees of St. Leonards	Freehold	One messuage and 60 acres of arable, pasture and meadow 16/6d
The Lord of the Manor		'One great wodd — as parcel of his wast' 96 acres
— Cheyney Esq.		5 acres 15d (This entry is too faded to be fully legible)
Henry Sandwell		Messuage, Cottage 57 acres, 20 acres of pasture, 8 of meadow 23/8d

St LEONARDS
~About the time of the 1581 Field ~
~ Survey ~

KEY

——	Roads
- - -	Footpaths
·····	Field Boundaries
■-■-■	Parish Boundaries
+++	Woods
✝ ◦	Churches & Bldgs

Chivery

One Great Wood Common

7

ndover

Chapel Farm

Kyrke Lade

5

3

4

Cherche Lands

Jenkins Lane

2

1

Stony Croft

6

Jenkyn's Lands

Ryddings

8

Broad St. Lane

Dundridge Manor

Stone Hills Wood

Archard Field & Wood

Widow Croft Wood

Old Bruns Farm

Lady Grove

Browns Farm

Cindery Bottom

N

1 Grover's ~ Henry Baldwin
2 Pleydells ~ Sylvester Baldwin
3 Blackmere Close Sylvester, John & Thomas Baldwin
4 Grove Meade
5 Possibly belonged 1st Parson of Aston Clinton
6 William Batchelor's Cottage
7 Probable Site of Cottages
8 Robert Plaston's Messuage

Map 3

Rent

William Bringginsham	Freehold	Messuage, 3 cottages, about 86 acres of arable, 8 pasture, 5 of meadow and 3 of wood 25/4d
William Bate	Life tenancy in his wife's right	Messuage and about 27 acres of arable, pasture and meadow 3/4d
Robert Plastow	Freeholder	One messuage, garden, orchard, 8 acres of wood and pasture and 2 pightles
William Batchelor	Freeholder	One cottage and one acre of pasture
William Stonehills	Copyhold	Tenement or cottage 20d
John Pratt	Copyhold	Tenement 2/6d
Richard Lashmells	Copyhold	One tenement 12d
Robert Kingham	Copyhold	One tenement 8d
Katherine Webbe	Copyhold	One cottage 8d
Parson of Aston Clinton	Unknown	One little pightle — 1 acre

One or two of the entries are worth repeating in full to show the sort of detail which enables us to reconstruct from this survey a reasonably accurate map of the greater part of St. Leonards at the time (see page 93). For example,

> 'Henrie Baldwin holdeth by copy of court rolls Two closes of pasture called Grovers containing 6 acres 7 perches, Buckland Wood north and east, a Lane called Brode Street South, a close parcell of Downridge and ye land belonging to St. Leonards west.'

Next to him:

> 'Silvester Baldwin next ye same holdeth freely one cottage and two acres of pasture called Pledells, Buckland wood east and ye high way west and south ye land of John Cheney, Esq., north.'

Turning to the occupants we see that the Batchelors have almost disappeared, the only one remaining, William, having no more than

> 'One cottage and one acre of pasture adjoining.'

Their decline may have been due to the loss in a lawsuit with Robert Playstowe who accused a William Batchelor of cutting down timber standing on his land and eventually won the case, being given £40 damages (he had claimed the large sum for those days of £100) and costs. [18]

Both at Chapel Farm and at Chivery they have been supplanted by the Baldwins who now dominate the village, farming Dundridge, Chapel Farm and part of Chivery. Parts of the present Dundridge Manor may have been built about this time and the Baldwins may have extended their building activities to Chapel Farm the oldest part of which is thought to date from about 1580. [19],

The three farms which are not clearly identified by description are those belonging to William Bate, William Brigginshaw and Henry Sandwell, but from the order in which entries appear in this survey it seems likely that Bate was a tenant at Chivery, Brigginshaw held the freehold of Brune's Farm and Sandwell that of Browne's. Chivery, therefore, was retained firmly by the Lord of the Manor, divided between two farmers William Bate and Silvester and John Baldwin who only enjoyed life tenancies.

The copyhold properties were held by a yearly rent 'suit of court and herriott', and the freehold mainly 'by rent and suit of Court', but there are two survivals in these of an old custom, a token addition to the rent in recognition of dependent tenure. In some Manors this was a red rose or a gilly flower; in Aston Clinton the appropriate payment for which De la Vache and William Brigginshaw were liable was,

> 'one pound of peper.'

The details from this Field Survey add to the information obtained from Wills about the agriculture in the village. Chapel Farm had some arable—we are not told the acreage—but apart

Fig. 14 Twentieth-century Cholesbury

from this the only areas of arable were at the two farms in Arrewig Lane Brune's and Browne's, both enjoying a reasonable amount of flat land along the top of a ridge. Apart from this and possibly part of Dundridge, the area was still devoted to sheep and cattle. The main change in 60 years, therefore, was in land ownership. Three of the main farms, Dundridge, Brune's and Browne's now belong to resident yeoman farmers instead of to eminent, but distant, Lords of the Manor or Missenden Abbey. The change seems to have been accompanied by some growth of population for the Field Survey names twelve resident families, omitting Cheney and counting the Baldwins as one; this may be an underestimate, as the occupants of four farm cottages are not mentioned.

Looking at the map again, perhaps the most surprising feature is that if one of these 16th century Baldwins were to return today he would have no difficulty in finding his way around. South of the Church, this area must still look, except for a few new houses along the road, almost exactly as it did in 1582 and the names of fields and woodlands are virtually unchanged too. Coming out of his house at Dundridge, our reincarnated Baldwin would look first to the Dundridge hedgerow marking the southern boundary of the parish and then west across the valley which dips down into Cindery Bottom to the outlying farms of Brune's and Browne's. He would still cross the 'Lane called Brode Street' and walk over Jenkins Fields to the Chapel and Chapel Farm where, at the time that Henry Baldwin owned Dundridge, his brother Silvester was the tenant. Opposite Chapel Farm he would see the first sign of change for he would miss Black Mere, the familiar watering spot, filled in since 1923, and would no doubt feel that the school was a poor substitute for the little group of cottages which probably occupied this corner.

Going north towards Chivery, where Silvester's sons, Silvester and John, were tenants of the Lady Winifred Hastings, Lord of the Manor of Aston Clinton, there has been much more change, for the extensive area of common was only enclosed in 1816 and in 1582 was dominated by

> 'One GREAT WODD adjoining upon St. Leonards Chappell belonging to the lord as parcel of his wast cont. 96 acres. The copyhold lands of Silvester Baldwin and the demesne lands of Chivery now belonging to John Gage Esq. upon the north side

lands holden of De la Vache and St. Leonards Chappell and others South, yt abbutt upon ye wodde of Buckland at east and upon the parish of Wendover towards the West.'

Cut off by this wood, St. Leonards must still have been pretty isolated from its parent village of Aston Clinton.

Before we move on to our other villages, there is just one more change to record—in 1587 the Chapel is referred to as [20]

'the decayed Free Chapel of St. Leonards.'

We can only guess at the reasons for the 'decay' of a Chapel which, 38 years earlier, the village had saved from dissolution. If it had not been for the Field Survey we would have guessed wrongly that St. Leonards had been depopulated in this age of enclosures. Without this obvious reason we can only suggest that the Baldwin family, the largest landowners on whom the Chapel would have been dependent for financial support, took little interest in a Chapel which they could not control as they never had the advowson, and preferred to use Cholesbury, like St. Leonards only half a mile away, where the family had the right of presentment. Silvester Baldwin was married there in 1590 and Richard two years later. A sprinkling of other St. Leonards names appear in the Cholesbury Parish Register and it was to be nearly 80 years before the Chapel, then a ruin with only the bare walls standing, was to be restored. As an aside we might mention here that the '2 closes of pasture called Grovers' of which Henry Baldwin held the copyhold were later to become a Charity for the poor of St. Leonards who received £1 a year. The charity still exists.

Notes and References

[1]Julian Cornwall, 'An Elizabethan Census of 1563' in *Recs. of Bucks*. Vol.XVI (1959) p.270.

[2]30 Aug. 23 Hen.VII –B.A.S. 111/17.

[3]1 Sept. 23 Hen.VII – B.A.S. 112/17.

[4]We are fortunate that the Muster Roll for Aston Clinton shows St. Leonards under a separate heading.

[5]A. Vere Woodman 'The Baldwins of Dundridge and Chesham in Co.Bucks.' in *The New England Historical and Genealogical Register* Oct. 1959. This is the source for many of the ensuing references to the Baldwin family.

[6]*Subsidy Roll for Bucks. 1524* Ed. by Prof. A. C. Chibnall and A. Vere Woodman (Bucks. Rec. Soc. 1950) p.96.

[7]Bucks C.R.O. Will no. D/A/We/2/126, Bacheler, Andrew 1527. This will was transcibed by the late Mr. F. G. Gurney of the B.A.S.

[8]*A Subsidy Collected in the Diocese of Lincoln 1526* Ed. by Rev. H. Salter (B. H. Blackwell and H. Frowde 1909). The names of the Chaplains of St. Leonards at this date are unknown, but in the subsidy a second name. Dom. Thomas Sheparde is included after the Rector of Aston Clinton. The value is shown as vi 1. assessed q. t. (one fifteenth) at viij s. This could apply to a Curate at Aston Clinton, but seems more likely to refer to the detached Chapel at St. Leonards.

[9]25 Hen.VIII. B.A.S. 113/17.

[10]20 May 33 Hen.VIII. B.A.S.114/17.

[11]V.C.H. *Bucks*. Vol.II, p.316.

[12]B.A.S. 121/17 Copy dated 28 Nov. 13 Chas.I of Interrogatories and Deposicons 3 Ed.VI.

[13]Bucks. C.R.O. D/A/We/6/376 Bacheler, Richard 1548 D/A/Wf/2/78.

[14]Probably a brother or nephew of Andrew as he mentions a brother, Robert, who does not appear in Andrew's will.

[15]Bucks. C.R.O. D/A/We/8/110 Batchelor, William 1555 D/A/Wf/2/219.

[16]V.C.H. *Bucks*. vol.II, p.313.

[17]S T 42 Bucks. Aston Clinton Field Survey 1581. We are grateful to the Huntington Library, San Marino, California, for photographic copies of this survey and for permission to publish extracts.

[18]Information from the Plaistowe family history compiled by Mr. D. W. Plaistowe 1945. We are indebted to Mr. D. W. Plaistowe of Chesham Bois for the loan of this manuscript and permission to publish extracts.

[19]For the approximate dates of this and other buildings mentioned in Chapters X and XI we are indebted to Mr Guy Beresford.

[20]Lipscomb, Vol.II p.93. The Chapel with other lands in the district were granted by Elizabeth to Will Tipper and Robert Dawe in 1587. These names do not appear in any local records.

X

'HE PLAYED FOOTBALL IN HIS SHIRT'

Hawridge and its people as the village develops—
1520–1640

A notorious parson; the local farmers and their lands; evidence for enclosure of old open fields; a grand funeral for the Lord of the Manor; Dame Dorothy Packington and her claim to control the Election at Aylesbury; the parsonage and its lands; 16th century cottages.

The Elizabethan census[1] gives the population of Hawridge in 1563 as 15 families, double that at St. Leonards. Its development in the 16th century is a much more complex story involving the conversion of the open fields into enclosed farms, a story, moreover, which is poorly documented. The Muster Roll has disappeared, there is no helpful Enquiry or Field Survey and our only sources of information are Wills and ecclesiastical records. We start with the latter, for in 1520 the parson of Hawridge was a notorious character.

By the beginning of the 16th century the Bishops had many problems to worry them about the state of the Church for, along-side recurrent heresies, they were trying to combat the general lowering of standards both in monasteries and among parochial clergy. In 1516 Bishop William Atwater of Lincoln had already ordered the Rector of Hawridge, who had left his own parish to serve one in London, to reside. Three years later another visitation disclosed that the Buckinghamshire clergy generally were in a bad state, for in only 22 of the parishes was it possible to make the return *Omnia bene*. One of the worst was Hawridge where the report reads:[2]

> 'The Lord Richard, the curate there, is a common player at foot-ball in his shirt, and on Good Friday the same Lord Curate said all Divine Services before the hour at 8 a.m., even compline and he did the same on Palm Sunday, Easter Even and Easter Day. The same curate was not living in that parish but at Cheham. The

same played at dice with the common people. The rector did not reside but served a cure in London at St John the Evangelist. The rectory is in ruins.'

The Curate was promptly suspended and the Rector instructed to attend his cure. This time he could not ignore the stern warning and the Procurator could report a little later:[3]

'That the Rector of Hawridge now resides and intends to reside henceforth and promised that all the ruin in the said three benefices and other irregularities will be fully repaired by pentecost and under penalty of sequestration.'

This Rector, Christopher Mychell, has disappeared by 1526 when the Clerical subsidy was levied and the new Rector of Hawridge, Richard Thomson, had to pay 16/11d.

Though far from wealthy, Hawridge was not one of the poorer parishes, assessed at £8.13.4d having to pay the subsidy at the higher rate of one tenth. This valuation presumably included lands at Marsworth, as the Rector of Hawridge appears on the Muster Roll for that village in 1522 with a tenement valued at £1.0.0. This land consisted of one small close and 25 acres in strips lying in the three open fields at Marsworth which were only enclosed in 1811.[4] The donor of this land is unknown; though mentioned in the early Terriers, the Rectors do not try to explain how they obtained the land and by the 18th century they can only say,

'Donation of a lady unknown to the Rectory of Hawridge ...'
'Time Immemorial.'

We have already met two of the parishioners, mentioned in Andrew Batchelor's Will (see Chapter IX), for the lands which Thomas inherited in Cholesbury, Hawridge and Chesham had been bought from William and Thomas Bennyng, and Clay Acre, bequeathed to Andrew Jun., had come from William Hollyman. Thomas and Andrew Batchelor were both under 18 when their father died and may not yet have occupied their lands. We have not sufficient information to identify Thomas's inheritance at this stage, but before pursuing this we should first meet two other families, the Gearys and the Putnams.

The Gearys were a family we were keen to discover because they have given their name to a lovely little wood which delights us every time we look out of the window. It is reputed to be

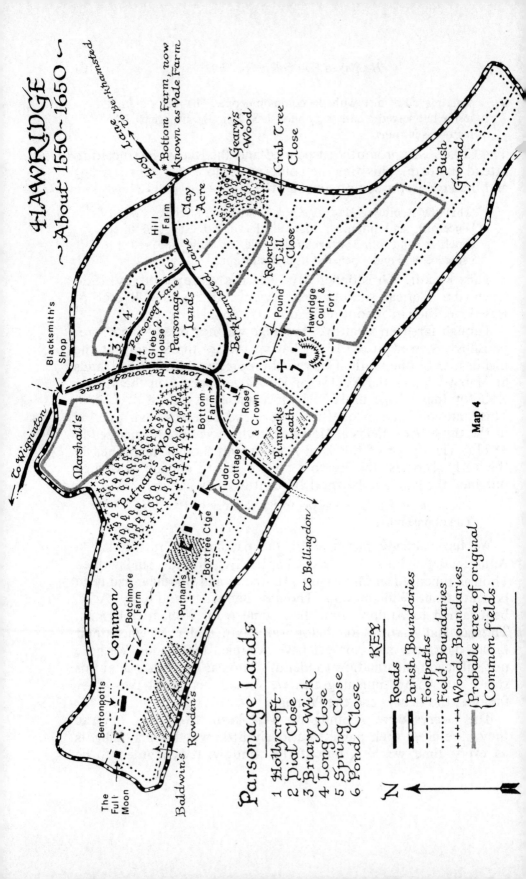

HAWRIDGE
~ About 1550 ~ 1650 ~

To Berkhamsted

Hog Lane

*Bottom Farm, now known as Vale Farm

Geary's Wood

Crab Tree Close

Clay Acre

Hill Farm

Roberts Dell Close

Berkhamsted Lane

Parsonage Lane

Parsonage Lands

Blacksmith's Shop

6

5

4

3

Glebe House 2

Pound

Hawridge Court & Fort

Lower Parsonage Lane

To Wigginton

Marshall's

*Bottom Farm

Rose & Crown

Pinnocks Leath

Putnam's Wood

Tudor Cottage

Boxtree Ctge

Botchmore Farm

Putnams

Bentonpotts

The Full Moon

Baldwin's Rowden's

Common

To Bellingdon

Parsonage Lands

1 Hollycroft
2 Dial Close
3 Briary Wick
4 Long Close
5 Spring Close
6 Pond Close

KEY

— Roads
—·— Parish Boundaries
– – – Footpaths
·········· Field Boundaries
+ + + + Woods Boundaries
Probable area of original Common fields.

Map 4

N

named after Jasper Geary, who died in 1624, but we have seen no evidence for this and it may have been earlier as the family had been at Hawridge a hundred years before. In 1521 John Geary[5] of Chesham Woburn left 3/4d for a Church in Hawridge, so he must have had some stake in this village, though he only mentions land in Drayton Beauchamp and Cholesbury. Other Geary wills during the 16th century tell us nothing about Hawridge, but the family were certainly established there in 1597 when 'Old Richard Geary late of Hawridge' was buried in Chesham. Though the Geary land, as we learn shortly afterwards, was tucked away in the most sheltered spot in the parish at Bottom Farm, in the hollow where the road starts to climb to Heath End, 'Old Richard' may have decided in his old age that Hawridge lacked certain sophisticated comforts and retired to Chesham while his sons carried on the farm.

Our third family, the Putnams, have also left their name about in one field and one small piece of wood. The Batchelors and the Gearys may have been descendants of the old husbandmen in a medieval Manor; the Putnams are typical of another strain which appears among the yeomen of the 16th century, the descendants of the younger sons of a Norman family. The Putnams[6] took their name from the village of Puttenham held by Roger, son of Anschill, of the Bishop of Bayeux in 1086. Roger's grandson William adopted the village name as the family name and throughout the 13th and 14th centuries branches of the family are found in at least 13 Buckinghamshire villages, including Drayton Beauchamp and Chesham.

The first we hear of the family's arrival in our villages is in 1552 when John Putnam owned in Hawridge:[7]

(a)   A House and lands and one other close on Hawridge Hill occupied by John Coyston and left to his son Henry.
(b)   The 'house wherein I nowe dwell' left to his son William after the decease of his wife Agnes
(c)   Two closes called Pinnocks Leath and Garrett's Wike, the former bequeathed to Henry and the latter presumably to William though he is not specific about this
(d)   Land held by indentures i.e. by lease left to William.

The field name Pinnocks Leath still exists and, as the map on page 102 shows, is in one of the areas which we have assumed to be those of the open fields. Garrett's Wike is not identifiable, but on field name evidence one of the Putnam houses can only have been the farm (now demolished) alongside the field still known as Putnam's and assumed to be one of the newer farms which developed as the waste was brought into cultivation.

In 1561, John's brother William also acquires lands in Hawridge,[8] identifiable as Marshall's, probably part of the third open field at Heath End.

John Putnam was determined that the lands he had acquired should if possible remain in the family; he makes detailed provisions for the brothers to purchase each other's bequests if the inheritor should wish to sell. This will also illustrates another problem of the 16th century, the worry that farms might be broken up into fragments too small to form an economic holding. Two of his sons, Richard and Edward, receive no lands, but in compensation his eldest son William is to pay each of them a life annuity of 3/4d; or, if one of them should die, the annuity for the survivor was to be increased to 6/8d. This figure of 6/8d was a statutory ancient yearly rent and there were certainly Manors where provisions of this kind were part of the customs of the Manor. There are no surviving documents to show whether this was the case in Hawridge, but these provisions in John Putnam's Will may well illustrate the link between medieval and modern customs in providing for the sons.

The exact descent of the Putnam lands in Hawridge are a little complicated; by 1600 they have all been acquired by Richard's son, another John, and on his death in 1592[9] by his son Thomas, then under 18. This Will adds to our knowledge of the Hawridge farms, for Thomas was to inherit at 18, with the 'landes, howses and tenements' in Hawridge,

> '2 acres of wheat, 2 acres of barley, 20 sheep, 2 milch beasts, 2
> horses [the Will is damaged—only 'Ho' remaining of this word] a
> plough and plough gear, a cart and cart gear, a folding table a
> round table, a stool and a feather bed.'

We shall meet Thomas Putnam again shortly in Cholesbury as well as Hawridge. In the meantime we must go back to the Batchelors.

We have seen from Andrew Batchelor's Will (see page 84) his sons John and Thomas settling in Hawridge, though it is not until the end of the century that we can start to discover their location.

John's lands were inherited by a nephew John the Younger son of Richard of St. Leonards, who may have been taken ill rather suddenly. 'Lying on his death bed,' as he tells us, John could only stammer out these few words to the attendant parson John Walweyn: [10]

> 'God bless my son Anthony and send him of his grace to whom I give all my goods, my debts being paid, and my funeral expenses defrayed.'

A Thomas Batchelor who dies in 1598 describing himself as a Yeoman of Hawridge makes some interesting bequests,

> 'To the repairing of the church of Hawridge 3/4d, to repairing of the highway to Berkhamsted and Hog Lane 3/4d, to the poorest of Cholesbury to be distributed at the discretion of my executor 3s. To my daughter Cicely 3 score pounds, two pairs of sheets, the long table on the frame that standeth in my last farm in Hawridge, a blanket, a feather bed, 4 ewes, a new brass pot, 4 of the best pewter dishes and two of the lesser, a Christening sheet, the best carpet.'

The rest of his goods and chattels go to John his son and heir, but again he tells us nothing about his lands so we are not much further.

The helpful will is from another Thomas Batchelor who dies in 1602 describing himself as a yeoman of Porters in Hawridge. [11] He owns 20 acres of wood pasture and arable in Wendover, which were obviously profitable as he left instructions that the executors were to make £10 from this within two years, but are otherwise of no interest to us. In Hawridge, however, he owned a close called Rowdens, 6 acres, which went to his son Thomas. From this he directed that three loads of wood should be delivered annually to,

> 'Joane now my wife to maintain a fire for her, one acre of land, 4 closes in East Field, a house and lands wherein William Mead now liveth,'

Of this property Rowdens is a field, probably then a wood, near the Cholesbury end, the field name still existing. East field may have been in the Hill Farm area (see page 79) and might be the first record of Batchelor ownership of that farm, and Porters, though the name has disappeared, is traceable from later evidence as the house now known as Bentonpotts another house which has been dated about 1580. This was the period of 'The Great

Fig. 15 "The Full Moon" Chelsebury Cottages

Rebuild' when yeomen farmers like the Batchelors and the Baldwins were prosperous enough to build themselves good solid houses which still survive. Leonard who is Thomas' heir disappears from our history, but his son Thomas and his heirs are prominent in both Hawridge and Cholesbury for the next 70 years.

They are not the only members of this family. Wills suggest at least one other line, possibly descended from Anthony, but this is a complicated family which needs a genealogist to disentangle it. The mere historian is constantly up against the problem that time does not permit the tracing of every family through all its ramifications and the Batchelors are both one of the easiest and one of the most difficult. They help by writing informative Wills; they are awkward because some of them are unusually long-lived and produce families of ten or more.

By this time, in addition to the brass, pewter and feather beds, it is not unusual to find pairs of sheets mentioned in Wills; they are precious enough to be bequeathed especially and not just included under 'the rest of my goods and chattels.' There is one yeoman in Hawridge, however, Nicholas Dell, who seems to have been a step ahead of his neighbours in sophisticated living. He not only had nine pairs of sheets, his wife getting five pairs, but three table cloths and thirteen table napkins divided between his wife and two sons. Though he says he is 'of Hawridge' the only land he mentions is in Northchurch and the family does not reappear in our history despite the fact that Dell is a common enough name in these parts.[12]

From the evidence of these Wills it appears that the partition and enclosure of the open fields of Hawridge had started by 1550, if not earlier, and the shape of the modern village is beginning to emerge. The outlying field at Heath End may already have been broken up; the western field on Hawridge Hill has been divided into closes, one of which, at least, has been sold to John Putnam, while the others may have been leased. The second field at Hawridge, however, still belongs to the Lord of the Manor, together with some of the pasture at Heath End, and possession of the former makes it possible for Hawridge Court to develop as an enclosed estate, possibly a sheep farm, growing later into the 18th century type of park. It may have been this which in 1574 attracted Thomas Tasburgh to buy the Manor.

Thomas Tasburgh was a gentleman who played his part in county affairs as High Sheriff in 1580, and Knight of the Shire nine years later. His wife, formerly Dame Dorothy, was even more prominent, or at least notorious. The daughter of Sir Thomas Kitson and the wife first of Sir Thomas Packington, a grandson of Chief Justice Baldwin and another prominent man in the county, she obviously had big ideas, for R. Gibbs, whose only fault as a chronicler is that he never bothers to quote his sources, tells us in *Bucks Local Occurrences* a collection of colourful extracts that Sir Thomas's funeral in June 1572 was very grand:[13]

> 'There were trumpeters and heralds, and led horses all caparisoned and the officers of the college of arms attended, there was Robert Croke, Esq. Clarenceaux King of Arms: Hugh Cotgrave Esq., Richmond Herald and a vast retinue. The mourners were John Pakington, Esq. son and heir; Sir W. Cordell, Knight, Master of the Rolls; Sir John Spencer, Knight; John Burley Esq., and Richard Cooper, Esq., and the ceremony was witnessed by a great concourse of people.'

But Dame Dorothy had not bothered to wait until her late husband was buried before making herself felt. On 3 May 1572, claiming to be 'lord and owner of Aylesbury', she issued the following proclamation:[14]

> 'To all Christian people to whom this present writing shall come. I Dame Dorothy Packington, widow, late wife of Sir John Packington, Knight, Lord and owner of the town of Aylesbury, send greeting. Know ye, me, the said Dame Dorothy Packington, to have chosen, named, and appointed my trustee and well beloved Thomas Litchfield (son in law) and George Burden Esqrs. to be my Burgesses of my said town of Aylesbury. And whatsoever the said Thomas and George burgesses shall do in the service of the Queen's Highness in that present Parliament to be holden at Westminster the eighth day of May next ensuing the date hereof, I the same Dorothy Packington, do ratify and approve to be my own Act, as fully and wholly as if I were or might be present there. In witness whereof . . . '

Her instructions were apparently obeyed, and it is perhaps as well for the future of democracy in Buckinghamshire that she died in 1577. Whether Thomas Tasburgh and Dame Dorothy lived in Hawridge is unknown, but it seems likely that they spent some time in their new Manor as she was buried there and there is a brass plate in the Church inscribed: [15]

'Here lyeth the body of Dame Dorothe Pakyngton. A Daughter of
Sr Thomas Kytson, late of London, Knight, and the wife, first, of
Sr Thomas Pakyngton, Knight and last of Thomas Tasburgh,
esquier.
She lyved very vertuously, and departed this lyfe a mooste
faythfull and godly Christian, the 2de of Maye, when she had
lyved xlvj year[e] and vij monethes, Anno dni 1577.'

We shall never know whether Thomas Tasburgh had his tongue
in his cheek when he compiled or approved this inscription. Any-
how, he married again and seems to have been involved in a family
wrangle when descendants of Thomas and his second wife Jane
married, were given the Manor and then failed to pay Thomas and
Jane the annuity which had been promised to them.

Thomas Tasburgh would have found the Church well equipped
and his parson — a more reputable character than our friend of
1520 — John Walweine had duly subscribed to the three articles in
1584[16] and seems to have met the requirements of the Episcopal
enquiry the next year as he managed to produce his letters of
orders and letters of institution.[17] He was a licensed preacher
though his degree is not stated and his educational qualifications
described in the cryptic remark 'Bred in the Schools.' The remark
suggests an old fashioned type of University learning. His successor, Peter Bate appointed two years later by Tasburgh had the
formal degree of Master of Arts, and by 1603 when there was a
further enquiry Hawridge could muster 62 Communicants.[18]

Twenty years later, when the first Terrier is available the Rector
appears as a landowner. This Terrier is very brief and tells us
mainly about tithes, but one sentence is revealing, for the Rector
speaks of,[19]

'a certain grounde of John Geary over against ye grounde of ye
parsonage of Hawridge.'

The parsonage ground is not specified until the next Terrier in
1639, but there seems little doubt that by 1620 and probably
earlier, the Rector had been given the '25 acres in 5 closes,'[20] the
closes 'all joining together,' as he proudly says later, which are
named and can be fully identified from a later Terrier, and consist
of Dial, Spring, Pond and Long Closes with Briary Wick, Holly
Croft and an acre of garden adjoining the house. These closes, with

the Rectory, are at Heath End. It is hardly the most convenient location half a mile or more from the Church and one wonders whether the Rector may have been 'persuaded' to move by the grant of a nice little compact and newly enclosed farm leaving the area near the Church and Hawridge Court for the Lord of the Manor to enjoy in privacy. Whatever the reason, the Rector was also wealthy enough by 1639 to substitute for a Rectory which in 1520 was 'Ruinosa' a substantial residence consisting of [18]

> 'A hall a citchin and two Buttreys below and two chambers. And
> 5 chambers above. Two Barnes containeing 3 bayes apiece. A
> stable, a lay house. A hen house, A hogsty.'

This Terrier shows the greater part of the Heath End field enclosed. It also places the Geary lands where from later evidence we expected to find them, round about Bottom Farm. From architectural evidence we can fill in one or two more gaps, as the first two cottages along the Cholesbury road, Tudor and Mildmay Cottages, clearly date from the late 16th or early 17th century, as does part of Botchmore Farm. This last farm is probably much older. A freehold property, when the first of our Court Rolls in 1767[21] record a change of ownership, it consisted of two holdings of 25 and 15 acres at rents of 2d or 3d. These very low rents are unlikely to be later than about 14th or 15th century, probably fixed at the time when this farm was a piece of scrub land to be cleared at the expense of its new owner.

This survey has therefore shown the conversion of Hawridge into a land of the five or six farms which still exist, Bottom Farm, Hill Farm and the Glebe Farm over at Heath End and Botchmore and Putnam's on the Cholesbury Road. The freeholders have exchanged their strips in the open fields and part of their share in the common pasture for these enclosed farms. They do not, as in some villages, go the whole way for at least 80 acres of common remain open.[22] At Hawridge, for lack of records, we can only piece together a picture of the changes after they have occurred. For a closer look at the process, we must turn to Cholesbury.

Before leaving Hawridge there is one point which should be mentioned and which suggests that the changes here were not as straightforward as appears at first sight. The 18th century Court Rolls record at least 16 houses held of the Lord of the Manor, enough to accommodate the whole population two centuries earlier. Of these, only one is copyhold, the rest are freehold, an unusual proportion. It is just possible, though unlikely, that Hawridge was a village which had never had any copyholders. The number of freeholders at a later period suggests that there was little conversion of copyhold tenure of cottages to leases, though such conversions may have occurred in the fields, and there is no evidence either for wholesale eviction. We can only assume, therefore, that when the open fields were broken up the copyholders managed to make a good enough bargain to obtain a freehold tenure of their cottages, or of areas on the waste where they could build new cottages, in exchange for their holdings in agricultural land. The average amount of land attached to these cottages is a mere 20 poles, as compared with the four acres which an Act of 1589 tried to lay down as a minimum, the 20 poles presumably being supplemented by the retention of common rights.

Notes and References

[1] Op. cit. Note (1) Chap. IX p.268.

[2] *Visitations in the Diocese of Lincoln* Vol. I Ed. by A. Hamilton Thompson (Lincs. Rec. Soc. 1936) p.44.

[3] *An Episcopal Court Book for the Diocese of Lincoln 1514-70,* Ed. by Margaret Bowker (Lincs. Rec. Soc. 1967) p.131.

[4] B.A.S. 1/59 Field Survey of Marsworth.

[5] Bucks C.R.O. D/A/We/1/52 Gery, John 1521.

[6] Much of the early information on the Putnam family is taken from unpublished papers of Mr. F. G. Gurney and Mr. A. Vere Woodman of the B.A.S.

[7] Bucks. C.R.O. D/A/We/6/113 and 16/85 Putnam, John 1551 D/A/Wf/2/131

[8] B.M. Add. Ch. 5165

[9] Bucks. C.R.O. D/AWf/12/243 Putnam, John 1592.

[10] Bucks. C.R.O. D/A/Wf/8/182 Bacheler, John the Younger, 1577.

[11] Bucks. C.R.O. D/A/We/22/211 Bacheler, Thomas, 1602

[12] Bucks. C.R.O. D/A/We/23/99 Dell, Nicholas 1604 D/A/Wf/16/39

[13] R. Gibbs, *Buckinghamshire A. Record of Local Occurrences* (hereafter referred to as Gibbs) (1878) Vol.I, p.51.

[14] Gibbs, Vol.I, p.52.

[15] Inscription in Hawridge Church.

[16] *The State of the Church I* Ed. by C. W. Foster (Lincs. Rec. Soc. 1926) p.51.

[17] Op. cit. (16) above p.117.

[18] Op. cit. (16) above p.268.

[19] Lincs. Archives Office (abbreviated hereafter to L.A.O.) Terrier Bundle for Hawridge—Terrier of the time of John Blackwell the Elder—about 1620.

[20] Bucks C.R.O. D/A/GT. Hawridge Terrier 1639.

[21] Hawridge Court Book 1767-1923.

[22] 80 Acres of common still existed at the Title Survey of 1838. The area may have been larger in about 1620.

XI

'FOUR CLOSES CALLED HALFACRES'

*Cholesbury spreads across the common in the late 16th
and early 17th centuries*

The misdeeds of a Canon from Missenden Abbey who eventually arrives in
Cholesbury; the Edwardian Inventory of Church property; Court Rolls and their
picture of the development of the village.

Here, as at Hawridge, it is the wills of Andrew Batchelor (page 84) and John Geary (page 103) which introduce us first to the new generation of yeomen farmers; but before tracing their development, we once again go to the Church to discover the topics which our friends would have discussed over a mug of ale.

Of their own Curate early in the 16th century we know nothing but his name, Thomas Stryton,[1] that the Curacy was valued at only £3 6s. 8d. and, on this, his share of the Subsidy of 1526, as for in all benefices valued under £8 0s. 0d., was calculated at one-fifteenth, amounting to 4/5d. Whatever his defects, he must have been harmless, or the Bishop's Commissioners would have reported on him on their way to Hawridge.

Even in these remote areas gossip would have spread, and the irregular proceedings at Missenden Abbey can have been no secret, though the official visit to that Abbey by Thomas Jackman, one of Bishop Longland's Commissioners in 1530 may have been intended as no more than a routine check.[2] He found a situation which was anything but routine. The Canons were uneasy about the management of their affairs by a lay Bailiff who went his own way without let or hindrance, including felling trees around the Abbey itself. The Refectorius, Roger Palmer, reported that there was no reading during meals and he himself was reproved for wearing unseemly clothes. None of this was very serious, but either during or after the visitation further information was produced of a grave enough nature to convince Bishop Longland that he should pay a personal visit.

Longland arrived at Missenden in June 1531, and the charges against Roger Palmer and the Abbott himself were that they had been familiar with Margaret Bishop. It was difficult to obtain evidence against the Abbot, but he himself was forced to give evidence against his Refectorius and the other Canons joined in avidly with their own testimony. Dates were given when Roger Palmer was found in Thomas Bishop's house in the middle of the night in Margaret's company; he was said to have keys to every door in the Abbey and to have gone out by night in lay clothes. The Abbot's Latin was insufficient for all the details and in the middle of his evidence, in the best Latin he could muster, the description appears in English:

> '*Et dicit quod habet claues adulterinos pro qualibet cera monasterij, ac etiam quod incedit nocturnis temporibus habitu laicali, et apprehensus erat noctu predictu* in his doublett and jerkyn with a swerde by his side, *et quod . . .* '

There was no escape from the weight of the evidence. Roger Palmer confessed and was imprisoned during the Bishop's pleasure, the Abbot himself being suspended, though this was probably a nominal sentence of short duration.

The records do not relate whether Roger Palmer had been released from prison by the time that Missenden Abbey was dissolved in 1539, but in 1554 he turns up again at Cholesbury where an enquiry into the state of ex-religious and Chantry priests mentions.

> 'Roger Palmer pr. of Chollsburie formerly canon of Great Missenden with a life pen. of £6 13s. 4d. He was never married and has no eccl. preferments.'[3]

Perhaps he had had enough of women.

The Church at Cholesbury had belonged to the Knights Hospitallers. When this order was dissolved, permission was given for the appointment of a Curate and Richard Norman held the appointment until his death in 1546.[4] We do not know whether Roger Palmer, finding a vacuum, just took over. There is no record of his appointment, but as Parson he must have been versatile enough to survive the rapid changes from the Protestantism of Edward VI, to the Catholic revival under Mary and the new Protestant regime of Elizabeth, and he was buried in the Church in 1568.[5] Even in his secluded village retreat he can have found no

real peace, for Edward VI's Commissioners had demanded a full
inventory of Church property before they appropriated it to fill
the national exchequer. In 1552 Cholesbury Church poor as it was
owned property at least as valuable as that of its wealthier neighbour Hawridge (see Appendix B). The Cholesbury list reads[6]

> won challyse of sylver
> ij lenan clothese for the tabull in the chorche
> ij coopes won of blue sattyn and a nother of frene
> syllke
> a westement of darke tawny sykle
> ij surplescys
> a lattyn pyx that honge ower the awter
> ij candylstyx of lattyn
> iiij lytell bellys of brase
> a peyre of sencers
> a hally water stoke of brase wt a handylle to yt
> ij paueter platteres
> xviij trene platters
> x trensheres
> ij wyne cruattes
> iij tuelles to wype handes on
> ij brase potts and a pan

The next time we have an inventory of its property in 1709 it
had been reduced to[7]

> A Bible
> A Common Prayer Book
> A silver Communion cup
> One bell.

The bell, which still exists, is engraved.

> 'Com and praye.'

It can never have been easy to find a Curate for this poor living
and Roger Palmer's successor, Thomas Castle, had suspect
qualifications. He was orthodox enough, as he subscribed to the
three Articles in 1584. But one of the objects of the enquiry the
next year, which resulted in the return known as the *Liber Cleri*
was a check on the qualifications and education of the clergy. As
early as 1559 there had been a Royal injunction that the clergy
were to study. In 1577 Bishop Cooper of Lincoln followed this up
with a detailed set of injunctions[8] requiring that every Parson or
Vicar below M.A. not a licensed preacher and

'Every Curate serving in a benefice where a preacher is not resident shall before 1st Sept. next coming buy the Decades of Bullinger either in Latin or English (being now for that purpose translated) and every week to read over one sermon in such sort as he be able to make reasonable account of it, and likewise every day in the week with like diligence to read over one chapter at least of the Bible taking some notes in a paper book of such wholesome sentences and good matter as he shall observe in the reading as well of the Bible as of the Decades mentioned, that he may show them when he shall be thereunto called.'

This injunction was more than a pious hope. To ensure its implementation the Bishop's Commissioners were told to take with them on their next visitation one or two 'of the best learned and most discreet preachers'. These worthy gentlemen were to ensure that the parish clergy had their own copies of the Bible and the Decades 'with every man's name written in the end of their said book' and to require the parsons 'to show some account of their task in reading the aforesaid book.'

Thomas Castle may have tried to evade this enquiry. He was marked as absent[9] and that 'he has to exhibit'—i.e. to show his letters of orders and institution. The remark against his name is even more cryptic that that of his opposite number at Hawridge. 'A paris clerke' he was called. We suspect that it was not exactly complimentary.

The population of Cholesbury was recorded in 1563 as 16 families.[10] We have already discovered three of these, the Batchelors, the Gearys and the Putnams (see pages 101–3). The Baldwins were a fourth. In 1541 the Cheyne family, owners of Drayton Beauchamp, had disposed of this outlying Manor, probably to Lord Justice Baldwin. Here, as at St. Leonards, the tenants were connected with the Dundridge Baldwins and in 1564 John Baldwin of the Hale (the one who gave evidence at the St. Leonard's Chapel Enquiry) left to his namesake John of Lynslad,[11]

'Six silver spoons, a mazer, a feather bed that was his father's and the lease of the manor Cholysbury.'

He does not refer to this John Baldwin as his son; he had six others who are mentioned as such in his Will, so the relationship is obscure. Nor is it known, as the Will refers to the 'lease' of the manor at the time, when John Baldwin bought the manor. In 1599, however, he appears in the Court Roll as Lord of the Manor and at this stage had styled himself not as 'yeoman' but 'gentleman'. This means that he bore a coat of arms, a right granted by Henry VIII through the College of Heralds to any man who possessed lands of at least £10 a year or movable goods worth £300.

To meet the other inhabitants, we have to skip to the end of the century and the first two existent Court Rolls dated 1599 and 1606, Rolls which reveal in considerable detail the development of the modern village. 'The Court Baron of John Baldwyn Gent.' met on 31 May 1599 and 7 August 1606. [12] Its meeting place may have been the Manor House, a house which retains this name, though for the last two or three centuries it has not been the home of the Lord of the Manor. Architectural evidence suggests that this house was built in the 16th century and was probably much larger than it is today, as its impressive roof would have been an unlikely superstructure for a small cottage. It is not unreasonable to assume

Fig. 16 The impressive roof of the Manor House, Cholesbury

that it was built by John Baldwyn for his own use or that of his family or steward.

The Homage at this Court Baron consisted of

Thomas Putnam	William Putnam senior
Richard Baldwyn	Robert Myles
Thomas Batchelor	John Wright senior
Richard Gearye	Henry Etinge

The officers were Richard Baldwyn and John Wright sen., and the steward John Style, whose son was later to become Lord of the Manor.

The business of the Court is recorded in standardised phrases, perhaps of necessity; fifty years later certainly some stewards have insufficient Latin to translate anything unusual and may burst into English. But, though standardised, the phraseology has a charm of its own. Translated, the first two items in 1599 read,

'Who [the Homage] say upon their oath that Thomas ^{6d} Cheyne Esquire and William ^{4d} Stocken are free tenants of the aforesaid manor and owe suit of court on this day and make default. Therefore each is in mercy as appears above his head.'

'Item. They present that Henry Putnam who held freely a messuage, an orchard, a garden and four closes called Halfacres lying in the fields of Cholesbury died after the last Court. William Putnam is his son and next heir and is aged 20 years. Whereby there falls to the lord as a relief 5s. 4d.'

From the 1606 Court Roll we may quote two other examples:

'Who say that Thomas Batchelor who held freely a messuage a garden and orchard and 3 acres of land with their appurtenances by fealty, suit of court and 16d. rent enfeoffed by deed his son Thomas Batchelor in the premises, and has died since the last court. Thomas Batchelor is his son and next heir. Whereby there falls to the lord of relief 16d.'

'They present that Thomas Batchelor who held by copy of court roll a parcel of land before his house formerly part of the waste— rent 2d—has died seised thereof. Thomas Batchelor is his son and next heir and about 40 years of age. The aforesaid Thomas comes and seeks to be admitted, to whom the lord by his Steward grants seisin, to hold to him and his heirs by the rod at the will of the lord according to the custom of the manor by the yearly rent of 2d and the other services formerly owed and of right accustomed. And he gives to the lord of fine 4d does fealty and is admitted tenant.'

Words like this have been used for centuries; they are to continue in use until the Court Barons finally disappear in 1923.

In an open field village, the Courts would have been concerned with common agricultural problems such as the dates on which the pastures were to be used for grazing, or the common fields opened for this purpose after harvest. In Cholesbury in 1599 there is only one entry of this type:

> 'It is ordered that William Stocken shall make the mound between his own land and the adjoining land of Richard Baldwyn adjoining the lane there before the feast of All Saints next under penalty of 6s. 8d.'

The significance of the term 'Half-acres' in describing Henry Putnam's holding has already been discussed (Chapter VII). If Cholesbury had had open fields, they are certainly enclosed by 1599, though the William Stocken entry may indicate that enclosure was fairly recent, as the mound had not yet been made. The size of the fine suggests general disapproval of his negligence, and indeed he appears to have been a rather 'Bolshy' character. As we have seen, he failed to attend the Court and in that same year he was excommunicated, presumably for non-conformity. He must have been reinstated by 1606, when he was one of the churchwardens.

Piecing together the information from these Court Rolls and from Wills we discover that the Putnams owned Parrott's Farm, half in Cholesbury and half in Drayton Beauchamp, an 8-acre freehold at a rent of 1d. as well as the 15 acres mentioned above, tentatively placed in the fields between the Church and Parrott's. The Batchelors had three scattered closes, Dellwick, Kipping and Great Meadow, while John Wright is at Braziers End. The latter must have had some reputation as a businessman, for when Thomas Batchelor of Hawridge died in 1602 [13] he orders his son to make £10 out of a wood of his in Wendover called Windmills for his daughter's use, adding,

> 'And I will that John Wright of Braziers End shall be at the sale of the said wood . . .'

John Geary's lands may also have been at Braziers End, as we find the family there later, and Richard Baldwin's lands can be placed in about the Home Farm area as they are 'adjoining to the lane'. Apart from Thomas Batchelor's lands, these are the main

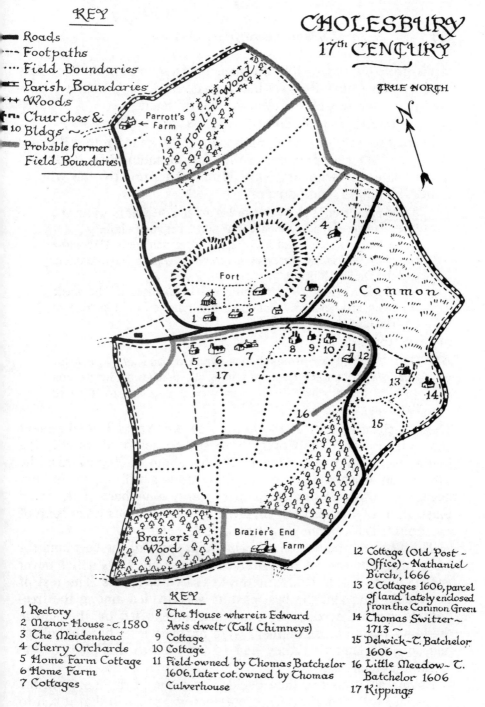

KEY

- ▬ Roads
- --- Footpaths
- ···· Field Boundaries
- ▬▬ Parish Boundaries
- +++ Woods
- 🏠 Churches &
- 10 Bldgs ~
- ▬▬ Probable former Field Boundaries

CHOLESBURY
17ᵗʰ CENTURY

TRUE NORTH

Tomlin's Wood

Parrott's Farm

Fort

Common

3

4

1 2

5 6 7 8 9 10 11 12

17

13

14

16

15

Brazier's Wood

Brazier's End Farm

KEY

1 Rectory
2 Manor House ~ c. 1580
3 The Maidenhead
4 Cherry Orchards
5 Home Farm Cottage
6 Home Farm
7 Cottages
8 The House wherein Edward Avis dwelt (Tall Chimneys)
9 Cottage
10 Cottage
11 Field owned by Thomas Batchelor 1606. Later cot. owned by Thomas Culverhouse
12 Cottage (Old Post ~ Office) ~ Nathaniel Birch, 1666
13 2 Cottages 1606, parcel of land lately enclosed from the Common Green
14 Thomas Switzer ~ 1713 ~
15 Delwick ~ T. Batchelor 1606 ~
16 Little Meadow ~ T. Batchelor 1606
17 Rippings

Map 5

farms probably where the old open fields were placed. The entry
in the 1606 Court Roll about Thomas Batchelor's holding, however, has a phrase which is even more significant,

'a parcel of land before his house *formerly part of the waste.*'

It is not the only one of the kind. In 1599 we learn that Richard
Edmonds inherits premises from his Grandmother, Elizabeth
Munn, 'late the wife of Henry Munn and formerly the wife of
James Hammond' consisting of

'three parcels of land 70 feet in length and 30 feet in width and
three parcels of land 4 perches long and 1 perch in width.'

'John Geary surrendered a cottage and garden—rent 1½d and a
parcel of land lately enclosed out of the common green rent ½d.
to John Darley. Fine 4d.'

'The lord grants to William Putnam a small piece of the waste
adjoining his messuage containing 4 perches to hold by rent of
8d. The lord pardons his fines.'

In 1606, too,

'. . . Robert Myles surrendered a parcel of land *lately enclosed
from the common green* containing 12 perches in length and
breadth upon which 2 cottages are now built to Richard
Batchelor. Rent 10d. Fine 20d.'

These enclosures start at the house now known as Tall Chimneys
and extend across the Common to the corner of Rays Hill, the
houses being built at varying dates from about 1600 onwards. The
subsequent history of many of these houses will appear in later
chapters, but it is perhaps worth mentioning here that, as an
illustration of the research involved, the continuous ownership of
one house, Tall Chimneys, is traced in Appendix C.

The Lord of the Manor probably kept some of the best land for
his own use or that of his family, for there are areas which never
appear in the Court Rolls for the next two centuries. The rest of
the arable land and the best pasture was divided among the freeholders while the copyholders were compensated by these little
'building plots.' Most of them were on the waste, but the village
had so little land that they had to nibble into one piece of the
'common green'.

Having got thus far, they decided to draw a firm line. Both the
farms and the land allotted to cottages was so small that it had to
be supplemented by use of the common and the exercise of the

normal common rights, pasturage of beasts, collecting wood and bracken. The insidious creepage on the commons and waste by encroachment, a time-honoured process which was to continue for a few more centuries, was for the moment sternly suppressed. In 1599 the Homage presented that

'William Gibbes, Cote widow, William Mertymer, William Eaton, John Wright, Thomas Darley, Richard Myles and William Putnam have encroached upon the lord's waste. Therefore each is in mercy 6d. And it is ordered that every one of them shall lay open his encroachment before the feast of St. Michael coming under penalties of 3s. 4d.'

This was a stiff enough penalty to ensure that the instruction was enforced, for none of these encroachments is mentioned again in the 1606 Court Roll.

The encroachers include one or two who were probably tenants rather than landowners. The number of families mentioned in the 1599 Court Roll is 17 and parish register evidence suggests that there were two or three more, so the population seems to have increased slightly since 1563. The mystery is how they all made a living in this tiny village. In addition to the farmers and farm workers, there was the blacksmith, John Pratt, and possibly a wheelwright, a carpenter and an ale-house keeper as well. Leonard and John Holyman,[14] from whom Richard Edmonds inherited his '3 parcels' were weavers, and it is possible too that Cholesbury provided some of the labour force for the sparsely populated village of St. Leonards. After making all allowances, however, the numbers at Cholesbury still look too large for an area of only 165 acres. Enclosure may have brought a measure of improvement and given some advantage in productivity over the still unenclosed villages in the Vale, as there was obviously enough money available for the building of new houses, but it must still have been a hard struggle to obtain a reasonable living in this village. Two of the more prominent inhabitants may indeed have decided that the battle was not worth fighting, for John Baldwin sold the Manor to Thomas Style, one of the Attorneys of the Court of King's Bench in 1618[15] and William Putnam disappears from the village after buying 'Moorings' with about 125 acres in 1616 from two other members of the Baldwin family. [16] The rest of the Putnam lands are acquired by Thomas of Hawridge and he and the other

Thomas, Thomas Batchelor, also of Hawridge as well as Cholesbury, stay with us for the next fifty years, though with the Batchelors this is in turn 'Thomas the elder' and 'Thomas the younger'. When the former died in 1624, his son was already 30 and working partly on his own, but he and his mother clearly did not get on. 'Thomas the elder's' [17]Will portrays a very human story as he tries to be fair to both of them:

> 'My will is that my son shall have liberty to work at his trade in the work house here at Cholesbury and to have convenient room for the housing and threshing of his corn yearly in the barns adjoining to my said work house from the time of my decease for and during his natural life, but yet upon this condition that he during his mother's life be dutiful to his said mother my wife and helpful to her and ready to look to all her cattle and to ensure that all her husbandry be well done and in due time to see that her ploughing and sowing be duly finished to thresh out her corn and clean it, to look to all the mounds and to be careful for her good in every respect for every thing; which if he do not accordingly then my will is my wife shall at her pleasure turn him out from the said work house and from laying his corn in the barns or elsewhere about this house.'

Notes and References

[1]Op. cit. note (8) Ch.IX, p.9.

[2]*Visitations in the Diocese of Lincoln 1518-31* Ed. by A. Hamilton Thompson (Lincs. Rec. Soc. 1940) Vol.III, p.18 - 27. The following extracts come from the same work.

[3]*The State of the Ex-Religions and Former Chantry Priests in the Diocese of Lincoln 1547 - 74* Ed. by G. A. J. Hodgett (Lincs. Rec. Soc. 1959) p.97.

[4]Op. cit. note (3) above, p.139.

[5]Lipscomb Vol.III, p.322.

[6]*The Edwardian Inventories for Bucks.* Ed. by F. C. Eeles from transcript by Rev. J. E. Brown (Longman's Green & Co. 1908) p.63 - 4.

[7]L.A.O. Ter. 19/37 Cholesbury Terrier, 1709.

[8]Op. cit. note (16) Ch.X – Introduction p.xix-xx.

[9]Op. cit. note (16) Ch.X – p.117.

[10]Op. cit. note (1) Ch.IX, p.268.

[11]Bucks. C.R.O. D/A/We/154/245 Baldwin, John of the Hayle 1565 D/A/Wf/6/228.

[12]B.A.S. 7-10/51 and 205/49. These early Court Rolls for Cholesbury are a scattered collection dated 1599, 1606 1644, 1666, 1713 and 1737. It seems likely that Courts were not held annually. The roll of 1606, for example states that 'Thomas Batchelor has died since the last Court' and both from the Bishop's transcripts for Hawridge and the will quoted on page   we know that he died in 1602. There is no

doubt that these two Thomas Batchelors are identical, the son of the Thomas (then under 18) who received lands in Cholesbury, Chesham and Hawridge from Andrew Batchelor in 1527. For the transcription and translation of these rolls we are indebted to the late Mr. A. Vere Woodman. From 1767 the Court Books for Cholesbury and Hawridge are intact and we are grateful to Mr. John Randall, the Lord of the Manor, for loaning them to us.

[13] Bucks. C.R.O. D/A/We/22/211 Batcheler, Thomas of Hawridge 1602.

[14] Bucks. C.R.O. D/A/Wf/7/191 Holyman, Leonard 1573. D/A/We/19/81 D/A/Wf/13/263 Holyman, John 1597.

[15] V.C.H. Bucks. Vol.III., p.334.

[16] Op. cit. note (5) Ch. IX.

[17] Bucks. C.R.O. Archdeaconry Index No.75 Batchelor, Thomas (Sen) 1625.

XII

'FOUR BRASSE POTTS'

The Civil War and its impact in our villages

Reactions of the villages to the imposition of Ship Money; fighting in the neighbourhood, emigration to America; encroachments.

We have been watching the villages growing quietly, immersed in their own affairs. Some news of the growing unrest in the larger world outside their own boundaries would reach them from the wealthier farmers who had land in other and larger parishes, but the majority, after shaking their heads gravely, would have returned quickly enough to discussion of the harvest or inspection of their new house now nearing completion. In 1636, however, even these quiet backwaters could no longer avoid entanglement with the larger affairs of state.

Their first news of a serious threat to their peace and pockets might have come from Robert Batchelor who, with lands in Ellesborough, was a near neighbour of John Hampden. So, it is not too fanciful to imagine Robert returning from Ellesborough one day full of the news of Charles I's attempt to raise Ship Money by an imposition on the whole country instead of on the ports only, and of Hampden's intention to resist this new and unjust tax. On his way back to Hill Farm he would feel that he must tell someone the news; when he reached Bottom Farm he could wait no longer and stopped for a chat to his friend John Geary. They would have sat in the kitchen round the large fireplace, with the copper and brass pots glinting in the firelight, a mug of home-brewed ale in their hands and a savoury odour coming up from the pot on the fire—a rabbit stew maybe, flavoured with wild marjoram, for with their piece of woodland the Gearys would be free to trap game without fear of poaching. They would be wondering whether, like John Hampden, they dared resist this hated innovation and the penalties they might incur by doing so. John's mother, Jasper's widow would be sitting in her corner advising caution; she would be supported by Thomas Putnam, who had looked in on the way

124

past and the Rector, Elidad Blackwell, may have joined them,
seeing the horses outside on his way back home from Evening
Service to his comfortable Rectory.

This would have been the first of many meetings. In the absence
of newspapers and radio the story which eventually percolated
down to the Putnams and the Batchelors and the Gearys would
have been so distorted that they would be incapable of weighing
up the merits of the case. Only the most prominent country
gentlemen or officials would have seen the very plausible writ sent
by Charles I to his sheriff and read his graphic plea:[1]

> 'Because it is given to us to understande that Certayne Theeves
> pyrates and Robbers at sea, Ass well Enemyes to the name of
> Christ, as other Mahomitans haveinge gathered togeather shipps
> and the goods and Merchandize not only of our subjects, but
> alsoe of the subjects of our freindes at sea, which by the English
> people in tymes past used to be defended, wickedlie takinge away
> and spoylinge them at theire pleasure, have carryed away, And
> the men in the same into miserable captivitie takinge, And
> whereas wee have beheld them daylie preparinge shipps, further
> to molest our Merchaunts and greive our Kingdome unless the
> sooner remedie be added and theire power more strongelie
> prevented, Consideringe alsoe the daungers which on every side
> these warlike tymes doe threaten, soe that it behooveth us and
> our subjects to hasten the defence of our kingdome, the Tuition
> of the sea, the securitie of our subjects, the safe conduct of our
> shippe, and Merchandize to our kingdome of Englande
> Comminge. And from the same kingdome to forraigne partes
> passinge. (by the help of God to provide) especially when as wee
> and our progenitors Kings of Englande alewayes heitherto have
> remayned lordes of the sea aforesaide, and it would much greive
> us, if the honour of this kingdome in our tymes should perrish or
> in any thinge to deminised, and whereas this burden of defence
> which toucheth all it ought to be borne of All, as by the Lawe
> and Custome of this Realme of England hath been Accustomed.'

Men in the seaports might understand this when they had heard
of their own friends taken away 'into miserable captivitie'. In the
country, it made little impression. Nor would the farmers realise,
because they had not seen the instructions to the Sheriff, that
Charles had explicitly instructed that the tax was to be assessed
according to ability to pay and that the poor were not to be
overburdened. These instructions, however admirable in theory,

were not so easy to implement and the Sheriff of Buckinghamshire, Sir Peter Temple, had these pertinent questions to raise with
the Privy Council:

> 'Weither I shall alter the Rates that be sett by the Assessors in
> every Parrishe concerninge the Riche men or to lett them goe as
> they be Assessed by the Assessors, for if I shoulde not Rayse
> them I knowe not howe to releive the Poorer sorte According to
> his Majesties desire.'

> 'Many men that live in the County furthest and most remote
> from me doe complayne that the Assessors have sett them too
> highe in their Assessments and unequallye what shall the Sheriffe
> doe in this Case. Shall he alter the Assessment or Releive them as
> he sees cause.'

> What to do with Assessors who refuse to assess 'Because by the
> writte and by your lordships Instruction I have nott powre to doe
> any thinge with those Assessors that shal refuse to Assesse but
> only againste those that refuse to Paye.'

Eventually an assessment was made and an attempt was made to
raise the money. For Hawridge, though appearing as Marsworth-
cum-Hawridge, we are lucky enough to have the full and separate
return for our own village, which shows a mixed reaction:-

Harridge	John Seere paid	2. 3. 6.
	Roberte Batchiler distrayned 4 Brasse potts not payd	0. 18. 6.
	Richard Scott distrayned 1 Brasse potte a brasse Kettle and Warmeinge panne not payd	0. 13. 4.
	Thomas Hallcye payd	0. 18. 6.
	Thomas Puttenham payd	0. 13. 10½.
	William Cokefield payd	0. 7. 8½.
	John Geerye 5 Kettles 2 skillets and 1 Brasse potte not payd	0. 18. 6.
	Thomas Gulliner distrayned a warmeinge Panne and 3 Pewter disshes payd	0. 9. 3.
	Peter Batchiler payd	0. 6. 2.
	Henry White distrayned 1 Brasse Kettle not payd	0. 3. 1.
	Thomas Batchilor payd	0. 1. 5½.
	Widdowe Geerye payd	0. 2. 6.
	Peter Munner payd	
	(Tho. Galliner Petty Counstable hath the distresses)'	7. 17. 10½.

Running through this list, we have already met John Geary of Bottom Farm, Thomas Putnam'of Putnam's and Thomas Batchelor of Porters or Bentonpotts. Robert Batchiler is at Hill Farm, Peter Batchilor presumably had some share of the family lands and John Seere must have been the occupant, if not the owner, of Hawridge Court—according to Lipscombe and the *Victoria County History* he did not buy the Manor until 1650. From the value of their property, Richard Scott and Thomas Hallcye were occupiers, if not the owners, of reasonably large farms, which we can only guess as being Botchmore Farm and 'The Limes' (we only know its modern name). As the Rector does not appear, he may at this stage have leased Glebe Farm; the other namcs may be those of the village craftsmen.

Those assessed for Ship Money did not comprise the whole population of Hawridge. The numbers in the Protestation Return[2] five years later indicate about eight more families and we can only assume that in this village the Assessor had carried out his instructions carefully and raised his quota only from those who were able to pay, thus avoiding the pathetic pleas for exemption which occur elsewhere in the Ship Money papers. William Lock of Chesham for example, assessed at 5/-,

> 'hath nothinge to be distrayned by beinge a poor man.'

John Hurley, it is stated,

> 'hath no money but will pay four shillings.'

William Brookes, who also,

> 'hath no money, assessed at seven shillings and will pay it as sone as he hath it.'

And the saddest of all from Princes Risborough:

> 'Henry Meade he rents 2 yarde lands and a halfe for which he is Assesste ii s that he complaynes of beinge a verrye poor man greatlye in debte haveinge no stocke but 4 poore Horses and 3 Beasts for which 2 of them he owes for upon his complaynte he hade Teares in his eyes beinge an olde man of 60 yeares of Age he did keepe himselfe in his House 7 years for debt.'

The inhabitants of nearby Chesham understandably were incensed with the assessor:

> 'They have neglected the constables direction and have imposed great parte of the money uppon poore tradesmen wherby except

your worshipp relive them therin they are like to be much
burdened. We the inhabitants of the towne Chesham manie of us
being poore tradesmen yett we are willing to paye according to
our abillitie but they have rated us five fold according to the rate
of parisioners . . . '

Cholesbury too was annoyed because it had been joined with
Drayton Beauchamp and called upon to pay a fourth share of the
levy, whereas, so the parishioners alleged, their lands comprised
only a tenth part. This complaint was treated in a thoroughly
modern way, being shuttled backwards and forwards between
quarter sessions, privy council and high sheriff. But from the
amount finally paid it looks as if Cholesbury lost.

Even when an assessment had been made, appeals settled and
attempts made to collect the money or distraints the Sheriff's
problems were not over. At Hawridge, as we have seen, the Petty
Constable was conscientious enough to distrain on himself, for,
allowing for the erratic spelling of the time, the Thomas Gulliner
who was,

'distrayned a warmeinge panne and 3 pewter dishes'

valued at 9/3d. must have been identical with the 'Galliner Petty
Counstable.' His neighbour at Ashley Green was a less satisfactory
character for,

'Nathaniel Rydeinge Counstable did make a Returne but he was
not sober to replie wheither the particular persons would paye or
not.'

Worse still was the problem of disposing of all the copper pots,
warming pans, brass kettles and skillets which had been collected,
as Sir Peter Temple, pressing the Privy Council to permit imprison-
ment rather than distress, explained,

'Because if he shoulde be onelye tyde to the way of Distresse he
feareth that he shoulde hardly fynde chapmen to buy all the
Distresses; so leavied, nor growndes of his owne to put them in
and is Informed by his Counsell that he cannot well carry them
into another county.'

The ordinary people of England might be up in arms, but the man
who had the really unenviable task was the Sheriff. In Buckinghamshire Sir Peter Temple seems to have tried to carry out his
instructions honestly and impartially. He got no thanks for his
efforts for after new sheriffs had been appointed and he had been

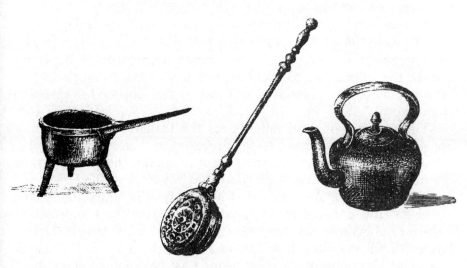

Fig. 17 Typical 'Brass Pots' taken as distraints — skillet, warming pan and kettle

ordered to hand over the list he received this rebuke from the Privy Council on 17th April 1636:

'After our hartie comendacions wee cannot but much marvaile at
your forgetfullness and greate neglect of duty.'

Two years later, he and his successor were still being summoned to the Privy Council as they slowly and painfully collected the arrears.

We have strayed a little from our hilltop villages in the last few pages because examples from the neighbouring parishes show us the sort of gossip and rumours which, by then, would have spread rapidly even to these isolated spots. The part our villages actually played in the Civil War is unknown, but the Yeomen of Buckinghamshire generally were on the side of Parliament and throughout the area strange and unusual scenes may have been seen on the Commons as the Yeomen and labourers prepared to fight. Gibbs tell us that:[2]

'It was under the woody brown of his own beauteous Chilterns,
that Hampden first published the ordinance to marshal the militia
of his native county. The parishes and hundreds, often with their
preachers at their head, mustered at their market-houses to march

forth to training. In the dearth of all the ordinary implements of
war, arms of the most grotesque fashion were brought into
service; the long bow, the brown bill and the cross bow resumed
their place among the equipments of men at arms.'

As elsewhere in this book, the author unfortunately does not
quote the source of this account, but those with memories of the
Home Guard 300 years later will hardly feel disposed to question
its veracity.

The strength of local support for the Parliamentary cause may
be gauged by the reaction to the Protestation,[3] an oath required of
all adult males in 1641, pledging them to defend the true reformed
Protestant religion, His Majesty's royal person, and the power and
privileges of Parliaments. In Cholesbury the inhabitants and
minister 'did conjunctly and unanimously take the Protestation,'
while in Hawridge the only refusals—23 having taken the Oath—
were John Seere, his son and two servants, and one other. Some of
those who trained on the Commons may have joined Hampden's
Green Coats and fought at the Battle of Aylesbury in 1642. The
conflicting accounts of this battle—its very date seems uncertain—
need not concern us, for the troop movements all took place in
the Oxfordshire plain and our hilltop villages could watch from
afar just as surely as in the Iron Age.

In 1643, they may have helped to barricade the streets of
Chesham, where, according to the fourth of Jeremiah Wharton's
nine letters, Prince Rupert sent off a detachment under Lord
Caernarvon which plundered Wendover before being routed by the
inhabitants of Chesham. With Aylesbury as a centre for the Parliamentary troops, it is not surprising to find that in 1654 these
forces were quartered at St. Leonards, The Lee and other villages
around Aylesbury, Amersham and Chesham, probably including
Cholesbury and Hawridge.[4]

The war only involved occasional interruption to the normal
flow of life and the small extent of its impact on the yeoman
farmer may be gauged from Thomas Putman's Will in 1644.[5] He
has by this time added Parrott's Farm, previously owned by the
Cholesbury branch of the family, to his lands in Hawridge and had
been living in Cholesbury before 1641, signing the Protestation
return for that village. His son, Thomas, inherited the Cholesbury
lands, his wife was bequeathed the 'house and commons' in

Hawridge 'wherein my son in law Richard Ware now liveth,' while
a second son was to have a 'mault mill'. In addition to the house
Thomas's 'loving wife' was well provided for; she was given

> 'One cow and six sheep . . . she to take her choice out of and
> among all my cattle for them. And I do further give my wife all
> my bees and poultry and also all my goods within my now
> dwelling house excepting one jointed bedstead in the Chamber
> over the hall . . . '

Thomas also decreed that his wife was to have

> '12 bushells of good wheat to be paid for by mine executor as she
> my said wife shall demand and at such time or times as she
> pleases . . . '

Thomas, her executor was also to

> 'pay and to deliver or cause to be paid and delivered unto my
> wife foure Loads of good woodd every yeare & from yeare to
> yeare duringe her naturall life out of Parrotts Wood . . . '

It was only when he went to Church that the ordinary man
would have noticed any difference during all the upheavals. Whatever his convictions or wishes, if he had any, he had probably seen
the Altar replaced by a Communion Table in the centre, listened
to an unfamiliar Service and looked at a parson who wore no
surplice or vestments. He had, too, watched the Church itself fall
into disrepair, even if it had not been deliberately damaged. At St.
Leonards the 'decay' of the Chapel was now complete, only the
bare walls remaining,[6] while three of the Baldwin brothers sailed
off to Connecticut in 1642, leaving the eldest, John, at
Dundridge.[7] Whether their motives were religious or economic we
do not know, but as strong non-conformists they would have
found a congenial home in New England, if they had reached their
destination. Alas, three of them died on the voyage leaving one of
their widows and her infant son to enjoy a grant of 350,000 acres
of land and found the American branch of the family.

At Cholesbury the village, profiting either from the disturbed
times or an absentee landlord, had indulged in another round of
encroachments. The 1644 Court Roll records,[8]

> 'That John Darvell has built part of the barn on the lord's waste.'
> 'That Thomas Baldwyn has built a carthouse on the lord's waste.'

This one was not approved, for

'he is ordered to pull it down the same under penalty of 20s.'
'that Thomas Baldwyn has ploughed the lord's waste, therefore in mercy 12d.'
'That John Marshall has encroached upon the lord's waste.'
'That Thomas Batchelor and Edmund Birch have encroached upon the lord's waste and made a pond and enclosed the same for their own use.'

No doubt they would have been popular enough if they had been content to make the pond without enclosing it—

'that Archibald Ogill clerk has enclosed the lane called Church Lane.'

From Cholesbury, too, we hear of another emigrant, Thomas Putnam, who went off to Virginia in 1647.[9] Again, we do not know whether his reasons were political or economic, but Cholesbury at the time may have been in some distress, for a survey of 1650 tells us that there was,

'No Minister for want of maintenance.'

The survey continues with the suggestion that,

'Cholesbury is about one mile distant from Hawridge and fit to be united with it.'

The implementation of this suggestion had to wait until the twentieth century.

Notes and References

[1]*Ship Money Papers and Richard Grenville's Note Book* Ed. by Carol Bonsey and J. G. Jenkins (B.A.S. 1965). All quotations from pp. 125–9 come from this book.
[2]House of Lords Record Office.
[3]Gibbs. Vol.I, p.132.
[4]Gibbs. Vol.I, p.160.
[5]Bucks. C.R.O. No.33 Putnam, Thomas 1644.
[6]Lipscomb, Vol.II, p.319.
[7]Op. cit. note (5) Ch. IX with additional information from research by Mr. A. Vere Woodman, Mr. Alfred Copps and Miss T. Matthews.
[8]Cholesbury Court Roll 1644 See note (12) Chap. XI.
[9]*A History of the Putnam Family in England and America* by Eben Putnam, (Salem Press Publishing and Printing Co.) corrected and verified by Mr. F. G. Gurney and Mr. Vere Woodman. The Thomas Putnam who emigrated must be a nephew of the Thomas who owned land in Cholesbury and Hawridge; the latter still appears in the Court Roll in 1666.
[10]V.C.H. III, p.335, Quoted from Ecton, Thesaurus Rev. Eccl. (Ed. 1742) 211.

XIII

'THE HOUSE WHEREIN EDWARD AVIS FORMERLY DWELT'

Village life in latter half of the 17th century

Episcopal Enquiries; houses and furnishings; property changes; parish offices; Sessions records.

Comparison of the 1644 and 1666 Court Rolls suggests that, at Cholesbury, some of the poorer families may have moved away during the war; only 7 of the 19 family names appearing in the former are repeated in the latter Roll. The family histories have one or two awkward gaps because the parish registers, badly kept generally during the Commonwealth period, are virtually non-existent at Cholesbury in the absence of a parson, and record only a handful of births with no marriages or burials.

Our main families, however, the Batchelors, Gearys, Putnams and Wrights are still there, as are the Baldwins at Dundridge even if they have moved from Cholesbury.

When they went to Church the older members of these families would see Church services gradually returning to the form they had remembered as children. For a short time in 1662, Cholesbury again had a Quaker Minister, William Dyer[1] who, describing himself as 'Preacher of the Gospel at Chesham and Chouldsbury, Bucks', treated his congregation to the gloomiest of sermons and wrote equally gloomy tracts. He can hardly have suited the mood of 'Merry England', but his parishioners did not have to suffer long before he was evicted for non-conformity. Like many other evicted Quaker Ministers he did admirable work three years later during the Plague in a London which had been deserted by most of its Anglican pastors.

St. Leonards, too, saw its non-conformist Minister, George Swinnow, ejected in 1661, but he must shortly afterwards have decided to conform, for he was reappointed two years later.

The churches were still in a poor state of repair; in Hawridge the churchwarden, Daniel Batchelor, had to report:[2]

'That the windoes of the Church of Hawridge are much broken
and the Church in decay.'

Cholesbury may have been no better off; neither we nor the
Bishop at the time can get much information because, it was
reported,[3]

'No Minister, no churchwarden.'

Even tiny villages like ours could not avoid an Episcopal
Visitation and the Bishop was not just concerned with the Church
buildings, for his officers delivered to the churchwarden a
formidable questionnaire to which he was sworn to make a
faithful return on the next visit.

The questionnaire[4] started with a section on the state of the
Church and its contents including such details as,

'Have you a comely large Surplice for the Minister to wear at all
times of his Publick Ministration in the Church? Provided and to
be duly washed at the Charge of the Parish?'

The second section on the state of the churchyards and parsonage
asked whether there was an up to date and accurate Terrier and,
among other things, demanded to know,

'Have any Inclosures been made in your Parish, to the detriment
of the Church, by the decay of Tillage and converting Arable-land
into Pasture?'

After a difficult section on the Minister himself, his qualifications and the orthodoxy of his views, the churchwarden was
confronted with an invidious series of questions about his fellow
parishioners—he was expected to say whether there were,

'Any heretics . . . '

or

'Any person that lyeth under a common fame, or vehement
suspicion of Adultery, Fornication or Incest.
Are there any common drankards within your Parish, or common
swearers or blasphemers of God's name, or any that are noted to
be railers, unclean or filthy talkers, or sowers of sedition, faction
or discord amonst their neighbours?'

An attempt was made too to probe Sunday observance, the use of
baptism and catechism and behaviour at Services, including the
query,

'Doth every person reverently uncover his head . . . '

Finally, there was a section on parish clerks and sextons and their performance of their duties.

Even the Inquisition could not have conceived a more awkward or unpleasant task, for the churchwarden was, after all, only an ordinary local man elected annually to an office he had little chance of refusing. In our villages he was probably a farmer, possibly barely literate, and these were his own friends and neighbours on whom he had to report in a small community where there could have been few secrets. Daniel Batchelor, at Hawridge, may well have thought the task beyond him, or decided to risk the displeasure of the Church rather than unpopularity with his neighbours, for he at first refused to take the oath. He was promptly excommunicated, but in penitent mood submitted a few months later and asked in humble terms for time to get the Church repaired. The excommunication was cancelled but he was landed with the costs of the visitation. One only hopes that his friends helped him to pay after his efforts to protect them. His Rector, Joseph Prettie was equally unwilling, refused to attend the second visitation and was suspended for his contumacy.

In these small villages it must have been difficult to raise money for Church repairs and St. Leonards was lucky in finding a benefactor, Cornelius Wood, a Loyalist who[5]

> 'Endowed it with provision for a Minister exempt from the jurisdiction of the Bishop and Archdeacon, receiving his appointment solely from the Patron without institution or induction.'

His brother, John Wood was appointed curate, and shortly afterwards appears as Curate of Cholesbury as well. There is no record of any attempt to combine the parishes, and they were separated again when Wood resigned in 1697. Probably as a result of this beneficence, the Trustees found themselves with savings from the sale of timber and with them bought land in Mentmore in 1665 and 32 years later a cottage in St. Leonards called the Pot House with a meadow which had belonged to John Tomkins.[6]

Cholesbury, though the living was only worth £8, had by this time been recognised as a parish separate from Drayton Beauchamp, though the living remained as a 'Perpetual Curacy'. With a poor living of this kind, the parsonage house was unpretentious. The Terrier in 1709[7] describes it:

'There's a house built mostly of oak, elm & brick, being covered with tiles; it contains a parlour floored with oaken boards, a kitchin and a wash or brewhouse floored with brick & 2 chambers above stairs, the one laid with oaken boards the other with beechen boards. There's also a barn consisting of 2 bays with a carthouse at one end & a little stable at the other, all of them built with oak & beech & covered with thatch.'

The parson at Cholesbury may have looked enviously at his opposite number in Hawridge who could report:[8]

'The parsonage House consists of four bays of Building; wherein are found; one Long Kitchin; two Butteries; one Long Hall; one parlour with four other small roomes below staires; And Above Staires there are 4 Lodging Roomes with two clossetts. This House is built of good oak; and it is covered with tyles; and walled about with some brick and some dirt walls.

'The parsonage Barn consists of 3 bays; which are covered with Thatch; and fenced about with boards; one Hay barn consisting of two Bays; one Stable: two or 3 small out Houses which are covered with straw; and built with ordinary Timber and boards; The yard where these buildings stand is pretty Large; and it is fenced about with pales.'

Houses of this type had been built in our villages from the beginning of the 17th century, houses built of local materials, their variety a sign of the complex geological structure of this district. The great beams which form the framework are cut from local trees—often unseasoned wood which in time will warp to cause the uneven floors and walls we find today in these old houses. The filling between the timbers is local clay—in the wealthier, like Dundridge it will be formed into bricks, for though there is no record of local brickworks in the area as early as the 17th century, sun-dried bricks must surely have been made here. One at Dundridge still bears the footmark of the pheasant which walked over it while it was drying, and the burial of Josiah Withers, bricklayer, of St. Leonards is recorded in the Cholesbury Parish Register in 1717. For the most part, however, the clay filling is less sophisticated, being whitewashed for protection with lime obtained from one of our innumerable chalk pits. A third local material, flints, would have been used extensively in the poorer cottages or even, perhaps, the lower walls of barns, just gummed together with some mixture of our sticky clay. These flint cottages are more difficult to date, because flint has the peculiarity that it does not weather like other stones.

Despite the distraints in 1636, these houses had not been denuded of the brass and copper pots, the pewter plates and dishes, the treasured possessions which are mentioned so often in Wills, and by this time furnishings were also becoming more elaborate. John Geary[9] of Bottom Farm, for example, bequeathed to his son Daniell,

> 'the featherbed whereon I now finally lye, the bolster pillows bedding in the chamber.'

and to his daughter Deborrah,

> 'bedding and a standing bedstead with silk curtains,'

while in 1668 Richard Edmunds of Cholesbury[10] mentioned, among other items,

> 'A ffeather-bedd and a sett of curtains of Wolland (being Hollands wrought with thred)[perhaps inherited from his Uncle John Holyman the weaver who was mentioned on page   ]
> 'My best boots
> A cabinett in my chamber
> A brass chaffing-dish, a great iron pottage - pott - a brass skillitt and an ingraven sword.'

A typical inventory, though for slightly later than the period covered by this chapter, is given in Henry Putnam's Will of 1735 [11] which mentions,

> 'One kettle one brass pot 2 skilletts, 2 brass candlesticks, a chafing dish, a mottle possett, one settle, one large spitone, one spit and jack, one large pewter dish, one deep pewter dish, four little pewter dishes, six pewter plates, one chest of drawers, one table, one great trunk, one little trunk, 4 pairs of flaxen sheets, one pair of pillows ... '

The cherished brass and copper pots, the pewter plates and dishes would perhaps have been bought at the local Fair. Much of the ironwork might be made by the village blacksmith and the furniture by the local carpenter, craftsmen who still had time to take pride in their skill and artistry. Chair bodgers may have been at work in the beechwoods overlooking Chesham Vale and their Windsor chairs would be familiar in every farmhouse.

Pottery was, perhaps, regarded as too common to be worth mentioning in Wills, but that too would have been made locally at

Buckland Common. This, the fourth of our hilltop villages has so far played no part in our story for the reasons explained in Chapter VIII but it seems clear that from the middle of the 16th century at the latest there was a small settled community in this hamlet living a life detached from that in the parent village of Buckland except for attendance at the parish church five miles away. As in our other villages farming would have been the main occupation, with one farmer at least sharing sufficiently in the general prosperity of this period to build a good new house, Folly Farm (later known as Kiln Cottage). Its owners even at this date could have been the Brackley family who lived there later and it seems possible that this family, and perhaps others, may have been astute enough to get permission to attend Church at Cholesbury to avoid the long walk to Buckland. All that is certain is that the name Brackley first appears in the Cholesbury Parish Register in 1601 and that by the end of the 17th century Richard Brackley, son of John of Buckland, and John and William Brackley, also of

Fig. 18 Folly Farm, Buckland Common (now called Kiln Cottage)

Buckland, appear amongst the burials in the Cholesbury Register.

This area, however, may not have been devoted exclusively to farming. The brickworks which we find at Buckland Common in the nineteenth century could well be of much earlier origin and the Pottery is known to have started work by 1701. Two examples of the work of this Pottery are illustrated below and are preserved at Chequers where the catalogue mentions,

'Jug, red earthenware, covered with dark manganese-brown glaze, globular, with short neck, small handle with three thumb-marks at its base, and reeded round mouth and shoulder. On the front "H K 1701" incised under the glaze. Probably made at Buckland Common, near Aylesbury. This jug has always been at Chequers and is of special interest as the work of a small rustic pottery hitherto unrecorded in the literature of ceramics.'

'Jug, red earthenware, with dark manganese-brown glaze, globular body, short reeded neck, small loop handle. On the shoulder, star shaped devices, and the inscription "JOHN REVET: ESQr, 1759 THOMAS BRACKLEY POTTER AT BUCKLAND COMMON, incised after the application of the glaze but before firing. Buckland near Aylesbury. H.133/8" diam. 10".'

Pottery historians mention both red-earthenwares and dark-brown wares and the pottery may have done a flourishing business

Fig. 19 Examples of pottery from Buckland Common Potteries; early 18th century (now in Chequers Museum)

in the local towns, for a Samuel Roeden of Hawridge who was buried at Cholesbury in 1728 is described as a 'seller of earthenware.' There may even have been a rival business in Cholesbury where Moses Middleton, a potter, appears in the Court Roll of 1713.

Our yeomen families are not quite as firmly rooted as might appear from this account of their houses and property. At Cholesbury Thomas Putnam is succeeded by his son James, [12] who leaves no male heirs, and his daughters sell the property in 1713 [13] to John Eayre, a grandson of Thomas Batchelor, whose only surviving daughter Martha Eyres inherits his lands in 1672. [14] Braziers End farm begins to take shape, for in 1713 we learn from the Court Roll [15] that John Geary owns freely,

'A messuage and certain lands—Rent 18d
Another messuage & lands. Rent 3/-.'

It may be that one of these was his original holding and that he had bought the other from John Wright who has disappeared from our records.

At Hawridge, the extent of the Geary's land, Bottom Farm becomes obvious in 1681 from John Geary's will. This farm was well endowed with woods and

'the price they can get for the game and the yearly profitt thereon'

is valuable enough to be worth specifying.

At Hill Farm, Robert Batchelor died in 1662 [16] leaving the farm to a son, Joseph (his other son John receiving the land in Ellesborough) and instructing his wife as Executrix to allow Joseph,

'So much as shall be necessary for his maintenance and to satisfy his Physician and keep him where he now is untill his rents come in next halfe yeare.'

We hear nothing more of Joseph, but by 1716 Hill Farm is in the hands of John, who sold it to John Putnam.[17]

The Mault Mill must have prospered, for John Putnam, or probably the son of the John who inherited the Mill in 1644, can not only buy Hill Farm but leave pecuniary legacies amounting to as much as £900.

These yeomen farmers were not wholly immersed in their own

affairs. John Geary of Bottom Farm was chief constable of the county in 1692, by then describing himself as a gentleman; while his namesake at Braziers End held the same office 20 years later. Inescapably they had to take their full share in the village offices, the jobs of churchwarden, constable, overseers of the poor and supervisors of the highways. Appointment to these unpaid jobs was by 'election', but they could not be refused and though literacy was not an essential qualification, the choice could only have been limited in a small village and the burden on the few qualified candidates considerable. The main candidates other than the yeomen came from the village craftsmen, such as Edward Avis the blacksmith. He had started life at Hawridge, signing the Protestation return there, but by 1663[18] had bought Tall Chimneys at Cholesbury, the original Richard Edmonds holding. He was suceeded by his son, and one of them made a considerable impact on the village because 250 years after their death this

Fig. 20 'The House wherein Edward Avis formerly dwelt' (now Tall Chimneys)

house could be described in Court Rolls as

> 'The house wherein Edward Avis formerly dwelt.' [19]

Of the village offices, none can have been less popular than that of supervising the highways. Since 1555 responsibility for the repair of the highways had been vested in the parishes, each householder being liable for six days work a year. It was an obligation which many tried to evade and offered scope for inter-parochial wrangles. Thus in 1678 the supervisors presented to Quarter Sessions [20]

> 'Samuel Graunge of St. Leonards, Thomas Ayres and Christopher Farmer, both of Aston Clinton with St. Leonards, and Richard How and William Nash, both of Chapel Farm in St. Leonards, for not "doeinge service with their teams for 5 dayes".'

As well as evading their obligations, the villagers at times went out of their way to make matters worse. In 1679 William Loch, senior, of Cholesbury was presented by the constables for,

> 'Laynge dunge in the high way and obstructing the way and spoyling the water.'

A few years later the Rev. Joseph Willis of St. Leonards (who surely should have known better) was presented by the Grand Jury for taking away

> 'the stones and flints gathered by the inhabitants of Aston Clynton for the repair of the Queen's Highways.'

It is not, therefore, surprising to find Peter Hill, Curate of Cholesbury, who we shall meet properly in the next Chapter, writing in 1723, [21]

> 'As for my coming to London, the badness of the Roads and the uncertainty of the Weather will prevent me from taking a journey so far from home . . . '

St. Leonards may have been involved in prolonged wrangles with Aston Clinton about their share of taxes and their responsibilities for repair of highways, but managed to settle any disputes with an agreement recorded at the Easter Session of the Buckinghamshire Sessions in 1679. This agreement reads:

> 'The following agreement entered into between the inhabitants of the parish of Aston Clynton and the inhabitants of St. Leonards, "a Hamblett within the said parish," is to be deemed to constitute an order of court. It was mutually agreed that St.

Leonards should pay one-fifth of all Taxes, impositions, and rates
which heareafter shall be imposed upon the said parish, to the
Church poor and Constables Bills, Kings bench and Marshallsea,
and all taxes to his Majestie, his heires and successors, and all
parochiall and public taxes.'

It was also agreed that the inhabitants of St. Leonards should
repair their own highways,

'unto the gate headinge from St. Leonards to Halton called
Hengrove Gate.'

However bad the roads, the parish officers could not avoid some
travelling, as Quarter Sessions were held not only at the nearby
towns of Aylesbury, Amersham, Chesham and Wendover, but also
further afield at Chepping Wycombe (High Wycombe),
Buckingham and Newport Pagnell. Occasionally the constables
themselves were presented for failure to return their own presentments of quarterly money. More often, however, they would be
dealing with a variety of petty offences.

The overseers of the poor were concerned with the inevitable
disputes about the removal of those due for relief from one parish
to another for, with responsibility pinned firmly by the
Elizabethan Poor Law Act of 1601 on the parishes where the
individuals were born, the overseers in every parish were vigilant in
trying to shift 'problem cases' to their neighbours and prevent the
next door parish from passing their own burdens on. Thus in 1717
Cholesbury succeeded in obtaining the removal of Frances Tomlin,
widow of Henry Tomlin with her seven children to Hawridge. A
few years before this the latter village had had a more complicated
case. The overseers had been ordered to pay 3/- a week to Mary
Lovett, a widow, but then persuaded her brother Daniel to take on
this responsibility. Three months afterwards he stopped payment,
but as funds seemed to be available from her late husband's
property it was ordered that the overseers should receive the
'rents, issues, and profits of all and every the Woodgrounds' of
William Lovett, and 'shall devote them to the maintenance of
Mary Lovett and her children.'

Daniel Lovett took exception to this order and a year later
there were two indictments,

'Daniel Lovett of Cholsbury, James Field, senior, of Chesham and
Charles Lights and John Glenister, both of Northchurch, co.

Hertford, for rioting in the woods of Mary Lovett, widow at
Choulsbury and breaking down and carrying away timber to the
value of 5s. 10d.'

Daniel Lovett of Hawridge, Charles Light of Northchurch, Co.
Hertford, and John Budd and John Francis, both of
Berkhamsted, Co. Hertford, for rioting in the woods of Mary
Lovett, widow, at Chesham, and breaking down and carrying
away 100 oaks, value £10.'

The case finally had a happy ending for Mary, with an order
that the overseers should reimburse themselves until the arrears
had been made up, but that the profits of the property should
then revert to her and the allowance cease. Daniel Lovett and his
friends were fined, though they were dilatory enough in making
payment and it seems to have been three years before the case was
finally cleared up.

The constables were concerned with a variety of problems. At
St. Leonards they had several times to present Thomas Parker and
Edward Ayres for keeping unlicensed alehouses; in 1703 the
former's was disorderly as well and he was fined 3s. 4d.

After the 1694 Act to suppress 'prophane curseing and swearing,'
there were various presentments of swearers. Edward Avis, blacksmith, John Lock and Samuel Springall of Cholesbury, Thomas
Dunston, fiddler of Hawridge, Thomas Eyres junior and Henry
Dawdy of St. Leonards were all convicted of this offence, the normal fine being 2/-. One cannot help thinking that there were many
more occasions when they and others escaped detection.

In 1699, the constable of St. Leonards had a rather more
unusual case. The shortage of water was another recurrent
problem, and we saw in 1644 Thomas Batchelor and Edmund
Birch making a pond on Cholesbury Common and enclosing it for
their own use. Mark Fenner, who had found his own solution to
the problem, was presented for

'Turning the water out of the water course which feedeth Thomas
Kingham's mill.'

He was lucky enough to find authority on his side; the
indictment was discharged as it did not appear 'to lye before this
court'. Generally, however, our villages seem to have been a law-
abiding community and in 27 years from 1678 to 1715 there is no
case of serious crime.

Notes and References

[1]Lipscomb, Vol.III, p.322.

[2]*Episcopal Visitation Book* 1662 Ed. by E.R.C. Brinkworth (B.A.S. 1947) p.58.
& 3

[4]Op. cit. (2) above pp.86-93, Appendix A, Visitation Articles.

[5]Lipscomb Vol.II, p.94.

[6]This information comes from a Statement of Facts in the case between the Attorney General at the Relation of Joseph Baldwin Gentleman against Dearing and another, 1754. We are grateful to Messrs Vaisey and Turner of Tring for permission to quote from these documents.

[7]L.A.O. Ter. 19/37 Cholesbury Terrier 1709.

[8]L.A.O. Ter. 19/83 Hawridge Terrier 1707.

[9]Bucks. C.R.O. Archdeaconry Index, Geary, John 1681.

[10]Bucks. C.R.O. Archdeaconry Index, Edmunds, Richard 1668.

[11]Bucks. C.R.O. D/A/We/71/103 Putnam, Henry 1735 D/A/Wf/80/210.

[12]See note (12) Ch.XI. Cholesbury Court Rolls.

15

[16]Bucks. C.R.O. Archdeaconry Index, Batchler, Robert 1662.

[17]Bucks. C.R.O. Archdeaconry Index No.57, Putnam, John 1716.

[18]See note (12) Ch. XI. Cholesbury Court Rolls.
& 19

[20]*Bucks. Sessions Records 1678 - 1712* Vol.I, Ed. by William le Hardy, Vol.II by William le Hardy and Geoffrey L. Reckett (Clerk of the Peace, Aylesbury 1933).

[21]See note (1), Ch. XIV.

XIV

'HAVING NOT WHEREWITH TO CLOATHE THEM DECENTLY'

Peter Hill: a country parson in the 18th century. [1]

The Neale trust; state of Church in Cholesbury; poverty of population; education;
distribution of books; Peter Hill as an individual.

In 1702 the poorly endowed curacy at Cholesbury received a welcome supplement by the creation of a lectureship. The donor, Joseph Neale of Gray's Inn, is a mystery character with no traceable connection with Cholesbury or Wigginton, the neighbouring parish in Hertfordshire which benefited to a lesser extent from this generous act.

The endowment consisted of lands in Cublington, a village still in the open field era, and the first Trustees included Frederic Slare, Doctor of Physic, Samuel Neale, possibly the founder's brother, the Rev. Henry Shute, Richard Seare Lord of the Manors of Cholesbury and Hawridge, the Ministers of Dunton and Cublington, six other worthy gentlemen probably from London and John Eyre, yeoman, a local representative. This impressive group of Trustees was instructed to pay the proceeds from the estate[2]

> 'Unto or to the use of such Grave, Good, Learned, and Orthodox Person, or Persons being a Protestant of the Communion of the Church of England, in Priest's Orders, and at least Twenty Seven Years of Age.'

The person to be appointed, the Trust deed continues,

> 'Shall be qualified as aforesaid, and be of a regular and sober Life and Conversation, and well qualified and able to Preach, Catechise and Expound the Church Catechism, and shall be duly Licensed to Preach, etc.'
>
> 'The Minister or Incumbent of Choulesbury may be elected and appointed Preacher or Lecturer as aforesaid . . . '

146

and his duties were to

> 'Constantly read the Offices in the Common Prayer Book appointed, and preach a Sermon in the said Church, every After-noon of every Sunday in every Year, and on every Christmas Day, and 5th Day of November. And shall after Sermon in the After-noons of every Sunday, Catechise in the said Church of Choulesbury, the Children of the Inhabitants of the said Parish, and such of the Children of Wigginton next adjoining as shall come to the said Church . . . '

In addition the Lecturer was

> 'To expound the Church Catechism in the Afternoons after Sermon . . . for the Space of Half an Hour at Least,'

on every Sunday in Lent and between Easter and Michaelmas. During this latter period, however, this was to take place on the first and third Sundays of the month at Cholesbury and on the second and fourth at Wigginton—on these occasions he was also to read Evening Prayer and preach a sermon at Wigginton,

> 'if the Incumbent of Tring [to which parish Wigginton belonged] shall give Leave for the doing thereof.'

This trust has been interpreted by some as a subtle attempt to infiltrate a Presbyterian bias into one corner of an Anglican Church. If this is so, the choice of two small villages with tiny, uneducated congregations for this attempt is a little incomprehens-ible. But for us the reasons for the benefaction are less important than the results. For the first time, Cholesbury had an endowment which was not derisory and an opportunity to attract a parson of some education and qualifications. In practice the offices of incumbent and lecturer were invariably combined and Joseph Neale, who had bought the advowson of the living ensured that the first holder of the lectureship was a man of his own choice by appointing Peter Hill as curate before his death. We shall meet him frequently in this chapter for, in addition to his other qualifica-tions, he was an assiduous correspondent who thought that his duty to the Trustees included information on the life of the parish. As historians we are indebted both to him and the Trustees who preserved all his correspondence.

Religious life at the time Hill went to Cholesbury was at a low ebb. We have already seen how poorly equipped his own Church was (page 114) and the wealthier Hawridge next door was not much better off. A Terrier of 1707 tells us that,[3]

> 'Wee have 2 Bells in our church; no clock; 2 Books; one Surplice;
> A little comunion cup weight about 6 ounces, one puter flaggon.'

An Episcopal enquiry between 1705 and 1723[4] into the state of all parishes, their population, the number of services usually held and the number of Eucharists a year discovered that, in Buckinghamshire there was nowhere where matins and evensong were recited daily in public, though nearly everywhere on Wednesdays, Fridays and Holy Days. Only in three churches, Buckingham, Hambleden and Newport Pagnell, was Eucharist held as often as once a month and in a few villages including Buckland only once a year.

In his answers to Visitation questions in 1720,[5] Peter Hill confirms that this general apathy was even worse at Cholesbury than in many other parishes. This was not because of inherent opposition to the Anglican Church. Of the twenty families in the village he tells us that there was 'one Presbyterian, one Anabaptist,' a proportion which must have been much the same thirty or forty years earlier, for in the three villages of Cholesbury, Hawridge and St. Leonards there were in 1689 no registered 'publick meeting houses for Religious Worship' and in the Sessions Records for these parishes there is only one presentment for absence from church, Robert Jones in 1684, who was a prominent Quaker. The Quaker Minute Book[6] records that Jones, with Edward Hoar were 'to visit Mary Belson of Chesham and reprove her for some disorders comitted by her.' They were able to report later that, 'they found her very tender, sensible of her miscarriage and sorry for it.' He must surely be the character whose death is recorded in the parish register in 1698 as 'Joans "Old" a Quaker.'

But despite this apparent lack of opposition, Peter Hill still could not get his parishioners to Church. As he told the Visitation,

> 'The public service I read in my Church as often as any of the
> Parishioners can come to join with me, which I find they cannot
> doe but on some particular festival, fast and solemn days; since
> they all depend, both men and women, upon the labour of their
> hands for their subsistence.'
> '12 or 14 communicants, no more than half that number did
> communicate last Easter.'

Sermons were popular at this time and lasted at least an hour, Puritan preachers often asking the consent of the congregation to turn over the hour glass and carry on when time ran out. Whether he had an audience or not, Peter Hill carried out his obligation under the terms of the Trust scrupulously, reporting in 1725 that he had not omitted the lecture 'nor the two Sermons to be preached on Gunpowder treason and Christmas Day' except on three occasions when he was ill and couldn't get anyone else to officiate for him. He added that the provision of deputies has

'Sometimes been very chargeable to me, and was particularly so the first year of this King's reign; in which being sick and indisposed for several weeks, the supply then procured stood me in a matter of 7/-.'

His second obligation, however, to catechise the children regularly was not so easy to implement, particularly with the detailed instruction that this should be done after the Sunday afternoon sermon, because, as he writes,

'Many will not stay to hear after the Sermon is ended.'

He got round this problem by expounding the catechism after the second lesson. Hard as he tried, the hearing of catechism from the children was an uphill struggle. He writes repeatedly and sadly about

'the children who don't come as they should.'

At times the reason for not sending children to church is the parents

'having not wherewith to cloath them decently.'

Other parents alleged, though Hill obviously doubts this, that the children say catechism at home, but,

'others are careless and will not take the pains to teach their children it; the rest would but cannot, because they never learnt so much as to read themselves, and being poor they have not the wherewithal to pay for their children's schooling.'

Up to this time we have had to look at our villages through the eyes of their wealthier members, the yeomen farmers. We have suggested once or twice that the farm workers and labourers were likely to be very poor; in these few extracts Peter Hill has more than confirmed this suspicion and he writes so dispassionately that there is no reason to think he is exaggerating. They were poor and uneducated.

Hill himself supplemented his income by teaching, excusing himself from attending one Trustee meeting in London,

> 'because some of my neighbours and acquaintances hereabouts having sent their sons to me lately to be instructed in the Latine Tongue.'

They would have been the sons of the wealthier yeoman farmers and craftsmen of whom, from the list of landholders taking oaths of allegiance in 1723 it appears that about two-thirds could at least write their own names. For most of the population in these country villages education was at best irregular. When there was a schoolmaster 'which sometimes we have not', Hill adds,

> 'but I am apt to think he will soon lay it down again, as some have done before him, there being but a very poor livelihood and scarce that to be got by schooling in this place.'

Despite this, Peter Hill was assiduous in carrying out the last duty imposed by the Trust, that of distributing 20s worth of improving literature to the poor. Most of the recipients would no doubt have preferred money, but the Trust decreed that they were to have books, whether they could read them or not. In 1724 Hill ordered

> '6 Testaments and 4 Common Prayer Books
> 10 Lewis's Exposition of the Church Catechism printed by Downing 3d
> 10 The Plain Man's Guide to Heaven by Dr. Lucas printed by Smith 1s
> 6 A Discourse of the Education of Children printed by Newborough 3d
> 6 Peer's Companion for the Aged by Downing 6d
> 10 Several methods for reading the Scripture by the same 3d
> 10 Lessons for Children historical and practical by the same 4d
> 10 A Conference Concerning keeping the Lord's Day by the same 3d'

The Testaments and Catechisms were given to the children, recipients of the latter ranging in age from 6 to 11; the distribution of the other books is shown on the following list, typical of many:

'Account of year 1749 ending Lady Day 1750

The 2 Bibles to	Mary Jeffs a Maid Servant
	Eliz. Hurnal a poor man's wife
8 Prayer Books	Ann Bishop a poor man's wife
	Mary Martin a poor man's widow
	Sarah Harwood a poor lacemaker
	Elis. Colby a poor maidservant
	Mary Horn a poor maidservant
	Mary Ayre a poor man's wife
	Lydia Taylor a d. of Tho. Taylor
	Francis Taylor 2nd s. of Tho. Taylor

6 Men's Duty	J. Beckley's son	Daniel Page
	J. Bishop	J. Warner
	T. Taylor's eldest son	J. Bunch

6 Bp. Wilson's Notes		
	J. Osborn	J. Bishop a potter
	Jos. Batchelor a shoemaker	Thos. Taylor
		another potter
	J. Beckley a smith	One to be disposed of

6 Whole Duty of Man		
	James Crook a day labourer	
	Sarah Horwood a lacemaker	
	S. Hill a Taylor's widow	
	4th to a Brickmaker	2 to be disposed of'

It should, perhaps, be noted that this list covers Wigginton as well as Cholesbury.

There was no problem in ordering the books; obtaining delivery was another matter. In 1715 Peter Hill used the Chesham Waggoner to send notes of receipts to London for a Trustee's meeting. In 1741 a letter for him,

'had layn at Aylesbury a week and would have been there longer but someone heard that there was a letter and had it conveyed.'

So he asks the Trustees to send his books to the

'Wendover Waggoner, who sets out from the Oxford Arms in Warwick Lane every Wednesday; his name is Willm More.'

and on another occasion arranges for letters to be sent to Mr. Hawards, apothecary, at Wendover.

Communications with Wendover may well have been easier at this time than with Chesham along the waterlogged Vale.

Peter Hill as an Individual

Despite the volume of his letters, it is disappointing to find how little Peter Hill tells us about himself. A bachelor, with a sister to support, a poor man, he tells us a little about his domestic problems. In 1720 he is living in Buckland because,

> 'I can't reside in the house belonging to my cure without turning housekeeper myself, which will not suit with my present circumstances nor can I meet with any lodgings so convenient for me in my own parish as in that where I am.'

Later he moved back to the Rectory, but in 1739 he is only living in an 'Upper Room and a Parlour' of the Rectory, having let the house to Mary Trumpet and her daughter Sarah, who got their living lace making, for a rent of 30/-.

Several times he mentions his health, which, in 1724,

> 'doth at present droop under a cold, which having invaded one part after another, is at last fallen upon my longs, and become somewhat troublesome to me, but the use of Pogeen remedies, accompanyd with God's Blessing will I hope ere long set me to right again . . . '

Fig. 21 Home Farm and Barn as Peter Hill would have seen them from near his Rectory

He must also have been a countryman and was well equipped for a task which occupied a good deal of his time, the local supervision of the Cublington estate, and his glebe land in Cholesbury. In one of his letters, writing about Priest's Grove he uses the phrase 'underwood ground'. The Trustees did not understand and asked him to explain

'what he meant by underwood Ground, whether he means Coppice Ground and if so how often it is felled and when it was last fell'd and how much in value per acre when fall'd.'

Hill could not only explain but retaliate with a brief essay on forestry. He means, he says,

'a wood of young trees coming up amongst and under those that are already shot up, from the roots of others that have been cut down. Priest Grove sometimes called underwood and sometimes springwood, differs from an underwood or a coppice in this, that a coppice every twelve years is all cut down at once with us, some low standards excepted.'

Priest's Grove, he explains, is cut 'here and there by parcels.' He gives a full description of the reasons for cutting—too thick, too close together, spreading hinders growth—and finally remarks,

'I have left it full of trees and in the judgement of some too full for the underwood to get up . . . '

He gives the impression of being a worthy, conscientious, honest and courageous man, quick enough to defend himself when the Trustees asked awkward questions about his performance of his duties and with no hesitation when asked to suggest names for appointment as Trustees of

'3 persons, either at Tring, or Cublington, that are Men of Temper and Charity, in good Circumstances in the World and well affected to the Government.'

in replying,

'As for the Chief Persons at Tring, whatsoever they may be in other respects, they are in their Principles what we call High Churchmen. At Cublington there is only one Person of note and he of the same Principles with those at Tring.'

It is difficult to discover how much influence Peter Hill really had on the village. Was the difficulty in getting people to Church only due to their lack of time, or was he perhaps somewhat uninspiring or even a bit dull? Perhaps he was too modest to write more about himself; he may have been too poor to help as much as he would have liked; but one suspects somehow that he was a little too worthy and rather lacking in a sense of humour. He is probably best summed up by one of the Trustees who, commenting on the letter we have just quoted, could write to one of his colleagues:

> 'I am well pleased with the candid answer and account of honest Mr. Hill ... He is a man who fears God and dares not to give under his hand a false report. I wish that not only all his neighbours but all the land were stocked with persons of equal Integrity.'

Notes and References

[1]We should like to thank the Trustees of Neale's Charity for access to the Trust records and permission to quote extensively from them. These records, kept by Messrs Halsey, Lightly and Hemsley of London, Solicitors to the Trust, comprise an extensive collection of Trust Deeds, Minute books and letters, the latter written particularly by Peter Hill, the first Lecturer and Henry Jeston, the fourth (see Chs. XVII and XVIII). The information and quotations in this and the two later chapters are taken from these documents and from the 'Buffed, Bossed Book', a copy of the Trust deed deposited in Cholesbury Church, which also contains some later notes.

[2]Neale Trust Deed.

[3]L.A.O. Ter. 19/83 Hawridge Terrier 1707.

[4]L.A.O. Spe. I – Speculum Dioecesseos Lincolniensis sub episcopis Gul. Wake et Edm. Gibson

[5]Peter Hill's entries in the Buffed, Bossed Book include a note of his replies to the enquiry.

[6]*Quaker Minute Book 1669-90* Ed. by Beatrice Saxon Snell (B.A.S.1937) p.5.

XV

'OUR OFFICERS BEING CONFUSED'

From yeoman to squire in the 18th century

Parish Register descriptions of the population; Hawridge—a new generation of the Batchelors—change in the Lord of the Manor; Cholesbury absorption of land by Brazier's End; St. Leonards—a local feast—the Baldwin's disappearance from Dundridge; general reasons for the decline of the yeomen farmers; the Plaistowe family and a letter on the Battle of Dettingen.

Peter Hill's entries in the parish register [1] supplement his letters in describing the state of the village. Robert Wright of Chesham is described as

'A housekeeper possest of many goods and chattels'

and John King as

'Possessor of a house and Orchd.'

Yeomen, farmers, bricklayers, potters, and even occasionally a day-labourer, are described by their occupations without further qualification, but for every one of these, there are two or three whose names are followed by the word 'poor,' or 'a pauper' or 'a collectioner'— the last indicating a recipient of parish relief. It was not only the labourers who were in trouble. William Johnson, 'a broken farmer', may have come from another parish, but there are many signs that our yeomen farmers are dying out to be replaced by the new type of landowner, the 18th century squire. Again, we must outline the changes in each village in turn.

Hawridge

At Hawridge, we have already seen the Batchelors disappearing as land-owners. They are still in the district but as tenant farmers not freeholders as the leading member of that family, Benjamin, Senior, does not appear in the Poll Books for 1722 and 1784.[2] He may already have been tenant at Hawridge Court as at the time of his death in 1813[3] and was not by any means 'poor, as he eventually accumulated enough money to buy not only 'The

155

Limes' but to re-acquire the old family property, Hill Farm,[4] and become a freeholder of some 120 acres. His Will gives the impression of a patriarchal old man who could instruct his executors

'not to cut more timber than shall be needed for repairs.'

After dividing his Hawridge land between two of his sons, Thomas and Benjamin, junior, he added:

'And I do desire my said wife to continue and hold the farmlands and premises wherein I now dwell called Hawridge Court, so long as she shall contine my widow sole and unmarried but no longer for the benefit of my said children.'

On Mary's death Benjamin, junior, took over Hawridge Court and alienated the rest of the property to Thomas, who spent the rest of his life alienating his lands by instalments.

Both our other yeoman families in Hawridge have disappeared by the end of the 18th century. At Bottom Farm the Gearys lasted until at least 1767,[5] but by 1784 Daniel Geary, the owner of this farm was living in Harrow-on-the-Hill,[6] the occupier being Bottom Joiner, and after this we hear no more of them except as owners of cottages. The Putnams disappear too. After John splits up his lands in 1717, they just fade out, keeping only Bentonpotts and an acre of meadow ground until William Putnam disposes of it in 1819.

One new family comes into the village in this century, the Wrights at Botchmore Farm, represented by a succession of William Wrights. The first was in possession of this farm by 1714, when William Wright leaves it to his son William.[7] Their own farm was a mere 38 acres,[8] but they had a lease of a further 52 acres in Hawridge in addition to lands in Bellingdon and Cholesbury. A non-conformist family, one of their houses was registered as a Chapel.[9]

The land lost or sold by the yeomen farmers was all reabsorbed by the Lord of the Manor. In 1748 Robert Dayrell had bought the Manors of both Hawridge and Cholesbury from the Seares. His son Edward inherited shortly afterwards, to be succeeded in 1814 by his brother-in-law, the Rev. John Jeffries, Rector of Barnes in Surrey, who in turn bequeathed them to his son. There is no evidence that the family, which remained until the end of the 19th century, were ever resident, though as will appear later they were generous enough when the village needed help.

Cholesbury

The build up of large country estates was even more pronounced at Cholesbury than at Hawridge. We have already seen the Batchelors and the Putnams dying out for lack of male heirs. By 1723 their successor at Parrott's Farm, John Eayres, is also dead. By 1781 Parrott's belongs to John Baker and Charles Orlando Gore, Lord of the Manor of Tring, and is farmed by Joseph Gurney, followed by his son John. [10]

Thomas Batchelor's branch of this family may only have survived in the female line, but in Cholesbury, as in Hawridge, this prolific family cannot disappear. From 1750 they are prominent enough to become, apparently, hereditary churchwardens at Cholesbury. The line starts with Joseph Batchelor, who kept an Inn, the *Castle*[11] for ten years and lived at Home Farm Cottage. [12] As churchwarden he was succeeded in 1790 by Thomas who in turn handed over to William in 1805. The family remained in Home Farm Cottage and turn up early in the 19th century as tenant farmers in the parsonage lands and at Parrott's. It is possible, therefore, that they were at Parrott's earlier than our records show.

Parrott's farm was so small that its absorption into a larger estate was inevitable. In the opposite corner of the parish at Braziers End, it was possible even in Cholesbury to build up a reasonable farm. When we last mentioned Braziers End we found that John Geary was the owner of [13]

'A messuage and certain lands   Rent 18d
Another messuage and lands   Rent 3/-'

Before 1767 this land had passed to a Joseph Burket of the parish of St. Mary Magdalen in Bermondsey; when he left his property to his niece, Elizabeth Hume of Masham Street, Westminster, it had also acquired as freeholds,

'A Messuage and certain lands in Cholesbury – Rent 1/-
Another messuage and certain lands thereto belonging – Rent 10/-

These holdings had presumably belonged previously to the Lord of the Manor, as there is no trace of ealier ownership. Joseph Burket had acquired, too,

> 'Three pieces of customary land with appurtenances, ½ acre.'

This was the plot next to the Edward Avis house which had belonged to Nathaniel Birch.

Elizabeth Hume died in 1776; her mother inherited the property and left it, when she died a year later, to 'My good Friend Fowler Walker of Lincoln's Inn in the County of Middlesex, Esquire.' He added to the property by making an encroachment near his house of about one acre, for which he was amerced 10/-; the line where the boundary has been changed can still be seen.

By this stage, architectural evidence shows that one of the new owners had started to convert the old farmhouse into a gentleman's country residence. But Fowler Walker only enjoyed it for 28 years; on his death in 1805 it was inherited by a George Hassell, who acquired the land adjacent to the copyhold plot described in the Court Rolls as

> 'Customary cottage or tenement with Appurtenances and out-houses ... and all Barns, Stables, Edifices and buildings to the same belonging Rent 2½d

> All that Orchard or Pightle of pasture or meadow or Mowing Ground to the said cottage or tenement belong or appertaining containing by estimation half an acre (be the same more or less) adjoining to the lands of the Widow Culverhouse on the East to a house called the Town House on the West and to the Common there on the North and to a pightle called Hunts Wick on the South.'

George Hassell, a magistrate, was Lord of the Manor of Buckland, a country squire, and had been Chief Sheriff of Buckinghamshire. With resources behind him he might have brought the village prosperity, but the first tragedy was about to hit Cholesbury. In 1821 he 'drowned himself in a fit of insanity.'[14] For ten years Brazier End remained in the hands of his solicitors, Thomas Atkinson and John Parkinson, who let it to a succession of tenant farmers. As we shall see in the next chapter, the tragedy could not have come at a worse time. It was followed by another.

In 1831 Braziers End was sold at last to a farmer, Thomas Lovett. Four months later he was dead. The parish register records that

'The verdict of the Jury was that the said Thomas Lovett was accidentally killed by the discharge of a gun that he had in his hands but that his death was accelerated by the administration of too great a quantity of opium.'

His brother, Richard Lovett, succeeded; he sold Braziers End within two years through the Rev. Francis Cole to Richard Albion Fellowes, who made two final additions, one small copyhold plot which had formerly belonged to the Batchelors and two more freehold plots of rents of 7d each. Fellowes stayed a long time by Braziers End standards—twelve years—and when he too was succeeded in 1846 by James Benners Parkinson this long story of rapid changes in ownership at last comes to an end.

This long succession of changes has been recorded at length because it illustrates the merger of small yeoman holdings into a country estate. To the initial small farm there were additions, first of two substantial freeholds, then of any small copyhold plots he could acquire and finally of two more freeholds. By the time the process was completed the owner of Braziers End was also the owner of more than half the village. He was not Lord of the Manor—that function had been bought by the Dayrells but by the middle of the 18th century they owned in Cholesbury little but the Manor House. In view of their acquisition of land elsewhere, it seems possible that the demesne lands in Cholesbury had already been alienated by their predecessors, the Seares, and were unobtainable.

St. Leonards – Dundridge

Of all the families in our villages, the Baldwins at Dundridge were the most firmly rooted. In their 250 years, they had made so many additions to the Manor that it is now impossible to trace the shape of the original house. In 1748, as yet another alteration was nearing completion, John Baldwin wrote to Mr. Senior, a Wendover craftsman who had been responsible for the work:[15]

'I intended, as you will have heard, to have met you at St. Leonard's on Sunday next but I am prevented, and I know not when I can contrive to be there. The London workmen told me

when I was last there that they should be able to leave me at
farthest in three weeks; I am desirous of parting with them and
the rest of you upon good terms; therefore propose that you shall
have one jolly day together; for this purpose order a handsome
buttock of beef from Parnham, let it be properly salted by
someone, and drest at Payne's upon Buckland Common, upon
the day preceding the Joiners' departure for London, adding to it
a noble plum-pudding, which it is probable Mrs Payne can make.
Tom Davis will be able to give you some cabbage and probably
carrots out of my garden. Turnips he will get for you. Besides the
London workmen you will invite yourself, Mr Tratt, Mr Smith and
such of you men as have worked at St. Leonard's in the late business, together with Tom Davis, and if you think the beef will hold
out Mr Gurney, Mr Payne and others of my neighbours that have
been employed for me in carriage or otherwise. Be merry and
wise; without stinting you I should suppose that two quarts of
beer for each man will be as much as you would wish. Let the
whole expence be collected and I will pay it when I go down.
I am your humble servant,

John Baldwin.'

The Disappearance of the Yeomen

Twenty years later, even the Baldwins had disappeared and the
Manor was added to the estate of Robert Dayrell, Lord of the
Manors of Cholesbury and Hawridge. By the standards in our part
of the Chilterns, Dundridge was not a small farm, and its
absorption into a larger 'country gentleman's estate' is more
surprising than that of the small holdings of Hawridge and
Cholesbury—the 25-30 acre plots inherited from a much earlier era
had ceased to be viable economic units. In our Chiltern Hills, they
could never have given more than a sparse living, partly because of
the untractable clay-with-flints soil which for most of the year is
either glue or concrete and is only easily worked on a few days
when the weather is especially co-operative. For most of the year,
as a local surveyor complained of Cublington, it was impossible to

'go over it without being bemir'd.'[16]

For a time the farmers of our villages may have gained considerable advantage from their early enclosure as compared with,
for example, the Neale Trust farm at Cublington which

'lay dispersed in small parcels, such as acres, half-acres and roods
amongst other man's land.'

Our yeomen were a tenacious breed, but mounting expenses were making things difficult. The cost of replacing

'ole ruinous barge 60 ft x 16 x 10½ height between joints,'[17]

at the Neale Trust Farm in Cublington was estimated in 1728 at £60,

'Requiring at least 14 load of oak and between 40 and 50 planks of deal and some of old material - oak @ 1. 8. 0 per load would come to 19. 12s and deal @ 3d per foot to £5. 12. 6 suppose planks to be 10 ft x 1. Workmanship and straw, spikes and other odd matters 3s.'

In 1732 a farmer at Little Gaddesden calculated that he made a loss of 10/9 on each acre of wheat sown, even on enclosed land.[18]

Once enclosure came to the larger farms in the Vale of Aylesbury, the disappearance of the small farms was inevitable. It was a slow enough process to permit survival for another 100 years to those who could still buy or lease enough land. Taking examples from the larger villages which have come into our history, Cublington was enclosed in 1770, Marsworth did not follow until 1811 or Aston Clinton until 1816, while Buckland was a late enclosure in 1844.

It is in Hawridge therefore that our yeomen farmers last longest, for Benjamin Batchelor and William Wright still have the mark of the old breed with freehold lands of their own, even if they have to supplement these with fields leased from the Lord of the Manor, and are described as yeomen in the Court Book. They marry into local families and they still attend the Manorial Court to acknowledge changes in ownership and pay the appropriate reliefs. Their right of inheritance is safeguarded by the custom of the Manor and recorded in the time-honoured phrases. There was no bar to a woman inheriting, provided her rights could be established through a Will and where necessary such documents are examined and noted fully in the Court records. Where copyhold property was involved, considerable efforts were made to protect the woman concerned and to ensure that if the property was sold later, the sale was approved by the woman and not just by her husband. Thus in 1791 the Hawridge Court Book tells us that[19]

'Mary Thorpe, Rebecca Wright and Sarah Smith are the three daughters and co-heiresses of John Horwood late of Wigginton

aforesaid blacksmith deceased and customary tenants of the said
Manor and being first solely and separately examined apart from
their said respective husbands by John Plaistowe Gentleman
Deputy Steward of the said William Mayton Capital Steward of
the said Manor and freely and voluntarily consenting thereto did
out of court surrender . . . '

Rebecca Wright was the wife of William Wright the second, who
inherited Botchmore Farm in 1767. It is still a community free of
class-consciousness where the farmers and the craftsmen inter-
marry.

At Cholesbury, as we have seen, the yeomen have disappeared,
their decendants being small tenant farmers or labourers. At
Buckland Common, when we first discover the farmers' names,
one, at Folly Farm, is a Brackley, the pottery family, and the
other Dorrien, whose farm is still known by his name, probably a
country gentleman. At St. Leonard's Dundridge, like Chapel Farm
is run by tenant farmers and the parish registers have only one
familiar name, that of Plested. This we would take to be a variant
of Plaistowe, the variation dating from the 16th century, though
there is no evidence two centuries later of any connection between
the Plesteds and the better known Plaistowes. It is a family which
wanders in and out of our history. Thomas Plaistow, it will be
remembered, was the founder of the Chapel Trust in 1509. 200
years later, William Plaistowe of The Lee is one of the Trustees, a
Richard Plaistowe becomes Rector of Hawridge and we have just
seen John Plaistowe, a Chesham solicitor as Deputy Steward of the
Manor at Hawridge. The connection of this firm (afterwards
Francis & How) with the stewardship of the Manors of Hawridge
and Cholesbury lasted until 1923. Lords of the Manor of The Lee
since 1635, the Plaistowes are typical of the wealthier country
gentlemen who are so curiously absent from the history of our
own villages, families which, after acquiring a Manor, would stay
in the village for centuries. Their absence has made the history of
our villages more difficult to piece together; the yeomen farmers
do not keep collections of letters, the country gentlemen sometimes do. But we feel that we have just enough connection with
the Plaistowes to entitle us to quote from their family papers one
letter of outstanding interest. Like all these country families the
Plaistowes had their wild younger sons who were sent off to the

army when they became too much of an embarrassment. One of these, Richard, writes to his father in 1742 bemoaning his fate:[20]

'Why should I be banished from the country I so dearly love. I neither robed nor killed any body, all that the Country say of me is I have been wilde and foolish . . . '

His plea had no effect, and a year later he was in the middle of the Battle of Dettingen. His graphic account of this battle is typical of the sort of news which would have filtered back to the villages and provided scope for gossip in the pubs. He writes:

'Mr Plaistow at The Lee near Great Missenden Bucks England
Honoured St   Frankfort Jun ye 28th. 1743.
    I should have wrought to you sooner since our last battle had I not been very much wounded, which had occasioned me some illness but by the blessing of God I am some thing better. I thought it my duty to write to you as soon as I was able. The 16th day in the morning we was ordered to strike our tents to march near Frankfort we have nothing in that part of the country for ourselves and our horses, both armies lying so close together enough to devour any country in the world, both armies now lye a mile of one another in some places there is only a river parts us which I can throw over, we water our horses head to head and are frequently a talking to them from one side of the river to the other. The 16th day we was marching along very unconcerned by the main side little did any body think of an engagement that day, his Majesty the earl of Stairs and all the general officers where with us, about eight we hears the first cannon go off which made all the army stand still being surprised the second cannon had life to have took his Majesty then we began to smell what they was about, their we was obliged to stand their cannon from several batteries for six hours, and do nothing for ourselves, which way we lost a great many men and in that time they got over the river threescore thousand men, but we drove them back a great deal faster than they came over with the loss of about 9 thousand and ten pieces of cannon besides standard and colours about two of the clock in afternoon we made our first attack with our cannon which did good execution and we began to march our army up towards them, they having taken their ground while we was adoing nothing at all, general Honiwood which is our second commander hear has got our regiment and he ordered our regiment up first which we was drawed up by ourselves almost, against the french gendarms which at that time was ten to

one against us, and our officers being confused one rode one way and the other another so that we had no officers to command us, by this time there was a regiment of dragoons come up and they seeing they had got the upper hand of us they charged us directly and fired upon us which confused our horses very much, and we could pretend to do nothing but ride in sword in hand but there being so many to one they drove us considerable but we still kept sloping them as well as we could, I received a slight wound or two but to no purpose, we was obliged to retreat and make our banks good and we charged them again directly with another regiment of horse and dragoons but in three minutes it was all over with me. My horse was shot and when I was down upon the ground I received several wounds in the head and lay down for dead for some time, our regiments were obliged to retreat a second time and the foot which was left of us throwed in a valeur of shot or two and defeated them quite which made them begin to run and when they once began, we soon drove them and drowned above two thousand a going over the river. We lost General Clayton and about fifteen hundred men with officers inclusive three of our regiment one Captain a Lieutenant and a Coronet besides several wounded two of the officers was Captain Reffet's acquaintance Merriden and Draper, there was the three battalion of guards four regiments of dragoons the bleurs Life Guards and horse grenadiers did not ingage, I wrought to you ten weeks agoe and have never received an answere from you about receiving the nine guineas which had been a great service to me since, for I lost every thing I had in the world in the ingagement from my hatt to my shew and have not one thing to shift myself, I even lost the boots of my legs for a man as soon as he is down he is stript directly by the plunderers, we expect another ingagement every day, the French would make a sessation of arms for six weeks but his Majesty told he would not for three days and he has given them liberty to build what bridges they will to come over to us and they have built three so we expect to engage every day, I am very much concerned that I cannot hear out of England from none of you all perhaps you may think I have not money enough to pay for a letter which I will assure you I always have and I desire you will write to me to let me know how you do so I remain your Most Obedient and ever dutiful son to command where you please

My love to all my brothers and Sisters and all friends.

Richard Plaistow'

Richard is wrong about the date of the battle which was 27 June not 16, otherwise his account is accurate. He recovered from his wounds, but on 7 September 1743, 'fell ill of a fever and bloody flux (haemorrhage) which carried him off.'

Notes and References

[1]Cholesbury Parish Register. The descriptions appear under Burials.

[2]Poll Books in the possession of Society of Genealogists. Benjamin Batchelor's residence in Hawridge is established from the Chesham P.R. which in 1745 records his marriage to Elizabeth Atkins.

[3]Bucks C.R.O. Archdeaconry Index No.42, Batchelor, Benjamin 1813.

[4]Hawridge Court Book 1795 - 1813.

[5]The Court Book records that Daniel Geary inherited Bottom Farm from his father John in that year.

[6]Poll Book, 1784.

[7]Bucks. C.R.O. Archdeaconry Index No.1714, Wright, William 1714.

[8]The Court Book in 1767 records William Wright as inheriting from his father William.

[9]Bucks. C.R.O. Dissenting Places of Protestant Worship - Registered in the Court of the Archdeacon of Buckingham 1781 - 1841.

[10]Bucks. C.R.O. D/A/We/105/31 Gurney, Joseph 1781. D/A/Wf/102/194.

[11]Bucks. C.R.O. V.128. Registers of Licensed Victuallers 1753 - 1827.

[12]The Cholesbury Court Book in 1767 states that Joseph Batchelor "held freely certain lands and hereditaments, late the estate of - Edlin." This cannot be accurate as Mary Edlin left this cottage to the Northchurch Poor, V.C.H. Herts. Vol.II, p.250.

[13]This and following quotations are from the cholesbury Court Book.

[14]Gibbs, Vol.III, p.93.

[15]Elizabeth Holland, *Old Wendover* - a booklet (Aylesbury 1944) p.20.

[16]Peter Hill's letters.
& 17

[18]Gibbs, Vol.II, p.66.

[19]Hawridge Gourt Book.

[20]Letters quoted from the Plaistowe family history see note (18) Ch.IX.

XVI

'THE HEALTH IS DOUBTLESS MUCH AFFECTED'

Sidelights on village life about 1750–1820

St Leonards, a local Gretna Green; 2 Parsons; population and employment; Inns and Ale-houses; straw-plaiting; gipsies.

While Peter Hill was having difficulty at Cholesbury in getting his parishoners to church, St. Leonards Chapel next door was having its heyday in an unexpected manner—it had become the local Gretna Green. In 12 years between 1739 and 1754 there were 77 marriages by licence and 6 banns,[1] none of them of local residents. The Chapel was especially popular with residents in Chesham and Wendover, but it was not only from the nearby farms and villages that they found their way to St. Leonards. From 51 Parishes they came, from Bletchley in the north to Kingston-on-Thames in the south, from Thame and Taplow in the west to King's Langley in the east, no mean journey on the roads of those days. 36 couples came together from these distant parishes, another 96 may have made the journey singly to meet their lovers from another parish.

The parson must have made a small fortune from fees until this enterprise was stopped in 1754 by an Act preventing clandestine marriages, in which St. Leonards got a special mention.

The Village, however, was not to settle down to a peaceful existence because it immediately became involved in one of the prolonged law suits which were common at the time. It started with a wrangle about the appointment of trustees, Joseph Baldwin bringing a case against Elizabeth Deering (née Plaistowe, whose father had been a trustee) and John Hely, the only survivor of a long list of trustees for their failure to add to their number or to account for the proceeds from the sale of timber on the trust lands. The 'Statement of Facts' in the case reveals certain peculiarities about the administration of this trust. The vagueness of the original trust deed was mentioned in Chapter IX and it will

Fig. 22 St Leonards Chapel

be remembered that in the Edward VI Enquiry into the chapel the witnesses maintained that their priest had

'been hired by the said inhitunts of the said hamlett of St. Leonards at their owne proper costes and charges.'

The statement revealed that where the chaplains had previously been maintained by voluntary contributions, the trustees[2]

'long before and ever since the year 1700 have permitted the Chaplain of St. Leonards to take the whole rents of the original Charity Estate as also of the additional purchases to his own use reserving only the Wood Ground and the Wood and Timber growing on the premises which Wood and Timber at seasonable periods of growth have been felled cut down and sold excepting only such part thereof as was wanted for repairs of the Chapel on the Estate and except other parts delivered to the Chaplain for firing.'

'And the Wood and Timber so sold has at some times produced considerable sums of money ...'

These sums had been spent in estate maintenance, repairs to

houses, buildings and the chapel, payment of quit rents, repair of the highway and the purchase of land.

The trustees may have exceeded their authority in using the money in this way. They were even more at fault in another matter and the 'Statement of Facts' continues:-

> 'nor does it appear that the inheritance of the Chapel ever vested in those Trustees or their Predecessors nor does their power or the right of the Inhabitants to appoint a Chaplain but that Mr Penn the late Chaplain was nominated by three or four Trustees as to a Donative or free Chapel . . .

The defendant, Hely had likewise

> 'appointed the Rev. Mr Smith Chaplain in the same mode as Mr Penn was appointed.'

This document called 'Statement of Facts' was dated 1754 but it appears that is was not until 1789 that the case was heard. This was much too quick by 18th century standards and the Master of the Rolls immediately appointed Mr Holford, one of the Masters of Court to make an investigation. While awaiting results new trustees were to be appointed and the estate was put into Chancery, Elizabeth Deering being ordered to pay the money from the sale of wood into the bank which was to invest this, with further profits, in 3% bank annuities. The interim judgement finishes with the ruling that the monies were to be devoted to the purposes indicated by

> 'the Original Foundation of the Charity in case the same can be discovered.'

Another 12 years passed before Mr Holford's report appeared and this was concerned particularly with the question of costs amounting in all to £439 17s. 4d. £153 18s. 3d. of this was due to the relator and the trustees were ordered to arrange for a survey of their woods and the subsequent felling of sufficient timber to pay both the relator and the balance of the £439 to cover costs for Elizabeth Deering and John Hely. The churchwardens' accounts for 1802 and the next few years give a most detailed record of the timber felled, numbering each plot and hedgerow and the number of feet which each had yielded and the proceeds from the sale. In 1802 the summary reads:-[3]

'2619 feet of beech	130.	19.	0
130 feet of ash	9.	15.	0
40 load and half of billet@			
£1.1.0 per load	42.	10.	6
4720 faggots @ £1 per 100	47.	4.	0
	£230.	8.	6'

Two fellings in 1803 produced a total of £392, and in 1804 there was an even larger clearance of woodland amounting to:

'3704 feet of beech @1d per foot	185.	4.	0
90 load of billet @ £1.2.0	99.	0.	0
6050 faggots @ £1.2.0 per 100	66.	11.	0
15 loads a foot of oak @ £6 per load	91.	0.	0
364 yards of bark @ 2/9d.	50.	1.	,0
720 oak faggots @ 1/7d. per 100	7.	18.	0
	£499.	14.	0'

The money raised from these extensive fellings also included £600 which the trustees had spent on their cottages,

'being in a very ruinous and delapidated state'

and unaware, apparently, that they had no right to authorise any fellings while their woods were in Chancery.

Even the cost settlement did not finish the case. Queries could still be raised on the respectability of the new trustees, involving a further report, and when these were satisfied the trustees failed to ensure the return of all their deeds, with the further problem of establishing their rights to these after the case had been closed and forgotten. It is not surprising, therefore, to find that the last documents are dated 1839, 85 years after the case had been started.

How much the Village understood of this protracted case it is difficult to say, but the retiring chaplain in 1801, Joseph Smith appears to have been too hazy about the trustees' problems to have appreciated their difficulties and wrote to his successor, Isaac King complaining,[4]

'Prior to my time of 5 loads of Billet Wood and 300 Faggots annually allowed to the Chaplain, but I fancy the whole is in great measure in the breast of the Trustees; I have never had any wood . . . on the winding up I have not been able to get a very large sum which I conceive is due to me, allowed for repairs.'

Two years later a belated payment of £100 was made to Joseph Smith, who finished in his letter to Isaac King, encouragingly -

'Wishing you better luck and a long enjoyment of your preferment.'

But the Rev. Isaac King was to have no luck. Shaken, no doubt, by the poverty of the living, he managed to obtain a temporary appointment at West Wycombe as stop-gap for an intended incumbent who was still a minor. This did not please the Trustees, and in 1805 King writes from West Wycombe to the Secretary of the Bishop of Lincoln about the inequity of their attitude:[5]

'I am now called upon to resign because it is not in my power at present to do the Duty, this place being 12 miles distant, and I have here Morning and Evening duty; it appears unreasonable I should leave a Parish of 1000 inhabitants for a hamlet in the Parish of Aston Clinton where there are not more than 20 persons reside, in addition to which I have procured a most respectable gentleman to perform the Duty, who resides within a mile of the Chapel.'

He queries the constitutional position of St. Leonards Chapel and asks whether the Bishop of Lincoln has jurisdiction.

'If not', he continues, 'this particular spot in a country where there is an Established Church will be subject to the same arbitrary and narrow policy which governs the Dissenters, who have the power of dismissing their Ministers at pleasure.'

After seeking advice about a solicitor to fight his case he concludes,

'It is not the Emolument which is trifling having only received about £50 p.a. but the injustice of requiring my resignation that makes me anxious to procure every information to resist this oppression.'

Isaac King is trying to make a good case for himself. A census of 1801 gives the population of St. Leonards as 137, so his statement 'not more than 20 persons reside' seems a little inaccurate.

In an age when pluralism was not unusual, Isaac King's attitude was not as unreasonable as it seems today, but the trustees had the last word and in 1805 he was forced to resign. For him, the story had a happy ending, as 21 years later he was elected mayor of Wycombe. By then he had developed advanced views for we hear that[6]

'The Rev. gentleman, after his election, announced that the petty
sessions and all courts at which he should have to preside, should
be thrown open to the public.'

It is a pity Isaac King left St. Leonards, as he seems to have
become as interesting a character as his opposite number at
Cholesbury, the Rev. David Roderick. Of Peter Hill's immediate
successor, John Ramsay, we know little, but Roderick, appointed
in 1784, was an eminent man, a famous Greek scholar and a
master of Harrow School who resigned in protest with his great
friend Dr. Frederick Parr when the latter was not appointed Headmaster. Dr. Parr mentioned Roderick in his Will as one 'whose very
name refreshed his soul'.[7] Like Isaac King, he was a pluralist, but
unlike King he attended to his duties at Cholesbury, and in
addition acted as Curate of Hawridge between 1792 and 1829.
One wonders what sort of a sermon this eminent and scholarly
man would have preached to his uneducated village congregations.

As already mentioned, the population of St. Leonards in the
1801 census was 137, Cholesbury with 122 and Hawridge with
121 being only slightly smaller.[8] Each village probably had about
25 houses or cottages. Assuming the Protestation return of 1641
to give us a reasonable measure of the population and allowing
about four to each family, Cholesbury had nearly doubled in 160
years, and Hawridge had increased by one-third. For St. Leonards
we have no means of even a rough count after the 16th century
when, it will be remembered, there were nine families in the
hamlet; in 1801 there would have been 34 or more. Buckland
Common cannot be estimated for 1801 as the official statistics do
not separate the hamlet from the main village.

Apart from the few farmers, the majority of the men in each
village were labourers, but as time goes on a greater diversity of
occupations keeping to emerge.

In the middle of the 18th century we find in Hawridge, Martin
Miller a victualler (*The Mermaid*) and two Thomas Horwood's, one
a blacksmith, the other a wheelwright; in Cholesbury, John Cock
is the carpenter and William Culverhouse, who had acquired the
land which was previously Thomas Batchelor's, a butcher; as well
as the Brackleys, there is another potter at Buckland, John
Hopkins, and at St. Leonards we find Josiah and Thomas Wilkins,
both bricklayers.[9]

The village craftsmen were an essential part of any farming community, the shopkeepers and publicans equally necessary. The latter, indeed, were a numerous class for, whatever else our villages lacked, they were richly endowed with Inns or alehouses. Some of these must have existed before we hear of them in records, but by the middle of the 18th century we know of at least nine.[10] At St. Leonards, the unlicensed and disorderly alehouses have already been mentioned; one of them was probably the *White Lion*, where Samuel Baldwin was the first licensee in 1714, followed by various members of the Geary family—it has not been possible to trace the connection between these Gearys and the branch which has disappeared from Braziers End. *The Plough* at Chivery is not recorded until 1766, but the *Boot and Slipper* at Buckland Common dates from 1698, the Brackleys, not content with the potteries and farming, being the licensees for 50 years from 1776. The other two Inns in Buckland Common, the *Britannia* and the *Rose and Crown*, may not have opened until the 19th century, but Cholesbury, at least, was not restricted to one. By 1753, there were three in this tiny village, the *Castle*, the *Blue Ball* (later possibly the *Nine Pin Bowl*) and the *Maidenhead*. The first two of these seem to have lasted for less than 10 years, but if the inhabitants of Cholesbury wanted a change from the Maidenhead they had not far to go. Just over the boundary in Hawridge, there was the *Half Moon* (now the *Full Moon*) and the *Mermaid*, the former claiming to date from 1693 and the latter in the hands of Martin Miller 60 years later. Just across the Tring boundary there was a third, though it also may have opened later; it was locally known as the *Slip Inn*, a sign of the value of varying licensing hours. One other pub in Cholesbury, the *Queen's Head*, next to the Maidenhead, may again be of later origin, but on the road to Hawridge there was one more, the *Rose and Crown*, also licensed not later than 1753.

With this plethora of pubs, it is surprising that Peter Hill's letters have made no reference to the problem of drunkenness; we can only assume that he never enjoyed a mug of ale with his parishoners.

For those who had to travel, there would have been two other popular resorts, the *Swan* on the road to the Lee and Wendover and the *Black Horse* in Chesham Vale, two of the oldest inns in

Fig. 23 One of the old Inns – the Black Horse, below Hawridge

the district.

Apart from home-brewed beer and ale, these pubs may also have sold local cider. The existence of this industry is perpetuated in the name 'The Ciders' at Buckland Common, dating from at least the nineteenth century. 'The Ciders' is next door to 'The Potteries' which has already been mentioned (Chapter XIII). The Brackleys too may have tried to expand into Cholesbury as, after the failure of Moses Middleton in that village, we hear of Thomas Brackley making an encroachment,[11]

'By erecting part of a furnace or Pott Kiln and a little stable'.

The third of the local industries at Buckland Common, brick-making, is again of uncertain date but in some form or other may have been of great antiquity. The two bricklayers of St. Leonards mentioned above (page 136) are of the early 1720s, but we have no further evidence of this trade for another 100 years. By that time, Job Brown of Buckland Common was recorded as a brick-maker[12] and his may not have been the only brickfield.

Straw Plaiters

By the early 19th century there are some signs of cottage industries, men and women who worked at home for factories or salesmen in the nearby towns. The parish registers record a razor-grinder, a chairmender, two shoemakers and a few lace-makers. [12] These only employed a few individuals. The one cottage industry of real importance, an industry which occupied most of the women and children and some of the men as well in their spare time, was straw-plaiting. Introduced into England by Mary, Queen of Scots, who brought French plaiters over from Lorraine to teach the Scottish and provide employment for the women and children, it was transplanted to Luton by James I. Some of the credit for its spread amongst the villages may possibly go to William Cobbett who had advocated its introduction in his *Cottage Economy* and had given detailed instructions, [13]

> 'From the information collected by my son in America.'

When he reached Tring in 1829 which, he wrote, 'is a very pretty and respectable place', Cobbett was delighted:

> 'At the door of a shop I saw a large *case*, with the lid taken off, containing *bundles of straw for plaiting*. It was straw of spring wheat, tied up in small bundles, with ear on; just such as I myself have grown in England many times, and bleached for platting . . . I asked the shopkeeper where he got this straw; he said that it came from Tuscany; and that it was manufactured there at Tring, and other places, for, as I understood, some single individual master-manufacturer. I told the shopkeeper that I wondered that they should send to Tuscany for the straw, seeing that it might be grown, harvested, and equally well bleached at Tring; that it was now, at this time, grown bleached, and manufactured into bonnets in Kent . . . '

Whether he was successful in persuading the local farmers to grow the straw is uncertain, but it is a pity that his ride did not take him off the beaten track, up the muddy, stony roads to our villages where by this time he could certainly have seen the plaiters at work. Plaiting had indeed become so common an occupation that schools were set up where the children could learn the trade. There was one at St. Leonards, another at Cholesbury [14] and a third at Wigginton. Children went to these schools at the age of four and were expected to make five yards of plait at the morning

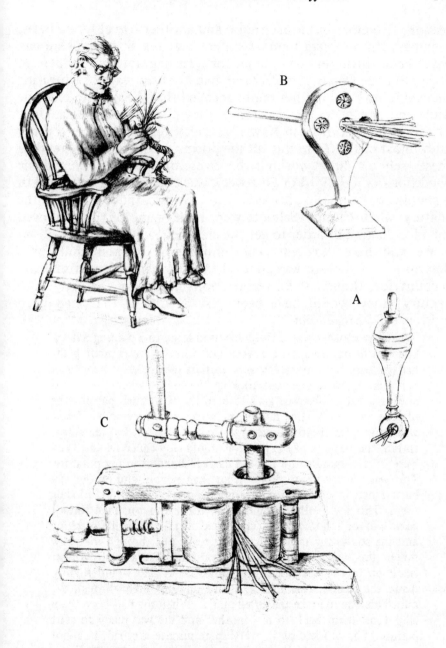

Fig. 24 A Straw Plaiter at work and her implements
A. Splint Mill
B. and C. Straw Splitters

session, five more in the afternoon and another five at home in the evening with an extra yard at dinner and tea breaks, There can have been little enough time for learning letters, though at Wigginton the Dame, Mrs Osborne, had her own ways of educating the children.[15] One of her pupils recalled that she used to read the Bible and poetry to the children as they plaited, and the daughter of this pupil who lives in Hawridge today recalls that her mother knew most of the Bible and 'all the poems' by heart. For attending these schools and working in overcrowded and unhygienic conditions, a fee of 1d or 2d a week was charged, but as a child of 8 could earn 9d a week, it was still worthwhile. Indeed, later in the century when Church Schools were built, some of them allowed time for plaiting in order to get the children to attend.

We still have residents who know how to plait and for a description of the life we cannot do better than quote a first-hand account for, though these recollections date from the early 20th century, they would have been just as true if they had been written 100 years earlier.

'When my mother was a child she used to go to a plaiting school. She had to pay twopence a week and while she was plaiting she had to learn her letters. My very earliest memories of her are of her plaiting with one foot rocking the cradle where there was always a baby. She was glad to earn the very small pay for the plait as we were a large family and wages were very poor. When I was quite a small girl I used to go to the other end of the village to buy the bundles of straws from an old lady called Dinah. They were 2½d. a bundle and I could carry 3 bundles in my pinafore. This was usually in my dinner hour from school and on the way back I had to collect from my granny the machine for splitting them. This my mother would do in the afternoon, then when I came out of school at tea-time I had to take back the machine and the straws my mother had split to be put through the straw miller; this was a small polished wood mill like a small wringer fixed on to the back of my granny's door. She would slightly damp the straws, a handful at a time and put them through the mill. This was to make the straw pliable. When she had done them all I took them back to my mother and she was ready to start plaiting. She worked at it every spare minute she had. I cannot remember all the kinds she did, some 4 straw, 8, 12, 16, Satin, Feather-edge, Brilliant, also an open pattern made over a match-box. It was sold by the score, 20 yard lengths, but first it had to be clipped, quite a long job, then wound from thumb to elbow and made quite smooth, then piled up in a clean cloth ready to take to the Friday market, piled up one end of the pram and walked into Tring where the dealers from Luton were waiting to buy. Sometimes these men would come up the hill to meet the women and offer to buy on the way, but prices varied and they liked to see what was being offered in the market. I wish I could remember the prices but I had nothing to do with the selling as I was at school. My grandmother died in 1912 at the age of 76 so it is a long time ago. My mother used to tell us such stories about the plaiting school. She said that some of the old dears used to have a device called a chad-pot. This was a pot with a lid with holes in it; they put in hot cinders and sat with it under their voluminous skirts to keep warm.'

The damping of the straws was done by mouth, and a commentator on this practice remembered that it was not only injurious to health because it was a sedentary occupation,

'But when double plait is made, the health is doubtless much affected by the great loss of saliva, as each pair of straws is passed through the lips before being used.'[16]

The women would work at this for 12—14 hours a day; even the children were expected to do their quota. A friend of Mrs Kingham's mother, for example, had to do ten yards every night, when she was ten, before she was allowed out to play and in some cottages there were two notches marked on the mantelpiece to measure off the yards.

At the beginning of the 19th century, however, this was not an unprofitable occupation. Plaits with single straws sold at 1/- a straw for 20 yards—in other words a five-straw plait sold at 5/- for 20 yards and a good plaiter could earn 20/- a week. In 1827 it was recorded that not only was lace making earning a better price but,

'The plait trade too has much improved; within the last month plait has been advanced to the retail trade from a shilling and fourteen pence a score to eighteen pence and in other sorts the advance is still more considerable.'[17]

By 1874 the price had fallen to 8/- when cheap plaits were imported from China.

Straw plaiting might be wearisome but it was profitable enough for the men to join in too, often working late into the night hoping that their earnings from this extra work would be concealed from the relieving officer. Some of the women and children would also have joined in more strenuous ways of making money. The most back-breaking of these must have been flint breaking— collecting flints from the fields and splitting them for road making. At other times they would go 'a chalkin' —collecting chalk from the disused pits for the fields and pigsties. Those who were fortunate enough to possess Common rights—probably some who didn't—would find time somehow to exercise the right of estovers, the right to gather dry wood lying on the ground for fuel and to cut bracken for fuel or cattle bedding. In Cholesbury and Hawridge, where the Commons have never been enclosed, these rights, along with that of common pasture, would have remained throughout the 19th century. In St. Leonards they disappeared in 1811 and in Buckland Common in 1844, when the Commons were enclosed.

The Enclosure of St. Leonards Common

At St. Leonards[18] the commissioners started by surveying the whole of the area specifying the boundaries in detail. Enclosures had already taken place on parts of the common as the commissioners referred to a number of old enclosures, but these were generally thrown back into the common pool so that the commissioners referred to a number of old enclosures, but these were compact holdings compensating each owner both for the loss of common rights and for the old enclosures they had given up. The results were that the following acreage was allotted:

	Acres	Roods	Poles	Old Encs	Wood
Aston Clinton Church Wardens	4	-	35		
Baldwin's Trustees	50	3	15		
Joseph Bradley			27		
Farmer Bull				77	5
John Burgess				59	
Joseph Chapman			20		
Colet Estate	13	2		9	
Stephen Dwight		1	25	3	
Assignees of Jones Gomm (Bankrupt)		3	20	5	8
Rev. John George	24	3	31		
Rev. John Jeffries			13	340	63
Lake					
St. Leonards Chapel	16	1	22	141	26

Where sensible, the owners exchanged plots, thus the trustees of St. Leonards Chapel were given an old enclosure Parsons Wick of about 1½ roods, which had belonged to the parson of Aston Clinton, the Rev. John George, who in exchange was given a plot on the common of 1 acre, 11 perches while there was another swap between the St. Leonards trustees and Joseph Baldwin's trustees. The Rev. George's allocation also compensated him for the loss of tithes to which he had formerly been entitled in this area.

The final table looks like a neat enough redistribution; the background arguments and bargaining which may have taken place are, unfortunately not recorded, but the result was the virtual destruction of the old common and its conversion into enclosed farmland. The larger owners clearly benefited; the cottagers, as we have seen before were no more than a handful and of these only four could claim even a small allocation in compensation for their loss of use of the Common. The Buckland Common enclosure is described in the next chapter.

The Gipsies

To finish this survey of the village at this period, we must just mention those visitors to the district, the gipsies or travellers—the name Braziers End, indeed, is said to have been derived from a tinkers' settlement nearby. In the 19th century they turned up when they wanted to be near a Church for christenings, marriages and funerals. Norris and Abigail Hearn had a son, Josiah, christened at Hawridge in 1813; Charlotte Hearn married Samuel Leatherhead and Emanuel Hearn, Elizabeth Leatherhead there, and both couples turned up again for the christening of their own children. Thomas and Sarah Cary also chose Hawridge for christenings, while Thomas and Rise Beldon and Edward and Mary Brill went to Cholesbury. [19] The biggest gathering, however, was at St. Leonards for the funeral of Abigail Norris, when—

> 'nearly 300 of the tribe were present and many of them in mourning.'[20]

The village may not have been pleased by this massive invasion, but there is no account of any trouble.

Notes and References

[1]St. Leonards Parish Register transcribed by the late Miss J. Fletcher.

[2]This and the following quotations come from the case Attorney General against Deering and another – see note (6) Ch.XIII.

[3]B.A.S. St. Leonards Churchwardens' Acts.

[4]L.A.O. Ben. 4/36.

[5]

[6]Gibbs Vol.III, p.151.

[7]Lipscomb Vol.III p.323.

[8]V.C.H. Vol.II, pp.97-9.

[9]This information comes from Wills, Parish Registers and Court Books.

[10]Innkeepers' Records, Kelly's and deeds seen by courtesy of Benskins Watford brewery.

[11]Cholesbury Court Book 1767.

[12]Cholesbury Parish Register.

[13]*Cobbett's Rural Rides*, Vol,II, p.273 (London, 1893).

[14]A Select Committee on Education of 1819 mentions the Cholesbury School.

[15]Information and following account from Mrs. Kingham of Hawridge, born and brought up in Wigginton.

[16]History of Wigginton, unpublished.

[17]Gibbs, Vol.III, p.160.

[18]Bucks, C.R.O. I.R. 51, St. Leonards Common Enclosure Report.

[19]Cholesbury and Hawridge Parish Registers.

[20]Gibbs, Vol.III, p.151.

XVII

'THIS RATE COULD NOT BE COLLECTED'

The village that went bankrupt 1820—33

A period of depression. the system of poor relief; Hawridge-increase of population—new houses—encroachment—a "take-over bid"—the Vestry and poor relief; Cholesbury—the rising burden of rates—the village goes bankrupt.

The first half of the 19th century was a period of acute depression, and by 1800 the labourers were already beginning to suffer from the effects of the Napoleonic wars and particularly from the rise in the price of corn. Wheat rose from 43 shillings a quarter to 126 shillings in 1812 and when, at the end of the war, prices started to fall, the farmers themselves faced bankruptcy and the protective Corn Law of 1815 was passed to restore agricultural prosperity—at the expense of the consumer. But, wages did not follow the upward trend; instead, and to prevent actual starvation, a system was introduced of supplementing them out of the parish rates, the 'dole' tending to rise with increases in the cost of the loaf. The effect of this system can be traced in parish records throughout the country, but nowhere does it appear in more dramatic form than at Cholesbury, the village that achieved national fame by bankrupting itself. Before turning to Cholesbury, however, it is worth looking at the effects in its more typical and wealthier neighbour.

Hawridge

Between 1801 and 1821 the population of Hawridge had increased from 121 to 208. The reasons for this increase are a matter for conjecture; there was no decrease in the amount of farmland and no sign of any industrial type of activity. It can only be assumed that communications with Chesham were improving as a result of extensive clearance of woodland and that we have the beginning here of a 'commuter' type of inhabitant. Nor is it certain how the newcomers were accommodated. In the 1810 Court Roll we hear of two new cottages built by George Franklin

of the *Rose and Crown* and William Horwood on land obtained by
encroachment on the waste. Both were fined 1/- and the cottages
were allowed to stand, George Franklin's, curiously, being granted
as a new *copyhold*. In 1819 we hear of another 'newly erected'
cottage belonging to William Wright.[1] No others are mentioned in
the Court Rolls, so the remainder must have been built by the
farmers on their own land rather than on the waste. The Court,
during this period, was pretty thorough in recording encroachments and imposing the appropriate fines and, after all, the fine
was usually higher when the encroachment was made for building
purposes than when it was used for a garden or orchard!

Even if the waste was not being occupied for building purposes,
however, it was by no means sacrosanct and the cottagers had
obviously discovered that they could mitigate their poverty a little
by extending their gardens. Between 1765 and 1810 it is rare to
find a *new* encroachment mentioned in the Court Rolls; the outstanding one was made by Moses Wooster of Wigginton in 1795
who,

> 'Had dug up a quantity of waste soil belonging to the Lord of the
> Manor about a Rood in measure.'

The fact that he was an outsider may have influenced the Court, as
it was ordered,

> 'That he should forfeit and pay to the Lord of the Manor for such
> offence the sum of 20 shillings'—a steep fine.

From 1810 to 1842, however, there is a spate of new encroachments. John Maple, in one of the cottages at Heath End, takes
about 15 poles in 1810; in the same year Stephen Dwight, in one
of the cottages which replaced the old *Mermaid Inn*, made two
separate encroachments,

> 'A small piece of ground for breeding and keeping of pheasants,'

and another piece for a garden. Daniel Mayo, three years later,
extends the orchard of the *Rose and Crown* by a further 3 poles
and makes a garden, and in 1819 little bits of waste ground are
being taken in all along the road from Tudor Cottage to the *Full
Moon*. Two successive occupants, John White and John Saunders
of Bentonpotts, added to their land in this way, as did William
Gardener and William Howes, who shared one of the *Mermaid*
cottages. In general the Court accepted all this philosophically and

fines were small, usually 3d or 6d, only rising to 1/- for the larger ones of about 15 poles.

No doubt the Court felt that little harm was done by these encroachments and the members, who almost invariably included one or more of the Batchelors and William Wright probably approved of this amount of self-help by those who might be in need of contributions from the parish rates. For the 'Homage' at the Manorial Court always included some members of the select Vestry which ran the parish. Before going on to their other duties we must turn aside for a moment to record an encroachment which was emphatically not approved. On 24 July 1827 the Court was a high-powered one, the members being William Wright (son of the William mentioned earlier who had died in 1810), Thomas and Benjamin Batchelor (sons of Benjamin the first mentioned in Chapter XV) and Thomas Franklin (landlord of the *Rose and Crown*). The Court had a good deal of business and it was not till the end that it came to the most important item—a 'Takeover Bid from Tring'. It is not difficult to imagine the general indignation as they agreed the following Minute:

'Forasmuch as a public perambulation of the Boundaries of the Manor of Tring hath recently taken place and the Circuit of the Boundary comprised therein took a considerable Portion of Land both old-inclosed and Waste lying within the Parish of Hawridge, the Homage therefore present that such Perambulation—so far as it extended to and comprized any part of the Parish of Hawridge is wholly new and unprecedented and altogether incorrect and that the Entirety of the Parish of Hawridge and all the lands both old inclosed and commonable lying within the same are parcel of and comprehended within the Boundary of this Manor and are within the Limits and Jurisdiction of this Court.'

We hear no more of this attempt by Tring to annex some of the Hawridge lands and can only assume that the protest was passed on and noted. In any case the village had other worries. The Manorial Court was only concerned with land ownership. Other village affairs were managed by the Vestry, a predecessor of the present Parish Council, and in Hawridge this was a select Vestry, a body which managed to avoid elections and simply filled in the vacancies by nomination.[2] Between 1822 and 1836 only nine members of the parish ever served on this Vestry. Thomas and

Benjamin Batchelor, William Wright and Thomas Franklin, with Thomas Weedon the tenant at Vale Farm were the regular attendants, supported by Walter Carpenter the wheelwright, Daniel Horn and James Collins and James Horn infrequently. This seems a small proportion from a population of 208, but of approximately 40 houses in the village 25 were not rated until 1833, so the Vestry actually included three-fifths of the rate payers.

The main task of the Vestry was parish relief. This included both the payments to those entitled to receive it and the imposition of the necessary rates to raise the funds. The first recorded meeting on 20 May 1822,

> 'Resolved that all the Cottages in the parish shall for the future be
> legally taxed to the poors rate',

and

> 'That no poors rate shall exceed one shilling in the pound for the
> future.'

The first of these resolutions must have caused some heart searching, for the parish was not obliged to support the poor who had not been born there unless they had established residence by contributing to the rates or taking one of the parish offices for a year. So they were faced with the dilemma that, by trying to increase the income by adding to the number of rate payers they might also be adding to their burdens; having passed this resolution it was ten years before it was implemented.

At this first meeting the Vestry decided that seven men and one woman should be granted 6d per week, another woman, Sarah William, '2d per week while proper lodgings are provided', and that 'Susannah Mably be allowed no money'. On 1 July most of the same men received allowances of 2/- or 1/6d a week; a fortnight later these were reduced to 1/- or 9d. Where possible the men were put to work, usually on the highways. Charles Horwood was allowed 4/- a week while unable to labour; this was increased a fortnight later to 6/-, then 7/-, but in October it was down to '2/- without labour and 4/- with labour' and by November he was fit to work, for the Minute reads,

> 'That Charles Horwood and John Axtel labour on the Highway
> from 8 o'clock in Morning While 4 o'clock in afternoon when the
> Weather permits and to receive 8d per day each from the
> Overseer.'

Often the Vestry preferred to give help in kind rather than in cash. John Axtel was to be provided with 'A swandown Waiscot an Round Frock': James Mably received 'A round frock: and 'A pair of high shoes'; David Aldridge was given '1 pair of High Shoes and a Jacket', Thomas Hart '1 pair of Small Clothes' as well as a pair of high shoes and a round frock, and James Maple '1 shirt and one pair of stockings'.

The Vestry also attended to the health and comfort of the poor. In 1822 it was agreed that

> 'Mr William Sutthery have the Offer to Contract to Attend the poor of Hawridge With Advice and Medecines in All Cases for the sum of five pounds pr Annum.'

The next year the overseer was instructed to

> 'Provide a flock Bed and Straw bed tick and flock bolster for the poor house.'

In return for aid the poor had certain obligations, though there were glimpses of humanity in enforcing these. In 1822, for example it was decided that

> John Joiner attend some place of Worship every Sunday when his health permits He now being 87 years of Age.'

John Joiner was a genuine old-age-pensioner who had certainly been in Hawridge since 1767 when we find him with a freehold cottage, one of the cottages opposite Vale Farm, at a rent of 2d. He only vacated it in 1810, possibly when too old to work. In 1833, however, they were in tougher mood and resolved:

> 'That all paupers that are found Drinking and Smoaking in Any Publick House or Alehouse be Stopped one weeks pay,'

and that,

> 'All paupers Attend Divine Worship Either in the forenoon or Afternoon Every Sunday Except prevented by Illness. And then to Give Notice to the Overseer or be stopped one week's pay.'

Perhaps the members of the Vestry had been fond of old John Joiner.

It may be, however, that the tougher attitude that they had adopted in 1833 was symptomatic of the rapidly increasing burden of poor rates.

In this year the Vestry decided that 25 cottages which had so far been exempt from paying rates should at last be rated. The

majority of these were assessed at £1.10.0 a year, but Charles
Horwood, who had been set to work on the roads was one of three
rated at only £1 and William Howes one of two who were to pay
£2. The Vestry may have been influenced by his effrontery, a few
years earlier, in not only encroaching on the waste but also
'erecting certain Outhouses' on it. By 1 October 1832 they had
been pulled down, but Howes may have delayed too long to avoid
having them included in his rating assessment.

By this time poor rates were having to be levied with increasing
frequency. There were six demands in 1833, including one where
the 1/- limit had to be increased to 2/6d, and the total for the
following year 8/- was even higher. This, however, was the end of
the real troubles, for the next year the whole system was changed
and the parish poor law functions were taken over by the
Aylesbury Poor Law Union with its Board of Guardians.

Unfortunately, for Hawridge the records are not detailed
enough to tell us either the total amount paid annually in relief or
the actual rates demanded from individual farmers. The highest
figure of 8/- in the pound in 1834 must have involved some
hardship, but the Vestry may have been even more worried about
the change of system the next year and the possible dissatisfaction
with a new and tougher policy, for in that year they obviously
decided that any unpopularity resulting should be shared as widely
as possible and took the unusual step of nominating six of its
seven members described as 'substantial householders' as overseers
for the year. Thomas Franklin was the member who managed to
avoid nomination.

Cholesbury

At Hawridge the number of ratepayers might be small, but it
comprised the 'substantial householders' of 1833, farmers with
sufficient land to provide a reasonable living for themselves and
some employment for the labourers in the village. The burden of
rates, even at its highest figure of 8/- in the pound, might be an
unwelcome burden, but it was not intolerable.

At Cholesbury the situation is very different. The number of
ratepayers was no higher; the farms, it will be remembered, were
tiny and could have offered little employment to anyone except
the farmer and his sons, and even for them the standard of living

must have been low. A few labourers might find work at the Brickyards at Buckland Common during the summer, but in the winter these closed down and the men were left without jobs. The result of all these factors in a time of acute depression was disastrous. By good fortune it has been recorded in some detail in the Vestry Records from 1820–33, and from these we can trace the progress of the village towards bankruptcy.[3]

In Cholesbury only 11 out of the 24 houses were rated, though rates were also levied on certain fields as well. Of these 11 houses, the occupants of 7 seem to have established a right to membership of the Vestry, and a typical meeting about 1824 would consist of

> The Rev. Roderick,
> Daniel Norris from Hone's Farm[4]
> John Batchelor from Parrott's Farm, one of the leading figures in the village who held the offices of church-warden, overseer and constable, sometimes more than one of these in the same year.
> William Batchelor from Home Farm Cottage, who also continued the family tradition in the churchwarden's post.
> Thomas Hawkes, licensee of the *Maidenhead*
> Robert Wright the butcher.

As at Hawridge, therefore, membership of the Vestry was not only restricted to the ratepayers, it was confined to a specific group of about two-thirds of these ratepayers. The only difference is that in Cholesbury these were not 'substantial householders,'– apart from the parson, the publican and the butcher, they were small tenant farmers. Hone's Farm had no more than 35 acres, Parrott's 11 and even Braziers End only 57, including 13 acres of garden. The omission of the latter from the Vestry is not surprising remembering that from 1821–31 it was owned by the solicitors, Atkinson and Parkinson, who were represented only once.

These small farmers, meeting as the Vestry in the Church had an unenviable task, to consider the likely needs for relief in the parish, and the rate which should be imposed to raise the necessary funds. The proposed rate was then approved by two Justices and the overseers took over to collect the money and distribute it. It was a hand-to-mouth business, with no question of an annual assessment; a rate was fixed, the overseer spent the money as long as it lasted and, as soon as the funds ran out, the

Vestry had to meet again to agree a new rate. The following list shows how frequently these meetings were necessary and rates demands for the year:

Year	Rates	Level of Rates for Year	Approx. Yield £
1820	4 @ 2/-	8/-	66
1821	9 @ 2/-, 1 @ 3/-	21/-	172
1822	1 @ 2/-, 5 @ 4/-	22/-	181
1823	1 @ 2/6, 5 @ 4/-	22/6	185
1824	1 @ 2/-, 5 @ 4/-	22/-	181
1825	3 @ 4/-	12/-	99
1826	5 @ 4/-	20/-	165
1827	1 @ 3/-, 5 @ 4/-	23/-	190
1828	1 @ 1/-, 1 @ 4/-	5/-	43
1829 & 30 Unknown			
1831	4 @ 4/-	16/-	131
1832	5 @ 4/-, 1 @ 4/6	24/6	201
up to September			

Records of expenditure are not available until December 1832, but from the annual sums required it is clear that the details for that year can be taken as representative of the demands on the parish purse facing the Vestry during the 1820s. In the week of 15 December the payments were

Old Men and Widows and Fatherless Children

Charles Batchelor (79)	3. 0	
Ann　　　　"	3. 0	
Widow　　　"　　and child	3. 0	
"　Carpenter	3. 0	
"　Norris	3. 0	
"　Sills (née Mary Culver-house see page　)	3. 0	
Sarah Carpenter	1. 0	
Jane Corbet	1. 6	
Richard Cox, Cripple	2. 0	
Mary Gates	2. 0	
Rhoda　"	1. 6	
Edmund Gurney, idiot	4. 0	
Mary Ann Gardner	2. 0	
Patience　　"	1. 0	Total £1. 13. 0

The Married Men	Children		
James Cox		6. 8	
Richard Cox		8. 0	
Thomas Griffin	4	9. 6	
David Newton		8. 0	
John Norris		7. 0	
William Spittel (Prob'y ill)		8. 0	
Thomas Thorn		9. 6	
William Thorn		8. 0	Total £3. 4. 8

Single Men and Boys		
John Cox	3. 6	
Joseph Cox	1. 6	
William Forster	3. 0	
John Gardner	3. 0	
William Thorn Jun.	3. 6	
John Thorn	3. 6	
Joseph Thorn	3. 4	Total £1. 1. 4

£5. 19. 0

The Poor Relief book, incidentally, gives the total as £6.10.0; there is nothing to account for the discrepancy.

This was the heaviest week, but only by a small margin for mid-winter when unemployment was rife, and shows how parish poor relief had to cover the whole range of what we should call 'Social Security payments'. The first group includes old age and widows' pensions; family allowance element appears in the first two and unemployment benefit in the second and third, though it is impossible to separate this last item from the payments needed to supplement inadequate wages.

These regular weekly payments were a heavy enough burden but still did not constitute the total liability for, as at Hawridge, additional help was given in kind and these extras could add substantially to the total bill. A few examples will show the cost of clothing and bedding and the inroads this must have made into the family budget for those who could pay and into Parish funds for those who could not:

1 Shift (1/-) for Ellen Cox and pair of shoes	6. 0
Gown and stockings for do.	2. 10
Edmund Gurney, Smock frock	4. 10
A rug and blanket for do.	7. 6
1 Pair of Shoes for do.	8. 0
(The Vestry had decreed a pair of "Stout shoes" for Edmund Gurney—hence the higher price compared with those provided for Ellen Cox)	
2 Shirts for Edmund Gurney	4. 0

Rents were sometimes paid as well, the board and lodging of Edmund Gurney cost 17/-, that of Mary Ann Gardner and Rhoda Gates £1.12.8, while 4/- was paid to Elizabeth Croft for the board and lodging of Patience Gardner. It is not clear, however, how many weeks these payments were intended to cover.

Funerals were another expensive item, and when William Forster died the Parish paid

'Bread and Cheese and Beer for Forster's funeral	2. 8½
Shroud for Forster	1. 8½
Expences for Doing for Forster	4. 6
Parish Clerk for funeral expenses	6. 6
	15. 5'

To this the cost of the coffin had to be added, in July 1833 Walter Carpenter being paid £2.19.0 'four four Coffings.' Medical attendance cost about 1/6d a time, and when Ann Batchelor died 3/6d was paid to the nurses, in addition to a few shillings of extra relief for the sick. In one case a payment was even made to an outsider, for on 29 December 1832 we find an entry,

'Relieved a sick man on the road   1/-'

Whenever possible the poor were set to work, stone-breaking being the usual occupation. Thus it was the Vestry,

'Agreed that Joe Cox be found work at the stone pit and that he be allowed 4d a load for breaking stone sufficiently small to be applied on the roads. And that he be paid partly in bread and partly in money. He beinge a drunken disorderly fellow.'

The poor and their children were sent away to work, too, the Silk Mill at Tring being their usual destiny. In the long term this may have been worthwhile, though the immediate effect was to add even more to the parish expenses. The Vestry had to pay,

'For the clothing of Richard Cox children that are gone
to the Silk Mill   19. 4d.'

and, a fortnight later,

'Paid the Board and Lodging of Cox's tow Children at
the Silk Mill for 3 weeks   £1. 1. 0.'

Payments for board and lodging to the Overseer at Tring for
Richard Cox and son or the Cox children continued for some
months. The Gardner children's transfer to Tring was a rather less
expensive operation costing only 8/1d.

In addition there were payments of travelling expenses for the
churchwarden and overseer, a journey to Tring usually costing 4/-
a time. Miscellaneous bills such as the blacksmith's and small sums
for stationery and postage had to be met; a new book and paper,
for example cost 1/11d, three new rates books 1/- and letters 6d
or 1/- each. All this had to come out of the poor rate.

If the village had had a squire during this critical period, the
story might have been different, but for a small group of tenant
farmers the burden was impossible. When they could no longer
pay, they just left their farms. At Parrott's, for example, where the
rates in the 1820s ranged from £4.14.0 to £14.0.0 a year, John
Batchelor gave up in 1824 and was replaced by Charles Brackley.
The village's bad luck was not restricted to Braziers End, for the
new tenant died a year later; his widow carried on for another year
and was then replaced by Benjamin Puddephatt. A year was long
enough for him too; then William Spittel took over and lasted four
years before he too was forced to give up, possibly through ill-
health as he was in receipt of intermittent relief after this,
sometimes being marked as 'ill'.

This bring us up to 1831 and by then the story of Parrott's
Farm has been repeated throughout the village. The demands for
relief grew, the number of ratepayers decreased, and despite the
record sum already raised in 1832 and loans from the new Curate,
the Rev. Henry Jeston, the coffers were again empty. The Vestry
might decree a further 4/- rate; its collection was more difficult
and in the list of October assessments only three names could be
marked as paid immediately—Jeston himself, William Mayo, who
had taken on Parrott's Farm, and John Reading, who was by then
farming at Braziers End. Up the side of the page Jeston minuted,

'This rate could not be collected except only a small portion of it
the land in the Parish being almost all abandoned.'

The village was bankrupt. On 29 November the Vestry met
again and the first minute reads:

'At a vestry held this 29 day of Nov 1832 the Perpetual Curate in
the chair, due notice of the said vestry having been given. The
following resolutions were agreed to by those present.
1st It appearing That the Overseer having used due diligence to
collect a rate of 4/- in the pound & owing to 94 acres of the
cultivated Land being unoccupied was not able to collect the
same: and two of his majesty's justices of the peace having
adjudicated the Parish to be unable to support its poor without
the assistance of a rate in aid on some other parish, & the said
magistrates having made an order on Drayton Beachamp for that
purpose—it is agreed by the persons assembled in vestry they
being willing to continue their exertions and to do all in their
power towards the support of their poor a rate of 1/- in the pound
be forthwith made.'

Three parishes were asked, or instructed, to help; Drayton
Beauchamp produced about £50, Aston Abbotts £26 and Grove
£15. Meanwhile Cholesbury itself continued to apply pressure on
its defaulters and eventually the greater part of the arrears from
the October assessment was collected. Other practical steps were
taken too. Arrangements were made for a new assessment of
rateable values and, to spread the burden more widely, it was

'Agreed that such cottages as are occupied by persons not
parishioners be rated.'

Cholesbury was singularly fortunate in its parson at this time.
Jeston reported fully to the Poor Law Commissioners and the
section of their report on the plight of this village was startling
enough for *Chambers' Edinburgh Journal*, whose readers would
normally have had little interest in a remote village in the middle
of Buckinghamshire, to publish an article on it. A quote from
Jeston's own report paints the picture in the darkest possible
colours;[5]

'The poor laws have produced so much dependence and
improvidence among them, that if, for a few weeks only, when
the funds are exhausted, they are deprived of parish aid, they
incur debts, and become behind in their rents, and, to avoid

discharging it, voluntarily quit a comfortable cottage for one much less so: thus a spirit of recklessness and dishonesty is promoted, detrimental to the moral character of the very best of them. I confess I now see no prospects whatever of the Parish being relieved from its present degraded and impoverished state.'

The *Edinburgh Journal* concludes the article by asking,

'Can such a thing acctually be in a country so long popularly known by the title of Merry England?'

Two years later, the old Poor Law had disappeared, and the New Poor Law transferred the responsibility from the parishes to Boards of Unions. We cannot, of course, claim that Cholesbury was responsible for the change; the evils of the old system were obvious enough for Parliament to set up a Royal Commission to enquire into the working of the Poor Law in 1832, but it may well be that the disasters at Cholesbury and the consequent publicity added impetus to the work of the Commission. Two years is a short enough time for a Commission to complete an enquiry, report and for new legislation to be enacted.

Notes and References

[1] Hawridge Court Book.

[2] B.A.S. Hawridge Vestry Records.

[3] B.A.S. and Parish chest, Cholesbury Vestry Records – In addition to Minutes of meetings these contain:

Complete lists of rating assessments 1820 - 7

List of money collected in rates 1831 - 2

Reliefs paid Dec. 1832 - Aug. 1833

Assessments, April 1838 - Jan. 1848.

[4] The modern name is Home Farm - it may be a corruption of *Hone*.

[5] Chambers Edinburgh Journal No.23, 1833.

XVIII

'A SMALL ORGAN WOULD REMEDY THIS EVIL'

Village life from 1832 to 1900

The recovery of Cholesbury; allotments; the Sunday School and the choir; the management of the Commons; road repairs; the Parsonage house. Hawridge, the farmers in difficulty; Buckland Common, enclosure; St. Leonards, a Shepherd's Grave; the end of the century; schools; the Queen's Jubilee; Jeston's death.

Cholesbury

Son of the Headmaster of Henley Grammar School, Jeston was 33 when he came to Cholesbury in 1830, and still inexperienced, his previous appointments being as Curate and, for one year, Chaplain to the Governor of Trinidad. A crisis of this magnitude within his first two years, when he would still be regarded as a newcomer and outsider, would have been a daunting proposition for an older and more experienced man and his fit of despondency, when writing his report, is understandable but he may not yet have understood the character of his Buckingham-shire parishioners, with their sturdy independence, or realised his own powers of leadership.

Expenditure on Poor Relief was still about £100 for the period of 27 weeks from Lady Day to Michaelmas and of this Cholesbury itself could raise only £15, the balance coming from a donation of £10 from Mr Dorrien, one of the Neale Trustees and a Buckland Common farmer, and rates in aid from other parishes including, by now, Marsworth, Mentmore, Slapton and Cublington. Outside help was no permanent solution, and already the first practical step had been taken to restore the village to some degree of self-sufficiency through the introduction of a cottage allotment system, the Agricultural Employment Institution taking over Hone's Farm and dividing it up amongst the village. In at least one case, Jeston himself helped by loaning to George Sills, his churchwarden, then occupying the Glebe land, £9.8.10,[1]

194

'To enable him to purchase potatoes to plant the same and also to
defray the expense of digging and planting the land and also for
the payment of the Poor generally.'

This sum was repaid on 21 November 1833,

'From part of the produce of the Glebe land given to the use of
the Parish from Lady Day to mich. 1833.'

This provided some occupation and some incentive to the adult
population, and the literate poor were further helped by a
Parochial Lending Library valued at £7.10.0. and established by
the liberalism of Lord Robert Grosvenor.[2] Two years later Jeston
decided to help the younger generation too, and established a
Sunday School which within a year was attended by more than 70
children. Realistically, he suggested to the Trustees that the
money allocated under the Trust for the purchase of books would
be better spent in paying a Sunday School teacher. The Trustees
felt they had no power to vary the conditions in this way, but
allocated the 20/- allowed for their own dinners after meetings to
a teacher's pay, Jeston himself contributing a similar amount.

Next, he decided to teach the parish to save by establishing
Clothing and Fuel Clubs. In 1839 deposits in the former amounted
to £37.9.2; two years later, they had risen to £73.6.9. Jeston
admits that what pleased him most was that,

'More than half the total deposits were subscribed by the children
of the Sunday School.'

These children could not have been earning more than two to
three shillings a week, presumably from straw plaiting and work in
the fields during harvest time. They must have put the greater part
of their earnings into the Clothing Fund.

Finally he decided to enliven the Church Services. Many
parish churches at this time had music from a church orchestra,
and one of these was Hawridge which owned a bassoon[3] made by
Geo. Aster in 1810 and illustrated below.

Cholesbury, presumably, had no orchestra, but, undeterred by a
story from a neighbouring church where, it was reported in 1827,[4]

'At Tring Church the singers mutinied and wouldn't sing, and the
Parson wouldn't preach till they had, so they had no service at
all,'

Jeston decided that he wanted a choir and in 1839 reported to the
Trustees,

Old Bassoon from Hawridge Church
Made by George Aster c. 1810

Displayed in County Museum,
Aylesbury, Bucks.

Verse on Brass
Mount

I hear some men hate music ● ● ●
Let them show in Holy Writ what else
the angels do;~ then those that do
despise such sacred mirth are neither
fit for Heaven nor fit for Earth~

Fig. 25.

Much pains have been taken to teach the children to sing, and they are now able to sing remarkably well and to chant the Communion Responses but the leader of the little quire is frequently prevented by indisposition from attending church and then the singing is often and the chanting of the Responses always necessarily omitted. A small organ would remedy this evil and so anxious is the Incumbent that his Church may have the advantage of one that he proposes to give £5 towards the purchase.'

By this time the village was pretty well restored to health. The rating of the cottages which had previously been exempted increased the number of ratepayers to 30 by November 1838, the yield from a 1/- rate rising to about £12.9.0. The rates were as low as 5/- that year and, more important, they were paid, some of the paupers of 1832 being included amongst the ratepayers. Thomas Griffin, for example, paid 15/- on a cottage, outbuilding and 4 acres of land, Thomas Thorn a similar amount on the Manor House and another 4 acres, and William Thorn 19/- on a

'Tenement and garden, outbuildings and land of 5 acres 3 roods 1 pole.'

Two years later these ex-paupers were taking part in parish affairs as overseers and Jeston could report to his Trustees that,

'Since the establishment of that [the allotment] system there has not been one able bodied pauper in the Parish, that the men still continue to maintain themselves and their families independent of Parochial assistance and with increased comforts.'

On the moral side he could add,

'It is with satisfaction he can state that with one single exception no complaynt during the last 7 years has been made of misconduct of any of the Parishioners of Cholesbury.'

If the village was healthy again physically, Jeston had had equal success on the spiritual side and told his Trustees,

'Owing to the Establishment of a Sunday school which has now for these three years been attended by about 70 children the Congregation many of which were previously either Dissenters or attended no place of Worship at all has become too large for the Church and almost every Sunday afternoon many persons go away for want of room.'

He attributed this partly to 'the attention paid to Church Psalmody', but the size of the congregation, and the fact that the Church was 'regularly filled', was also due to the decision by the inhabitants of Buckland Common to attach themselves to Cholesbury for 'spiritual services'. It was hardly surprising that, with a popular vicar and attractive services next door, Buckland Common residents should have decided to save themselves the five-mile walk each way to their own parish church. Their arrival added another '200 souls' to Cholesbury's 140. As well as his organ, therefore, Jeston asked for a new gallery for the Church in order to extend the seating. The Trustees agreed, he himself set about raising money and succeeded in getting £122, resulting in an increase of 90 free seats.

Meanwhile the village as a whole could turn its attention to other matters. Though the Manorial Court continued to sit inter-mittently in both Cholesbury and Hawridge, and at the latter was still concerned with the management of the Common, at

Cholesbury this latter important function had been taken over by
the Vestry. Even at the height of their troubles in 1832 they had
time to protest,[5]

> 'Whereas Richard Deverell has suffered his flock of sheep to graze
> on the common Agreed that notice be given to him to keep the
> same off otherwise he will be proceeded against as the law
> directs.'

Two years later, the Vestry,

> 'Resolved, That Cholesbury Common for the future be
> considered a Stint common, and that Richard Cox be appointed
> Howard, and that he be paid in the proportion of one penny per
> head for cows, horses &c.'

The next year, James Palmer was appointed, at the rate of 2d a
head,

> 'To look after the Stock turned out upon it, and to keep off the
> stock of persons having no right of Commonage.'

In 1847 it was resolved,

> 'That any person found picking up or carrying away dung from
> this Common be proceeded against according to the Law,'

The next year, they

> 'Resolved that no joisting be allowed on the Common. Resolved
> that a parish pound be erected on the Common under the
> direction of the Surveyor and paid for out of the Stone rates,'

and three months later authorized the Surveyor to buy,

> 'An Iron Pound similiar to that on Boxmoor Common, cost
> £6.10s from Tompkins of Tring.'

The pound was to be as near the Manor House as possible.
The basis of Common rights had been defined in 1844:

> 'One head of cattle for every four pounds at which he (the Rate-
> payer) is assessed to the Poor rates, and no more.'

Six years later, this was amplified in some detail—two calves under
one year were equal to one cow, donkeys or asses were considered
as other cattle and no sheep were allowed. Obviously, however,
members of the village were continually trying to evade the rules
and a few years later they had to restate them:

> 'at Publick Vestery helden in Pursistence of Publik Notice given
> on the 29 day of May 1856 for taken into consideration the Rits
> of Common and Payment of Howard to look after the Same.

Resolved that the same Rules be Carred into hopperation as was aggread to at a Publick vester[y] in the year of 1844.

Resolved that only one head be turned on the Common let ther age be wat it may.

Resolved that one Calf under one year of age Peay half pr head to wards the Peayment of the Howard as a full head does.

Resolved that Wm Weedon be Howard to look after the Common untell further notice be gevin at Eight Shillings Per week and be Pead by the Parisheners that turn cattle on the Common in the Perp[or]sion to wat the[y] turn out and peay as head money.

Resolved that no Pigs be turnd on the Common untell the[y] Have Rings in ther nose [   ] to Damage the Common.

Resolved that the Common be Cleared of Cattle from the 25 day of March to the 13 day of May.'

Common rights and their protection was no doubt the subject on which the village felt most strongly—it was still an important element in the general economy and similar Minutes appear for the rest of the century. But the Vestry was also concerned with the tiresome business of highway repairs. It will be remembered that in 1679 there had been trouble at St. Leonards about the removal of flints needed for the repair of the highways (Chapter XII). In 1832, the Cholesbury Vestry was not so engrossed in the problem of Poor Relief that it could overlook a similar attempt by an outsider, and it minuted,

'Whereas Joseph Philbey of Tring has carried away from the gravel pit in this parish a quantity of flints without the consent of the surveyor or other parish officer agreed that the surveyor forthwith demand payment for the same: & if refused a warrant shall be obtained against the said Joseph Philbey.'

In the 1848 the Vestry

'Resolved that the monies expended by William Collier on Shire-Lane road, & on that of Parrotts Lane, be not allowed: the former being considered by the Vestry as a disused road, and the latter as an accommodation road.'

A few years later they had to reverse this decision and cooperate with Tring and Drayton to 'make the required highway through Shire Lane', levying a rate of 10d for three years to meet that and general highway expenses. The responsibilities for the highway were not without their compensating advantages. Heaps of road

sand which were left over were worth buying and in 1849 the
Vestry divided these among themselves on the following basis,

'George Sills	1st Lot			3d
	6th "	110 heaps		2/6d
Daniel Bishop	2nd Lot	40	"	6d
Ezekiel Osborn	3rd "	33	"	5d
	4th "	33	"	4d
William Collier	5th "	20	"	2d'

Despite this, the village remained mutinous about these responsibilities and in 1864, after a new Highway Act had been passed,
could agree unanimously,

> 'That it is the opinion of this Vestry that it is not desirable to
> adopt for the Parish of Cholesbury the provisions of the
> afore-said act of Parliament.'

The Vestry who could adopt this independent attitude was not
composed of wealthy landowners. The owners of Braziers End
from 1834 did, it is true, play their part at last in village affairs.
Robert Albion Fellowes was for a time surveyor and his successor,
James Benners Parkinson, was often chairman at Vestry meetings.
But the others, apart from Jeston and Thomas Little who had
acquired 15 acres of 'The Limes' farm at Hawridge, were ordinary
villagers and small farmers.

Of the regular attendants, George Sills the churchwarden had
started life as a labourer, though he later became a butcher and a
farmer.[6] Daniel Bishop kept the *Queen's Head,* a beerhouse
next to the *Bricklayers' Arms,* where Ezekiel Osborn was the
publican. Matthew Puddephatt had failed at Parrott's Farm in the
1820s, while Thomas and William Thorn had both been paupers.
John Blake who appeared occasionally was a drover and others
such as Edward Wright, William Howes and William Keen probably
labourers. Intellectually, this is not a high-powered group, but
they filled the parish offices and could show a sturdy independence
of mind when aroused. They petitioned the Poor Law
Commissioners for relief from the

> 'Very heavy burthen that was thrown upon this parish by its
> connection with the union,'

disagreed with authority on the treatment of individual cases and claimed against the London and Birmingham Railway for compensation for David Cox, who had been crippled while working on the railway and become a burden on the parish. This case had a curious ending; in the meantime Cox had been convicted of a highway robbery and transported to Van Diemen's land, but he eventually got his money with interest when he had obtained a ticket for good conduct! By the middle of the century the village was in a healthy enough state to impose with equanimity rates, usually 6d, for the repair of the church.

We still do not know how the inhabitants of Cholesbury made a living in the middle of the 19th century. Though farming went through a good period from about 1850, after years of depression caused partly by a series of bad harvests, it still seems unlikely that the village could have supported its population without some other outlet for employment. That population had, it is true, started to decrease. From 124 in 1841 it had gone down to 113 in the next 10 years, continuing to fall gradually to 95 in 1891. Straw plaiting could no longer keep the family going—it can only be assumed that the development of the brickfields, with which this district abounded with the increasing demand for houses, filled a considerable part of the gap.

Jeston, meanwhile, had made time to attend to his own affairs. The Parsonage House at Cholesbury which he found, in 1830[7]

'In a most wretched state of repair',

was enlarged in 1849 by building a dining room and bedroom, at the cost of £400. Some of this expense was met by the sale of timber from Priest's Grove. 'The rest', Jeston says, 'was raised by my own exertions'. Nine years later, at a cost of £10, the

'Wooden Barn erected by Mr Roderick was removed by me from its present objectionable site, to the back of the parsonage house; to the great improvement of the premises,'

and in 1861 the front of the house was,

'Cemented with Roman cement to make it drier ... and the trellised verandah replaced with a new one.'

Hawridge

Meanwhile, in neighbouring Hawridge there are signs that the twenty years from 1830 to 1850 which saw recovery in

Cholesbury were a period of increasing difficulty in the next door parish, far more dependent on farming for its prosperity than Cholesbury. Thomas Batchelor, for example, was almost permanently in difficulties from the time he inherited Hill Farm in 1813. Under his Father's Will some of the adjoining fields came to him too, and on his mother's death his brother Benjamin alienated to him the rest of the family's freehold property: some 65 acres in all.[8] Almost immediately he alienated 15 acres to James Collins. In 1827 his 8-acre and 5-acre fields went to Robert Sutton, to be followed in 1840 with the rest of his property, described as 'a messuage and 40 acres' and 'part of the farm and land called Hill Farm'. Thomas Batchelor remained as a tenant farmer both to Sutton and to James Field who replaced Collins, but when he died in 1846 he could only leave to his widow,[9]

> 'The use and enjoyment of all my stock in trade and implements of husbandry ... for the purpose of carrying on my farming business or any other business she may think proper during her natural life for the purpose of maintaining herself and family in such manner as she shall think proper.'

He only limited her freedom of action in one respect:

> 'And I direct that my son-in-law George Pitkin and his wife and family shall not reside with my wife but shall find a home for themselves ...'

Thomas Batchelor was probably typical of the struggling farmers of this time who got deeper and deeper into debt until they had no alternative to parting with their freeholds to those who had lent them money. His brother Benjamin had already left Hawridge—as one of the Executors he is described in this Will as a farmer of Beaconsfield—and though the family never disappear completely, it is no longer the important family that it had been in the past.

The Wrights remain until towards the end of the century, the last survivor of the friends we first met 150 years earlier or more.

If the farmers were in trouble at this time, the cottagers claimed that they were equally short of money. In 1832, a second attempt was made to rate 25 of the cottagers who had not so far contributed to the parish funds.[10] Five years later, there was a reassessment; the next year Ann Parsley and Ann Dearing pleaded to be exonerated from paying the poor rate on grounds of poverty. Their plea was granted and was followed two months later by 31 other claims for exemption. The list included most of those who were newly rated and, curiously, the name of Thomas Batchelor, who was Chairman of the meeting. There may of course have been two Thomas Batchelors at Hawridge at the time, but the family tree does not reveal this. The Chairman himself may have had to plead poverty.

As at Cholesbury, highway problems appear occasionally in the Minutes, but there was only one of an unusual character. William J. Hobbs, the Surveyor had decided to help himself in the course of his duties and had put '70 loads of picked flints from his own land' on the roads and used his own teams for the purpose. This was regarded as improper; the Vestry sought a Licence from the Magistrates to cover Hobbs' past fault but minuted for the future that,

> 'Vestry are of opinion it is very important that Surveyors of roads, whoever they may be should contract with the regular dealers for supply and cartage.'

Hawridge seems to have been more reluctant than Cholesbury to raise money; church rates were granted unwillingly, if at all, and by 1855 when the church was rebuilt the fabric was in a deplorable state and had lost most of its glass.

However reluctant they might be, there was no possibility of evading Government demands and in 1845 the Vestry had to meet,

> 'To nominate 4 able men to serve as Essessors for the Land and Essessed tax.'

The names are not given at the time, but two years later the four who were appointed to this unpopular and invidious duty were Matthew Carpenter, William Wright, junior, Joseph Pitkins the publican, and Henry Philby.

Buckland Common and St. Leonards

To the outside world Cholesbury and Hawridge might appear as two quiet backwaters, isolated from the main developments of the 19th century. There was no need for the revolutionary changes which occurred elsewhere; the land had been enclosed for two centuries or more, and though an agricultural report of Buckinghamshire in about 1813 mentions the Chilterns, particularly in the

neighbourhood of Chesham and Amersham, as an area mainly
devoted to the fattening of cattle [11] for the London market, our
villages were mainly arable, the percentage amounting to over 70%
at Buckland Common, over 80% in Cholesbury and 90% in
Hawridge.

The Vestry records have shown that, for the inhabitants, life
was more exciting than the outsider would have expected, and the
records for Buckland Common and St. Leonards, or for many
other villages, would tell a similar story. These last two villages,
however, changed much more than Cholesbury and Hawridge,
because enclosure of the open fields down in the Aylesbury Vale
was also accompanied by enclosure of the large Commons up in
the hills. This is not just a question of little encroachments on the
waste; it involves the division of large areas of 90 acres or more
into hedged fields which change the appearance of the village
completely. At Buckland common, only 1¾ acres was left open as
a recreation ground, and even that had a footpath running across
it.

The Commissioners for Enclosure [12] in 1842 surveyed the
whole area dividing the result into three categories—'old holdings',
(all outside the actual common), land allocated in compensation
for the loss of common rights, and land to be sold. The second of
these categories resulted in the allocation of 15 acres to the
following 16 villagers, mostly, though not exclusively, the existing
owners.

	Acres	*Roods*	*Poles*
Job Brown (House and Brickkilns)		2	1
John Amsden (Blacksmith)			23
Joseph Bishop			28
Lydia Brackley (Folly Farm)		3	24
Job Brackley (The Potteries)			16
Hugh Cook			19
John Eayres (Dorrian's Farm)			39
John Garrett (Buckland Wood)			12
Elizabeth Newman		2	16
John Parkinson	5	1	9
William Prickett			23
George Sutthery	1	3	28
William Sutthery			5
Rev. John Sutton (The Big House)			29

Henry Weaver		27
Rector and Churchwarden of Aldbury	1	39
Surveyor of Highways for a Watering Place		12
Recreation Allotment	1	3	37

This list suggests that Buckland Common was a very different type of village from St. Leonards. The latter as we have seen consisted mainly of small farmers, but Buckland Common was clearly a community of cottagers, many of whom enjoyed common rights. The small allocation of lands may have provided little compensation for the loss of these rights where in the words of the Commissioners 'all rights of sheep walk and common were extinguished', but enclosure was an expensive operation and the greater part of the common lands, 70 odd acres, were sold to pay the costs. We can imagine an animated scene at the New Bell Inn, Aston Clinton on 2nd January 1843 when these lands went up for auction; where the successful bidders were:

Name	No. of Lots	Total Acreage			Cost
Edward and William Weller (White Lion)	2	2	3	02	£ 50
Edward Horwood	9	23	3	04	255
Richard Benson	4	8	0	27	107. 10. 0
Hugh Cook	2	2	1	26	42. 10. 0
George Sutthery	2	6	0	13	83. 0. 0
Daniel King	1	0	1	24	10. 10. 0
Thomas Collier	4	17	1	4	208
William Glouster	1	2	0	12	26
John Brown	1	1	2	08	21
Rev. Faithful	1	0	0	39	6
		64	2	39	
Plots Withdrawn		5	1	18	
		70	0	17	£809. 10. 0

As will be seen, there was only a handful of villagers, some three or four who couldn't acquire a small portion of the common under one pretext or the other, but henceforth its memory is only preserved in the name of the hamlet. Buckland Common is an area virtually without a common.

The Buckland Common population figures have never been separated from those of the parent village, but from parish register information it remained the most industrialised of the four villages, with two brickworks and its potteries until at least 1853. The larger houses by this time had been converted to tenements, three of them housing as many as 21 families [13].

The inhabitants, as we have seen (page 197), were already attending Cholesbury Church and in 1851 Jeston reported to the Trustees [14] that the Bishop of Oxford had proposed a permanent allowance of £10 to the incumbent of Cholesbury if the Trustees would allow him to take over Buckland Common with a population of not less than 260. The Trustees thought the

> 'Annexation would be decidely advantageous to the inhabitants of Buckland Common . . . but thought the £10 suggested quite inadequate.'

Nothing further seems to have been done, and by 1860 Buckland Common had both its own Church and a Strict Baptist Chapel. The former was pulled down in 1939, the latter remains today.

The St. Leonards enclosure has been mentioned in Chapter XV. The population in this village continued to increase, reaching its peak of 200 in 1871, but then dropped by a quarter in the next 20 years. Edward Owen, who followed the unhappy Isaac King, was Chaplain there for years; he married a wealthy woman, daughter of Robert Sutton of Rossway, and with her help converted his house into a charming building which has since unfortunately disappeared.

Enclosure would have changed the appearance of part of this village too, but moving off into the fields the villagers in about 1847 could still visit one of their favourite spots called the Shepherd's Grave. [15]

> 'It is a lofty eminence commanding a wide view of the valley below. Tradition says that a shepherd named Faithful (a common name in the area about this time), delighted with the panorama, used to make this spot his common resting place, while attending

his master's flock. Becoming at length so attached to it he exacted
a promise to his fellow shepherds that at his death, they would
bury him there. This promise they fulfilled, and cut in the turf
the following epitaph:-

'Faithful lived and Faithful died,
Faithful shepherd on the hill side,
The field so under the hill so round,
In the day of judgement he'll be found.'

Only the tradition remains; the site is thought to be on the summit
above Aston Hill where Alfred Rothschild built his Swiss chalet as
a showplace and retreat.

The End of the Century

The rest of our history is less dramatic. Though events might
occur which are important to the villages themselves and their
future, there is little that is unusual and would not be equally true
of any other English village.

Generally speaking the population dropped after 1850–60,
with a gradual drift towards the towns. Cholesbury, indeed had
reached its peak before this; from 132 in 1821 it fell steadily to 95
in 1891, when it started to increase again. The top figure in
Hawridge is 276 in 1861, falling to 209 in 1901. St. Leonards, as
we have seen, dropped from 200 to 150 in 20 years.

From 1853 Jeston, for health reasons was ordered abroad for a
few years, years, Cholesbury being in the hands of a Curate. He
had returned by 1861, when the Bishop of Oxford who had held a
Confirmation at Cholesbury reported that this was, [16]

'The most satisfactory confirmation he had held that year.'

Attendance at the Sunday School had dropped to 37, though it
now had a regular schoolmaster as teacher, as well as members of
the Jeston family. Jeston, finding the terms of the Neale Trust with
its dual duties and sermons at Cholesbury and Wigginton hard to
fulfil, told the trustees, he felt himself 'unequal to the three
duties'. He had left the Wigginton duty to the Curate of
Wigginton, Mr Snell, thus provoking a furious reaction from the
Trustees, who

'Were unanimously of the opinion that Mr Snell was not a fit
person to perform this duty . . .'

Reluctantly they agreed that Jeston and Snell should alternate at

Wigginton for the rest of the summer and that they would take steps to try to release the holder of the Neale charity from 'duties which are no longer needed'. The Wigginton duty was finally detached, with the Curate of that parish receiving a quarter of the income from the Trust. But at 75, Jeston was not finished. In 1872, he reported that

> 'The Parish Church of Cholesbury having become by length of years delapidated as to be almost unfit for Divine Worship, the Incumbent advertised for tender for its restoration.'

The tender accepted was from an architect who was said to have had experience of this work. It did not go smoothly: [17]

> 'There was delay in starting and torrential rain and a furious gale on Sunday night 8 Dec. 1872 caught the new work unroofed and caused the North wall with parts of the East and South walls to collapse . . .'

However, it was eventually finished, and the outside suits its position inside the fort well enough, though some of us may feel that part of the decor is unsuitable for a delightful old church. Jeston himself must have done a magnificent job to raise the £991 needed for the restoration.

In his closing years he saw two things which must have given him great satisfaction. During the 19th century proper provision had at last been made for education in these villages. The first was at St. Leonards, where [18]

> 'A commodious National School House,'

had been built in 1851 for the use of that and adjoining parishes. These premises were generously offered to Jeston for his Sunday School, which up to then had been held in Glebe Cottage. In 1878 a second school had been built at Hawridge on land given by the Lord of the Manor and conveyed to the Minister and church-wardens of Hawridge for the joint parishes of Hawridge and Cholesbury in trust for a public elementary school and subject to the condition that it should not become a Board School.

Finally, in 1887, he must have been delighted to see the parish for which he could see no prospects in 1832 in a happy and festive mood on the occasion of the Queen's Jubilee. Arrangements started in March when, [19]

Fig. 26 Cholesbury Church after restoration

> 'At a public meeting of the parishioners held at the parsonage
> March 28, it was unanimously resolved that a treat should be
> given to the labourers, and their families on June 21st and that
> the Guardian be requested to call on the owners of property in
> the parish to collect funds for this purpose.'

The menu, it was minuted, was to consist of:

> 'Dinner—Rounds of Boiled beef, Hams, Roast Beef, Plum
> puddings and Cornflour shapes with a pint of Beer for those who
> wish it. Tea—tea, bread and butter, cakes, Jams etc.'

The sum of £25.3.0 was collected in subscriptions, the list of
contributors together with the full accounts appearing in
Appendix D. But for a full account we can do no better than to go
to the local press report:

> 'In this little parish the celebration of the Queen's Jubilee was a
> great success. First of all there was a very hearty service in church
> at noon. This was followed by dinner arranged in two tents which
> had been pitched on the Common, and were prettily decorated.

All the inhabitants of the parish, three only expected, sat down together arranged in families, to an excellent dinner, which did much credit to the caterers, Messrs Pallett and Bishop. In the afternoon there was a cricket match between married and single, with sports and games for the children for gifts and money prizes. Presents were also given to the 27 children who had passed the record inspection at the district school. Tea for all was served at six, followed by sports and games. In the course of the evening an oak tree was planted on the common to commemorate the Jubilee; after a short but pointed speech by Captain Parkinson. At 9.30 there was a display of fireworks; concluding with a bonfire of furze and billets which lit up the whole Common and greatly delighted the onlookers, who separated one and all expressing the great pleasure and enjoyment they had experienced. The venerable and much respected Rector was able to be present at the service, and again at both dinner and tea. This is the third Jubilee in which he has taken part, that of George III, in 1809, his own Jubilee as Rector of the Church (since 1830) and now the Jubilee of our Queen.'

In 1887 Jeston was 90, and after 50 years at Cholesbury he asked if he could have a pension of one-third if he retired. The Trustees by now met infrequently and there seems to have been no answer by the time he died in 1889. There is no one left in the village who knew him personally, but his memory is still so fresh that he is spoken of with the affectionate respect usually reserved for a close friend. The memorial window in the church was the least the village could do in memory of a great man who had steered it through its worst ordeal.

Notes and References

[1] Vestry Accounts – Parish Chest.

[2] This and the following information except where otherwise noted is from the Neale Trust records, including Minute Books and Jeston's letters and reports to the Trustees, (see note (1) Ch. XIV).

[3] This bassoon is now in the Aylesbury County Museum.

[4] Gibbs, Vol.III, p.160.

[5] B.A.S. Cholesbury Vestry Records.

[6] Parish Register and Vestry Records.

[7] Jeston's letters.

[8] Hawridge Court Book.

[9] Bucks. C.R.O. D/A/We/144/93, Batchelor, Thomas 1846. D/A/Wf/211/138.

[10] B.A.S. Hawridge Vestry Records.

[11] Lyson's Magna Brittania.
[12] Bucks C.R.O., I.R. 89 Buckland Common Enclosure report.
[13] Tithe Survey 1844.
[14] Neale Trust Minutes.
[15] Gibbs, Vol.I, p.124.
[16] Jeston's letters and Neale Trust Minute Book.
[17] Report in the 'Buffed Bossed Book' – a record of the Neale Trust kept at Cholesbury.
[18] Jeston's letters.
[19] Cholesbury Vestry Records.

XIX

THE CHILD IS 'SOWN IN FOR THE WINTER' AND 'LORD ROTHSCHILD HAS CONTINUED AN ENCROACHMENT AND IS AMERCED 6d.'

Village life in the early 20th century

Roads, transport, food, employment, social conditions. A new Lord of the Manor, Mr H. J. Turner. The Rothschild and their contribution to the Villages. Medical arrangements. Village amusements. Postscript on the present day.

Village life as Jeston knew it in his later years, was to change little for another generation or more. Our Bronze Age founders had picked their sites carefully to provide a refuge when enemies were prowling about along the Icknield Way: 4,000 years later, the villages were still just as secluded on their cold hilltops. The railway, which came to Chesham in 1889, was no more than four miles away from Hawridge and Cholesbury, but the road down the Vale still turned into a river for three to four months every winter, when the bourne rose, and only the long way round via Braziers End and Bellingdon or the footpath across 'The Mountain', the local name for the hill behind the Black Horse, were passable. Going north the road to Wigginton and Shire Lane was still a single track lane with a grass ridge between the ruts and the hill down to Tring so stony and muddy that most villagers preferred to use the footpaths 'down the Downs'.

These narrow unmade roads, repaired in the traditional way with turf from the commons and flints from our fields, were all that the villages had to connect them with the nearby towns until the 1930s, and the inhabitants continued to live an isolated, independent, self-sufficient existence. It was still an area of small, mixed farms where a lad might start work as a ploughboy at 13 leading the horses, the family turned out to help with the harvest with the children eager to earn pennies by laying a band (putting out lengths of straw after reaping for tying up the sheaves) and hedging and ditching or hurdle making from the ash saplings which

212

still grow in our hedgerows would provide welcome winter employment.

The grain, meat and milk produced from these small farms with their difficult soil might be no more than needed for local consumption, with any surplus sold at the nearby markets, but there was at least one thing which could be produced in abundance from these fields—hay grass—and hay was needed in large quantities in London to feed the bus and tram horses. So, in the winter the hay tier would appear to break down the ricks, tie the hay into trusses to be carted away.

Another product went even farther afield than London. Our woodlands today still ring with birdsong at dawn and dusk, but there was one bird—the pheasant which could be made profitable and breeding and the export of eggs was big business in these parts. The export trade was organised on a large scale from outside our villages, but their supplies came from our woodlands. As early as 1810 Stephen Dwight, whose family ran this business from Potten End had made an encroachment in Hawridge for breeding and keeping pheasants. 100 years later pheasant rearing was continued at Brun's and Dundridge Farms, at Rays Hill by Mr Brown and William Brackley and on the former St. Leonards Common by John Collier, and their work helped to provide employment.

The woods contributed rabbits and pigeons to the local economy and poaching was something of a local industry, though, often the results were bartered for a drink at the 'Poachers' Paradise'—the old Plough at Chivery—before the wives could get hold of them for the pot. The fields and the commons contributed cowslips and dandelions for wine which was made both at home and on a larger scale at the cider factory, the children being sent to gather the flowers. Cider apples were not produced locally but were sent by rail to Tring station from where a steam waggon brought them to 'The Ciders', but there was a fruit farm at the house now known as Orchard End which provided some employment at picking time and most of the cottages, as we know from the Court Rolls had a garden for vegetables and small orchard in which the prune damson, a big black plum and the black Bucks cherries used for a special 'stir-about pudding' were grown.

Our last product in these hilltop villages is timber, used especially by the High Wycombe chair industry, and chair bodging (making legs) along with tree felling kept a few men employed.

The soil, therefore, was not unproductive but it had other values as well in the village economy. It is not surprising to find the clay still used for brick making, an important source of employment in the summer, but an equally important ingredient in our soil were the flints which we curse so heartily in our gardens today. The children could earn money collecting them from the fields, each picking a 'land', a strip in line with the furrows, with a firm rule that there was no trespassing on the next strip. For a cubic yard of flints the payment was 8d to 1/- and they were in much demand for road repairs, not only on the local roads but in Aston Clinton and Buckland where they do not 'grow' them as we do. They were split by the flint knapper, Teddy John Brackley and carted off down the hills a journey on which the horse would take eager advantage of its driver's somnolence on a hot day and wade into the pond at Dancer's End for a drink.

When the flint knapper had finished his work he left behind him a pile of road sidings, a sandy material which could be used in brick making as mould sand or as brick laying mortar. Occasionally, an unauthorised stone contractor would try to obtain a free supply of our flints and in 1901 the Cholesbury Court Book records

> "That stone carters George Bartes of Wiggington use the Common for the purpose of drawing stones'.

Even when they were local men, the contractors were often unpopular for their habit of just dumping the stones on the Common and in 1909 the Court records that,

> 'Mr Alfred Brown had placed three heaps of stones and one heap of gravel on the waste of the Manor and the Steward was directed to write to Mr Brown and ask him to have them removed.'
> 'Thomas Collier had deposited one heap of Road Siding on the waste of the Manor and the Steward was directed to Write to Mr Collier and ask him to have them removed.'

The first of these heaps is still there, though by now grassed over!

It will be remembered from Chapter II that our clay-with-flints top soil is often a thin layer over the chalk and the local farmers knew well enough how to make use of this geological formation, for they used the chalk as a fertiliser. The chalk diggers, like

Frederick Humphrey would sink a shaft in the field they were to fertilise and with a pick, shovel, bucket and windlass dig it out, load it on a wheelbarrow and distribute it over the field. When they had finished they roofed in the shaft with timber, covered it with the topsoil and went off to the next field, but we can still see signs of their work in shallow depressions in the fields and this old practice can still give an occasional surprise when the timber covering has rotted through and the ground suddenly caves in, taking with it trees and any unfortunate animal standing on the spot. It sounds strenuous work, but Frederick Humphrey was only a few weeks short of his 100th birthday when he died.

The early years of the 20th century were still a time when the villages expected to be self-sufficient, with the normal range of village craftsmen. There were blacksmiths at the Old Forge (now Orchard Cottage) and the Great House at Buckland Common, where Mr Hending the smith used to let the girls and boys go in to the warmth after tea for a sing-song, while at Hawridge the Tomlins combined the functions of wheelwright and undertaker. The Palletts at Cholesbury and Joshua Brackley at the Thatched Cottage and later George his son next to the White Lion were coal merchants. John Collier the carter used to take loads of chair legs to High Wycombe, or hay to London or flints to the Aylesbury Plain, while Joshua Brackley at Chivery not only owned a waggonette which a group of housewives might hire to go shopping in Tring, but he or his family were also foresters, joiners, builders of houses and farm buildings and timber merchants. With the miller, the shoe repairer and the village policemen the villages could be independent of outside help in running their lives.

The range of village shops, mentioned below, though these did not all exist at the same time, shows how well the day to day necessities were catered for in the villages. At Hawridge, Mr Free in The Row kept a little store and Mr Stanniford at the Village Shop sold ropes, buckets and chicken food. There was a butchers' and slaughterers' still at Cholesbury, though it had now moved to the Queen's Head while William Culverhouse's butcher's shop had become the Post Office and also sold sweets. In St. Leonards, Samuel and Phoebe Gilbert kept a general shop at Dundridge Cottage and delivered the post in the course of their rounds, the postman, Reed having walked up from Tring, left the post with the Gilberts before walking on to Swan Bottom, delivering letters en route, where he spent the afternoon doing odd jobs and gardening, walking back to Tring in the evening collecting from the boxes on the way. In Buckland Common, there was another slaughterer, Mr Bishop in Potteries Lane. Mrs Brackley at the Thatched House sold cigarettes and sweets, Mrs Gibbs at the Great House kept calico, tapes, cottons and sheeting while Mrs Nethercott at the Corner Cottage and later Charles and Henry Gilbert had a bakery. The most unusual of these local stores was Mrs Bowdery's at Kiln Cottage, with premises in an old horse tram. Nobody knew where the tram came from, but it was well supplied with bacon, groceries and snuff (sold by the pennyworth), and would sometimes offer delicacies such as bloaters which had been brought back from Tring.

The villages, moreover, were not dependent on local supplies alone. The tradesmen of Tring competed for the business of the Commons and the pony carts of the butcher, the baker, the grocer and the fishmonger came to the housewife's door to provide a service we miss today. From Chesham, Watts the grocers would call, too, while Patterson's ran a clothing club for which they collected from door to door. For extra sewing materials, there was the pedlar, a little man, it is remembered, who came up the hill with a box on his back stuffed with buttons and tapes and ribbons.

Supplies from the shops were supplemented by home-produced food. In addition to vegetables and fruit, everybody in these villages kept a few chickens and a pig, killed at the local slaughterer's. In a few of the larger houses the carcasses might be taken back home and the kitchen floor would be running with blood as it was cut up and the entrails sorted out for black puddings, while hams were smoked over an oak fire; but the villagers mostly preferred to take money and leave the sausage making to Mr Bishop, who sold them from a van near the Thatched Cottage.

Our Villages, therefore could produce much of their own food and provide most of the services normally needed by the community. If there were few in what would now be regarded as a 'steady job', opportunities for some sort of work were varied and the women helped to supplement the family income by straw plaiting while the girls normally went away into service as soon as they were old enough. In a bad winter when the brickyards were closed and work on the farms scarce some families undoubtedly had a hard time. Parish relief by now was only 1/- plus a loaf and with no money for proper food dinner could consist only of skimmed milk, bought from the farmers at 1½d a gallon and thickened with flour, while twice a week the children might walk to Wendover for a quart of soup. In the summer, however, though there were few luxuries most would have lived comfortably enough and the following recollections of life 60 years ago from one of our local residents, are probably typical

'I am 65, I can remember when I was 5 so it is 60 years, but it seems only yesterday when I think of Saturday bath night. The water had to be carried in buckets from a tap which supplied 6 cottages and was quite a long way from the house. Sometimes my Father would fill up the copper, which was also shared, then my Mother used to bring in her big washing bath which for some reason she called a tray and wash us each in turn including hair, then she trimmed our nails and dried and plaited my hair rolling the ends in paper, then off we all were sent to bed, then while she still had hot water she would scrub the stairs which were bare boards, then the kitchen where the bathing took place, the floor was blue and red bricks, then the step and a piece she called the pitchen just outside then she was ready to start her Sunday cooking.

She first chopped a huge lump of suet and made a basin of suet crust chopped up beef and kidney and made a meat pudding also two bacon dumplings. The Sunday dinner of those days was so different from today, we had one large cast iron boiler lined with white enamel it went on at eight o'clock in the morning on a clear open coal fire, when the pot boiled in went the huge pudding basin, tied up with strong calico cloth then in went the dumplings. Now we were got ready for Sunday school at 10 o'clock, hair all crimped at the ends, 1 hour in school, then two by two to church till 12.30. When Mother had got us off to School the vegetables were prepared, a bucket full of green or cauliflower and loads of potatoes which she put into a strong string net; out came the dumplings, in went the potatoes, then the greens, the dumplings were for Monday dinner warmed up in the oven, it was an open fire place with two hobs, a trivet for the kettle and the oven cooked quite well. But one awful Sunday the soot came down the chimney, the boiler lid was worn out, it filled up the boiler with soot, poor Mum she threw her apron over her head and wept, but my Father who was quite a clever man, made a new lid before the next Sunday. I can remember how proud I felt that my Father was able to make a lid to fit the boiler.

The cold dumplings were heated up in the oven on Mondays again with lots of fresh vegetables, we had a most wonderful allotment, in those days you almost had to fight to get one. When my father tried for one as soon as it became vacant it was because he was such a good worker and at 21 had 3 children to feed.

On Tuesday it was a meatless day, we did sometimes get an egg, Wednesday we used to get liver and muggin, that was the lovely curley fat, nothing today can compare with the flavour; sheep's heart stuffed, and melts sewed up like a small bag and stuffed, 3 or 4d worth of flare to make lard and the crimplings, all with bread, faggots and pease pudding. The food today is nothing like the old days.'

As a child, the author of these memories lived at nearby Wigginton, but the food she mentions would be typical of that anywhere in the area. The Saturday bath night ritual, however, would have been less common in our villages, where there was no piped water or taps and, in a dry summer, a scarcity of water from any source. The only deep wells were at Hawridge Court and Bottom Farm, though a few cottages had, and still have, surface wells fed by rain and surface water. Drinking water was virtually non existent. Every garden had its brick tank with a domed top to collect rain water and hoped that the winter rains would fill it enough to see them through a dry summer. There were a few ponds on Cholesbury Common—Old Gomm's pond outside Tall Chimneys was a duck pond, there was Clysbury's Pond opposite the old Post Office and in Hawridge others outside the Full Moon and Kingston Farm, with a third at Heath End shared by the forge and the wheelwright. The farmers had their own ponds for the stock, and when supplies ran out in the cottages the children were sent to wriggle their way through the fences and collect a bucketful. In a real drought even water for the stock was scarce and the sheep from Chapel Farm would be driven down to 'Ebspit Pond' below the modern waterworks to drink, usually returning as thirsty as ever by the time they had walked up the hill again.

Water came to our villages in 1935, but we still have no main drainage and as late as 1963, the Inspector chairing a public enquiry into the sanitary arrangements of houses near the Pumping Station, expressed more than a faint surprise at the details of the earth closets and pails which still existed alongside the cesspits and septic tanks.

Into this area with no roads, no water and no sanitation came two new families of special importance round about 1900. The Hawridge Court estate was sold in 1899, after the death of the second of the Rev. Jeffries' sons. The outlying property in the Parish of Chesham went to various new owners, including a Mr Nightingale, who bought the small 10-acre holding where we ourselves now live. Most of the Heath End farmland was bought then or shortly afterwards by the owner of Rossway, thus turning back to face east towards Hertfordshire as it had 1000 years before. Hawridge Court itself, with its land, was bought by Mr H. J. Turner, who already owned Braziers End and now became Lord of the Manors of Cholesbury and Hawridge and owner of Dundridge. So the estate extended right along the top of the hill to the south-west of the present main road, interrupted only by Botchmore Farm and a few small cottages. Mr Turner continued to live at Braziers End and was a familiar figure riding around on a great chestnut horse. At last our villages had a resident squire who enjoyed his position as Lord of the Manor and was interested in reviving the old Manorial Courts as an instrument of local government.

The two Manors, Hawridge and Cholesbury, it will be remembered, had shared a Lord of the Manor since the 17th century, but the mere accident of common ownership could neither obliterate their separate identities nor change the 'custom of the Manor' where this was slightly different. So Mr Turner and his Steward, Early Christopher Francis who had succeeded his father, John Dunkin Francis, held two Courts on the same day, at the meeting places which had become traditional, the Manor House for Cholesbury and the *Full Moon* for Hawridge. The Homage might by this time be reduced to one or two; at Cholesbury the Rev. Ferry was the regular foreman for some years, followed mostly by William Brackley and Albert Gomm, while at Hawridge George Redding and Frederick Fincher were normally present. These Courts were still concerned about the use

Fig. 27 The Manor House, Cholesbury where the Manorial Court may have met since the 16th century.

of the Commons; their disapproval of the dumping of stones has already been noted but they were also concerned, as their predecessors had been hundreds of years before, with grazing rights and enclosures. Thus in 1906, the Homage at Cholesbury presented that

> 'Mr Henry Bailey of Tring Grange Farm had during the past year turned out his sheep on the common without any right for so doing and the Steward was instructed to write to him to inform him thereof.'

While at Hawridge, as late as 1923,

> 'It was presented that cattle are still permitted to stray on Hawridge Common and that a house has been erected on one of the enclosures continued by Richard Turney.'

Four years before this there had even been four new encroachments at Hawridge, by Harris Brackley, George Free, George

Parslow and Thomas Rance, for the patriotic purpose with the scarcity of food in the first World War of growing potatoes. The custom of the Manor did not prevent the fine being increased from the usual Hawridge rate of 3d or 6d to 1/9d or 2/-, a reflection perhaps of the changing value of money.

These 20th century Courts had one other purpose, to collect 'Quit Rents', as they were referred to locally and in the notice which was posted giving the date of the meeting. Most of those who paid had no idea that these quit rents were mainly fines for 'encroachments on the Lord's waste' which dated back 100 years or more. The total sum involved can never have been more than a pound or two and was promptly disbursed in hospitality at the *Full Moon*.

Among the entries in both Court Books for the years between 1900 and 1923, appears the following:

> 'Lord Rothschild has continued an encroachment . . . therefore he is amerced 6d.'

Mr Turner must have enjoyed collecting this fine from his distinguished neighbour, for by this time the Rothschilds had settled in the area to the north of our villages. Baron Anthony was at Aston Clinton, followed by his daughter, Lady Battersea, Count Ferdinand at Waddesdon Manor and Mr Alfred, at Halton on the St. Leonards boundary, but it was the first Lord Rothschild, Nathaniel, who is remembered best in our villages. Inheriting Tring Park from his father in 1879, his lands included the greater part of Buckland Common, Parrott's Farm and Shire Lane and Tring Grange Farms on the north and north-eastern borders of Cholesbury.

It is difficult to say whether this concentration of lands in the large estates was an unmixed blessing to the people of the villages. Many a small farmer or smallholder must have been bought out in the process and the Bucks villager, retaining the traditions of his yeomen ancestors in his desire for land—his own plot of land—may at times have resented the loss of his own plot more than he appreciated the increase in opportunity for steady employment. Of the increase in these opportunities there was no doubt, the activities on the Rothschild estates including forestry, general estate work and at shooting parties, in horse breeding, particularly Shire horses, in sheep raising and shearing, in cattle raising, particularly Barrington shorthorns and in bee-keeping. Plantations of trees the length of Parrott's Lane from Buckland Common to Shire Lane provided work for the fellers, the tops being sold to villagers for 1/- a time and made into rick pegs and fold stakes, while in a 'pimp-shed' in the woods two old men made up bundles of firewood known as 'pimps'.

In a hard winter any able-bodied man who walked to one of the estates would be found work in the woods and as a bonus would be allowed to take away with him as much wood as he could carry for his own fire.

To his own tenants and estate workers Lord Rothschild was a model landlord, building new cottages let at a weekly rent of 2/6, providing a doctor and nurse who had a supply of blankets on loan and fitting out the daughters of his employees with a uniform for their first job in service wherever that might be. In the year of the worst unemployment he had the water tank at the top of the Crong erected and piped water from it in order to provide work, incidentally giving St. Leonards and Chivery a water supply long before it reached our other villages. There are many still alive who remember special acts of kindness; one tells how four young relatives with no prospects at home were helped to emigrate to Canada, another that, when left a widow with five or six young children, she found that her weekly meat bill was to be sent to Lord Rothschild. Estate workers received a haunch of venison sent specially from Scotland at Christmas; allotment holders on 20 pole plots let by Lord Rothschild at 5/3d a year were given a piece of beef and the return of the 3d. Some of our older residents still recall the discussions on the alternatives of eating this meat in one glorious feast or cutting it up into two or three portions to spin it out.

It was not only their own workers who benefited, because the Rothschilds took the villages under their wing in so many ways. They gave every encouragement to the farmers, particularly through their sponsorship of the Agricultural Show at Tring; they arranged a clothing club scheme at St. Leonards school to help poorer parents; and in hard winters they set up soup kitchens where for 1d a time the men could fill up cans for the family and collect bread.

The happiest memories, however, come from those who were children at the time. If they saluted him, they could be sure of pennies or sweets; even better was to man the gates along the Bridle Way at Hastoe when Lord Rothschild rode the estate on Saturday mornings, for the boy on each gate received 1/- from the groom and the lucky one at the last gate 2/-. It was at Christmas that the Rothschild generosity reached its height, when every child in the villages of Hastoe, St. Leonards, Buckland Common, Cholesbury and Hawridge, except for the unfortunate few who were illegitimate, knew that there would be at least one gift. Early in the autumn each child had to write its name, age and address on a label and hand it in at school. Excitement increased as the term went on and the date was announced; when the great day arrived there was no attempt to keep the children in school, they had gone out to meet the waggons as they came up the hills, great waggons with four horses and two traces, and the children ran alongside until they reached the school. The precious cargo consisted of Christmas hampers, one for each child, with its label attached and containing cake, chocolates, two toys and a new shilling. The wonderful smell of chocolate, an unusual smell to most of these children, is still remembered.

Life in these villages was simple and sometimes hard. The doctor when he was needed usually came from Wendover, if he could get there, but when the snow lay thick on the ground and his pony could not get up the hill the villages had to rely on their own resources. For confinements, the vicar's wife kept 'The Bag', but most women had their own remedies, remedies which were not necessarily approved by the medical profession. In winter, baths were thought to be dangerous and for some children indeed they were impracticable without destroying the traditional protection against colds. As late as the 1920s a young medical student visiting a sick child for the Wendover docter, who was snowbound, was a little taken aback after suggesting examining the patient's chest to get the answer,

'Oh, you can't do that, he's sown in for the winter'—and sown in he was, in good red flannel covered with goose grease.

Though life might be hard our villagers, like countrymen anywhere, knew how to amuse themselves in their own simple ways. They enjoyed their beer at any time and it sometimes constituted part of their wages. Harvest Festival was always an excuse for a celebration, called at Hawridge, 'Mugs and Thumbs' at the *Rose and Crown*. The men took their own mugs and cut the bread and cheese on their thumbs. On 5 November Mr Turner gave the children a bonfire party to which each child took his own mug with, apparently, no limitation on size. The village fêtes in the summer had stalls covered with home-made articles, jams, jellies, cakes and wine, as well as the results of months of sewing and knitting. The Cherry Fair at Chesham, and the Great Fairs at Aylesbury and Tring gave an excuse for an outing, the third of these, held in the Combe at the bottom of Tring Hill, had a traditional game, a game sometimes productive of tears when a child, given the first orange it had ever seen, found that it was expected to join in the fun and roll the orange down the hill.

Alongside these harmless, unsophisticated amusements, the earthier, cruder side of village life also lasted beyond the beginning of the 20th century. A man who felt lonely at night and decided he wanted a women's help—or company—would put a brush or broom by the door. For those who indulged in extra-marital relationships, the village had a harsher treatment in those days of the non-permissive society. Quietly a group would get together with all the old tin trays, pots or kettles that they could filch from their kitchens and would then go off to serenade the unfortunate couple with this 'rough music'. Great fun, no doubt—except for the victims!

We had proper music too. Apart from the normal Christmas carols, St. Leonards boasted a celebrated brass band. Started by a Mr Prothero about 1880, and carried on by George Brackley, who combined the jobs of churchwarden, organist and choirmaster with a multitude of other activities and later by George Brackley's son-in-law, George Gurney, this band won many prizes while taking part in nationwide contests such as the great music festivals then held at the Crystal Palace. It will be remembered even more, however, locally where it was called on to perform at nearly every public event. Perhaps the most memorable was the annual Sunday School treats when the band headed a great procession of the children of the villages to and from the special service in the church which preceded the feast. The band, alas, was never revived after the First World War, except for special cornet numbers in the

Remembrance Day services at St. Leonards with the British Legion.

The bands, treats, fetes and fairs were special events. For day-to-day amusements the boys played 'Fidguts', a simple game in which the first player cut a pointed faggot of wood, and threw it hard so that it stuck in the ground, while his opponent with a similar piece of wood tried to uproot it with a sideways throw. The men played bowls at the *Full Moon*, or on the Common opposite, or Quoits on pitches on Hawridge Common just below the *Full Moon* and at the *Boot and Slipper* at Buckland Common. This popular local game, matches being played with nearby villages such as Ballinger, Berkhamsted, Boxmoor and Hemel Hempstead and Wigginton, was played on a pitch some 18 yds long. A square of firm puddled clay about 3' by 3' at each end of the pitch contained an iron peg sunk level with the clay, the quoits being pitched to land as close as possible to this pin. In the top of the pin was a small indent, callipers were placed in this indent to determine which quoit(s) were nearest the pin. A fixed number of 'ends' were played in each game and the scoring seems to have been similar to bowls. Singles or doubles, again as in bowls, were played.

The size and weight of the quoits used was optional, the player using those most suited to himself; some players used only their own personal quoits and these were sometimes burnished with sand and water until they were smooth and shining.

Quoits disappeared in the early 1920s though bowls is still played at the *Full Moon*. Nobody, unfortunately, remembers when cricket started up here, but the local residents and their visitors, who enjoyed playing or watching village cricket in a glorious setting on a sunny Sunday afternoon, cannot help being grateful for the last enclosure recorded in our Court Rolls in 1919, an enclosure made by the Lord of the Manor himself. We can think of no better way of ending this Chapter than by recording the Minute which reads,

> 'It was presented to the Court that the Lord intended to erect fencing sufficient to protect the Cricket Pitch for the Hawridge and Cholesbury Cricket Club.'

Postscript

At the end of the First World War most of the villagers when they went to town still used the earliest form of transport, their own legs. The carrier's horse and cart went to Chesham twice a week, charging his passengers a 2/6. fare while Mr Pallett of Cholesbury had a brake which he used for Sunday School outings. Heavy loads still came up by waggon, with the trace horses still waiting at the bottom of the hills from Wendover and Tring to help the waggons up. The first bus service was a lorry with seats in it run by the brothers Grace who lived at the Mustard Pot (now a garage) which plied from Buckland Common via Cholesbury to Tring, charging 6d. down and 9d. up.

We crept, perhaps reluctantly into the 20th century but gradually between the wars electricity, telephone and made-up roads came to our villages and now we are no longer isolated—until the snow comes. Then, the snowplough may clear our roads, but many of us have a long dig down our own drives before we reach them, quite apart from the final effort through the mound that the snowplough has piled up at the end of the drive! I suppose we are more sophisticated now and more in tune with 20th century society, but it is not all gain. We have lost most of our own village shops, and the visiting tradesmen, and have to use a car or the infrequent local bus service to buy our food.

But we are still a self-contained community. Hawridge and Cholesbury Ecclesiastical Parishes were united in the 1920's and these two villages, with St. Leonards and Buckland Common, were combined into a new civil parish in 1932. Our hilltop villages, so closely linked geographically, have at last discarded the Saxon arrangements which tied each of them separately to one of the villages in the plains. We each retain something of our individuality, but together we hope we can continue to form a barrier against encroachments from the towns. We may become an anachronism, but we like being country villages.

We can amuse ourselves too, with our fêtes, flower shows, wine and cheese parties and the numerous societies which compete for our two village halls for their meetings. We think our yeomen predecessors would have enjoyed our social life as much as we do today. We are sure they would have shared vigorously in our societies and in our efforts to preserve their houses, their

Commons and their open spaces, to keep the villages as villages
and save them from degenerating into a suburban sprawl from the
neighbouring towns. They might even have come to the monthly
meetings of our Historical Society. We hope, at least, that they
will not disapprove of the way we have written up their story.

FARMER WITH TYPICAL STRAW PLAITED HAT

APPENDIX A

SOURCES and BIBLIOGRAPHY

I

Original Documents

Detailed references are given in the Notes at the end of each Chapter.

Court Rolls	Cholesbury	1599, 1606, 1644, 1666, 1717, 1737 and 1767 onwards.
	Hawridge	1765 onwards.
Churchwards Accounts ⎱	Cholesbury ⎱	19th century—particularly interesting for Cholesbury the village that went bankrupt in 1833.
Vestry Records ⎰	Hawridge ⎰	
Enclosure Award	St Leonards	1811
" "	Buckland Common	1838
Field Survey	St Leonards	1581
Interrogation and Depositions	St Leonards	1549
Innkeepers' Records ⎱ Brewery Records ⎰		
Muster Roll	St Leonard	1522 (these rolls are missing for Cholesbury and Hawridge).
Neale Lectureship	Cholesbury	Trust deeds 1710 Minute Books Letters from holders to Trustees —a considerable volume for periods 1710–54 and 1830–89.
Parish Registers	Cholesbury	From 1575 (Transcribed by M. F. B. Fitch, H. N. Peyton and Lt. Col. H. K. Percy Smith.)
(inc. B.T.s)	Hawridge	From 1600 (Transcribed by Lt. Col. H. K. Percy Smith and J. S. W. Gibson.)
	St Leonards	From 1737 (Transcribed by Miss J. Fletcher.)

228

Plaistowe Family Chronicle	St Leonards	A private collection of information about the family who owned The Lee, a nearby village and had some connection with St Leonards.
Poll Books		1722 and 1784—Society of Genealogists
Protestation Returns	Cholesbury ⎱ Hawridge ⎰	1641—House of Lords
Terriers	Cholesbury ⎱ Hawridge ⎰	A scattered collection from 1639
Tithe Surveys	Cholesbury Hawridge Buckland	1838 " 1843
Trust Deeds	St Leonards	From 1507
Wills		A considerable selection from 1550
Notes of author	Hawridge	References to a few early charters not mentioned elsewhere

II

Published Documents

Publications of the Bucks Archaeological Society and the Bucks Record Society

A Calendar of the Feet of Fines for Bucks
Ed. by M. W. Hughes   1940

The Cartulary of Missenden Abbey Volumes 1, 2 and 3
Ed. by J. G. Jenkins   1938

Episcopal Visitation Book 1662
Ed. by E. R. C. Brinkworth   1947

Pipe Rolls, Bucks and Beds
Ed. by G. Herbert Fowler and Michael Hughes   1923

Quaker Minute Book 1669—90
Ed. by Beatrice Saxon Snell   1937

Ship Money Papers and Richard Grenville's Note Book
Ed. by Carol Bonsey and J. G. Jenkins   1965

Subsidy Roll for Bucks 1524
Ed. by Prof. A. C. Chibnall and A. Vere Woodman   1950

Records of Buckinghamshire—The Journal of the B.A.S.

Publications of the Lincoln Record Society

An Episcopal Court Book for the Diocese of Lincoln
        1514–1520 Ed. by Margaret Bowker   1967

Visitations in the Diocese of Lincoln 1518–31
        Ed. by A. Hamilton Thompson   1940

Rotuli, Hugo de Welles Vol. II   Ed. by W. P. W. Phillimore   1913

The State of the Church I   Ed. by C. W. Foster   1926

The State of the Ex-Religious and Former Chantry Priests
        in the Diocese of Lincoln 1547–74
        Ed. by G. A. J. Hodgett   1959

Others

A Subsidy Collected in the Diocese of Lincoln 1526
     Ed. by Rev. H. Salter, B. H. Blackwell and H. Frowde   1909

The Edwardian Inventories for Bucks   Ed. by F. C. Eeles
        from transcript by Rev. J. E. Brown,
        Longmans Green & Co.   1908

Bucks Sessions Records 1678–1712
        Published by the Clerk of the Peace Aylesbury
        Vol. I Ed. by William Le Hardy
        Vols. II & III Ed. by William Le Hardy &
        Geoffrey L. Reckett   1933

III
General Reading

Lipscomb, George *The History and Antiquities of the*
        County of Buckingham, 4 Vols. London   1847

Victoria County History, Buckinghamshire,
        4 Vols. and Index   Constable, London   1905–28

Victoria County History, Hertfordshire,   4 Vols. and Index
        Constable, London   1902–37

An Inventory of the Historical Monuments of Bucks,   Vol. I.
        Royal Commission on Historical Monuments   1912

Report on the Charities of Bucks.   (Vol. 5 in series)
        House of Commons   1815

Records of Buckinghamshire–The Journal of the
    Buckinghamshire Archaeological Society (B.A.S.)

The Journal of the British Archaeological Association

AULT, N.	*Life in Ancient Britain*	Longmans 1920
BATSFORD, H. and FRY, C.	*The English Cottage*	Batsford 1938
BERESFORD, M. W.	*The Lost Villages of England*	Lutterworth Press 1954
BONHAM CARTER, V.	*The English Village*	Penguin Books 1952
BRIGGS, H. and JORDAN, P.	*Economic History of England*	U.T. Press 1967
CARPENTER, S. C.	*The Church in England 597–1688*	J. Murray 1954
CHAMBERS, J. D.	*Laxton, The Last English Open Field Village*	H.M.S.O. 1964
CHILDE, G.	*What Happened in History*	Penguin Books 1952
CLARK, G.	*Prehistoric England*	Batsford 1940
COBBETT, W.	*Rural Rides*	London 1893
COPPOCH, J. T.	*The Chilterns*	Geographical Association 1962
COULTON, G. C.	*Life in the Middle Ages*	C.U.P. 1929
DALY, R. A.	*The Changing World of the Ice Age*	Yale University 1935
DARBY, H. C. and CAMPBELL, E.M.J. (Eds)	*The Domesday Geography of South-East England*	C.U.P. 1962
DITCHFIELD, P. H.	*The Counties of England (Buckinghamshire)*	George Allen & Co. ˙1912
EMMISON, F. G.	*Some Types of Common-Field Parish*	N.C.S.S.1968
”	*Archives and Local History*	Methuen 1966
”	*Tudor Food and Pastimes*	Benn 1964

FEARNSIDES,W.G. and BULMAN, O. M. B.	*Geology in the Service of Man*	Pelican Books 1945
FINBERG, H. P. R. and SKIPP, V. H. T.	*Local History, Objective and Pursuit*	David & Charles 1967
FINBERG, Joscelyne	*Exploring Villages*	Routledge 1958
FOX. Cyril	*The Personalities of Britain*	National Museum of Wales 1933
GALBRAITH, V. H.	*The Making of Domesday Book*	Clarendon Press 1961
GIBBS, Robert	*Buckinghamshire—A record of Local Occurrences*	Aylesbury 1879
HAWKES, C. and J.	*Prehistoric Britain*	Penguin Books 1952
HEAD, J. F.	*Early Man in South Bucks*	Bristol 1955
HOLMES, A.	*Principles of Physical Geology*	Nelson 1945
HOSKINS, W. D. and STAMP, L. D.	*The Common Lands of England and Wales*	Collins 1963
HOSKINS, W. G.	*The Midland Peasant*	Macmillan 1965
"	*The Making of the English Landscape*	Hodder & Stoughton 1956
KUHLICKE, F. W. and EMMISON, F. G.	*English Local History Handlist*	Hist. Assn. 1969
LENNARD, R.	*Rural England 1086–1135*	Clarendon Press 1959
MAITLAND, F. W.	*Domesday Book and Beyond*	C.U.P. 1897
MASSINGHAM, H. J.	*The English Countryman*	Batsford 1942
"	*English Downland*	Batsford 1936
ORWIN, C. S. and C. S.	*The Open Fields*	O.U.P. 1967
QUENNELL, M. and C. H. B.	*Everyday Life in Prehistoric Times*	Batsford 1926
"	*A History of Everyday Things in England Vols. I and II*	Batsford 1918 and 1924
"	*A History of Everyday Things in England Vol. III*	Batsford 1967

ROUND, J. H.	*Feudal England*	Sonnenschein London 1895
SEEBOHM, F.	*The English Village Community*	Longmans 1883
SHERLOCK, R. L.	*London and the Thames Valley*	H.M.S.O. 1947
STAMP, D.	*Britain's Structure and Scenery*	Collins 1946
STENTON, D. M.	*English Society in the Middle Ages*	Pelican 1951
SUMMERS, W. H.	*The Lollards of the Chiltern Hills*	London 1906
TATE, W. E.	*A Hand-list of Buckinghamshire Enclosure Acts and Awards*	Aylesbury 1946
,,	*The Parish Chest*	C.U.P. 1960
TAWNEY, R. H. and POWER, Eileen	*Tudor Economic Documents*	Longmans 1924
THIRSK, Joan	*Sources of Information on Population 1500–1760 Unexplored Sources in Local Records*	Phillimore 1965
,,	*Tudor Enclosures*	Hist. Assn. 1967
TREVELYAN, G. M.	*English Social History*	Longmans 1945
,,	*History of England*	Longmans 1926
TROTTER, Eleanor	*Seventeenth Century Life in the Country Parish*	C.U.P. 1919
TRUEMAN, A. E.	*Geology and Scenery*	Penguin Books 1952
WELLDON FINN, R.	*An Introduction to Domesday*	Longmans 1963
WINDLE, B. C. A.	*Remains of the Prehistoric Age in England*	Methuen 1909
WOOLDRIDGE, S.W. and MORGAN, R.S.	*Physical Basis of Geography*	Longmans 1937

NOTE: It will be seen that this Bibliography includes both authoritative books and volumes of more popular interest. This is because we think that as wide a public as possible should be encouraged to take an interest in Local History.

APPENDIX B

PROPERTY OF HAWRIDGE CHURCH IN 1552

From *The Edwardian Inventories for Buckinghamshire* ed. by F. C. Eeles from a
transcript by the Rev. J. E. Brown (Longmans, Green & Co. 1908)

The Indenture made between the Commissioners and Rychard Gery and
Rychard Child listed: —

        ij small belles in the steple
        ij hand belles
        On challis with the paten parshall gylt
        On westment of sylke
        On surples
        On ater clothe
        A crose with the staffe of copper
        A crose clothe of sylke
        On candlesticke of latyn
        A pixe of latyn
        Sensers on pere of latyn
        A plated crose
        A holy water pot of brase
        iiij cruettes of peoter
        ij sacrying belles

APPENDIX C

THE HOUSE WHEREIN EDWARD AVIS FORMERLY DWELT
(Now Called Tall Chimneys)

Summary of Entries in the Cholesbury Court Rolls
and other local documents

1599   C.C.R.   Richard Edmonds inherits from his grandmother Elizabeth Munn, late of the wife of
Henry Munn and formerly of James
Hammound (her 3 daughters Joan Hammond
and Agnes Holyman and Elizabeth William
Edmond having all died, leaving Richard
Edmond as the sole heir)
(a) 3 parcels of land 70 ft. in length x 30 ft.
in width

(b) 3 parcels of land 4 perches long and 1 perch in width

At the same Court Richard Edmonds surrenders 3 parcels to John Pratt.

1644	C.C.R.	Surrender, made 16 March 1637, by John Prate blacksmith of his houses and orchards to John Putnam, is recorded.
1644	Will	Thomas Putnam bequeaths to his son John 'the sum of £8 which I lent him when I had bought John Pratt's house at Cholesbury'.
1666	C.C.R.	Surrender made 27 Jan. 1663 recorded. John Putnam Sen. surrenders a cottage in which Edward Avis Sen. then dwelt to Edward Avis jun. son of Edward Avis Sen.

Rent 8d. Fine 8d.

1713	C.C.R.	Surrender made 1 Aug. 1698 recorded. Edward Avis sen. blacksmith surrendered cottage in which he then dwelt to Edward Avis sen. and Johanna his wife for their lives and after their deaths to Edward Avis jun. and Rebecca his wife, the said Johanna being dead.

Rent 4d. Fine 8d.

1727	C.P.R.	John Horwood of Hawridge marries Mary Aves of Cholesbury.
1739	Ind.	Edward Avis, the sole survivor of the Trustees of the Poor's Plot mades an Indenture transferring the land to new Trustees. Poor's Platt is described as the

> 'Messuage or Tenement wherein Samuel Springwell and Benjamin Davis do now dwell, also all those 2 acres of Meadow Ground with Appurtenances abbutting upon the lands of the said Edward Avis on the East and upon the lands of Mr Burkett on the South and upon the lands of Matthew Geary on the

West and upon a certain Comon called Cholesbury Comon on the North'.

Note: This is the first clear evidence we have of the site of this house.

1750	Copy of C.R.	The Court records the death of Edward Avis, that Mary, the wife of John Horwood was his only daughter and makes proclamation for her to come forward and be admitted.
1756	"	Mary Horwood, through her husband is admitted by the steward, Thomas Plaistowe, Gent.
1789	C.C.R.	Mary Horwood, of Wigginton is dead and bequeathed to her 'Son and daughter James and Sarah Smith All my household goods likewise my Copyhold estate lying and being at Cholesbury . . . now in ye possession of Thomas Brackley'.
1801	C.C.R.	Sarah Smith surrendered the propery 'late in the tenure or occupation of Thomas Brackley and Young and then in the tenure or occupation of Moses Wooster and Thomas Brown . . .' to Moses Wooster, who the same year surrendered it to Joseph Gurney.

Rent 4d.

1808	C.C.R.	John Gurney inherited from his father Joseph.
1817	C.C.R.	John Gurney surrendered to the use of his Will 'All that Cottage or Tenement with appurtenances situate and being in Cholesbury . . . wherein Edward Avis formerly dwelt'. This property had previously been 1 cottage but was now two.
	C.C.R.	Later that year David Newton bought the copyhold for £100.
1819	C.C.R.	The house was sold again to Edward Johnson of Chesham, Draper for £97.

1832	C.C.R.	On Edward Johnson's death his brother William inherited
"	T.S.	The cottages were occupied by John Maunders and George Sills
1855	C.C.R.	William Johnson's heiress, his sister Elizabeth Pryor sold the cottages to Thomas Butcher Jun. of Tring, Gent. for £130.
1871	C.C.R.	On Thomas Butcher's death it was inherited by his two sons, Frederick of Tring and George of Aylesbury.
1875	C.C.R.	Frederick and George Butcher, who had inherited a good deal of other property divided it up, Frederick acquiring Tall Chimneys.
1919	C.C.R.	Frederick Butcher's son Arthur inherited the property—it was then in the occupation of Mrs Wright and Mr W. Goom.
1921	C.C.R.	The house was sold to Albert Gomm and Lucy his wife for £350.
1924		The last Court was held on 12th December of that year, Albert Gomm being the only member of the Homage. Old copyholds were by this time converted to freeholds.
		Though the subsequent ownership is known it is not recorded here as it is no longer part of the Manorial History.

Abbreviations

C.C.R.	Cholesbury Court Roll
C.P.R.	Cholesbury Parish Register
Ind.	Indenture
Copy of C.R.	The copy of the Court Roll entry which was given to the Copyholder as evidence of his title to the property. Most of these copies have been lost and Miss Piggott, the present owner, is the only resident in our Villages who seems to have a complete set of copies. For 1750 and 1756 the original Court Roll has been lost.
T.S.	Tithe Survey

APPENDIX D

THE CHOLESBURY JUBILEE CELEBRATIONS, 1887

Accounts

Dinner, Tea and Food distributed (Messrs Pallett and Bishop)	£14.	0.	0
Tents (King, Tring)	2.	0.	0
Fireworks (Pain, London)	1.	1.	0
9 Workcases (Aldis, London)	0.	17.	3
9 Writing cases (Aldis, London)	0.	17.	3
Toys, Knives and Work Boxes (Bird, Tring)		10.	10
Aunt Sally (Benefink, London)		16.	10
12 Dressed Dolls		4.	0
Carriage of articles		3.	4
Nuts, oranges and sugar plums (Glover, Tring)		11.	2
Money Prizes		19.	9
Additional Beer		6.	0
Music		5.	0
Jubilee Tree (Lane, Berkhamstead)		2.	6
Iron Railings for Tree (Wood, Berkhamstead)		14.	0
Journey for Tree and Railings		7.	6

Total Exp.	£23.	16.	5
" Receipts	£25.	3.	0
Balance	£ 1.	6.	7

Contributors–Capt. Parkinson	£1.	1.	0
Revd Jeston	3.	3.	0
+		9.	6
Canon Jeffreys	3.	3.	0
Lady Rothschild	5.	0.	0
Miss Jeston	2.	2.	0
H. E. Jeston	1.	10.	0
Mr F. Butcher	2.	2.	0
Miss Jones	1.	0.	0
Others in shillings			

INDEX

Note: This Index does not include the Appendices

'Abel', Parson of Cholesbury *1230*, 74

Agricultural Employment Institution, 194

Aldridge, David, poor relief, 185

Alehouses, unlicensed, 144

Archaeological finds:
Bronze Age, 20–2;
Iron Age, 48 ff.

Ashley Green, 76, 128

Aston Clinton: link with St. Leonards,
67–68; distance from St. Leonard's
Chapel, 88–9; enclosures in, 161;
Rothschild lands in, 221

Avis, Edward, blacksmith, 141

Axtel, John, poor relief, 184–5

Aylesbury: first battle of, *571* AD, 29,
64; second battle of, *1642*, 130

Bacheler, Bachelor, Batcheler, Batchelor:
William of Belenden *1468*, 83;
16th century
Andrew, 83–4, 91, 101;
Johane widow of Andrew, 89, 90–1;
John of Hawridge, 91, 104;
Richard, 91;
William of Chivery, 91;
William of St. Leonards, 94–5;
Andrew Jnr, Thomas, 101, 104;
John the Younger, Anthony,
Thomas, Yeoman of Hawridge, 105;
17th century –
Thomas of Porters, 105, 107;
Thomas the Elder, 107, 117–8.
Leonard, 107;
Robert of Hill Farm, 124, 126–7;
Thomas the Younger, 126–7;
Peter, 126;
Daniel, Churchwarden of Hawridge,
133–5; John, Joseph, 140;
18th century –
Joseph of the Castle, 157;
19th century –
Benjamin Sen. 155–6,
Benjamin Jnr., Thomas, 156, 161, 183,
202;
John, William, 187

Bailey, Henry, of Tring Grange, 220

Baker, John, Parrott's Farm, 157

Baldwin, Bawdewyn, 131, 133, 159:
St Leonards and Dundridge –
Robert, 82; John; Richard,
Robert, Robert Jnr, 83; John of the
Hale, 87 ff, 115; Henry, Silvester,
91 ff;
Cholesbury – John, Lord of the
Manor, 27, 116, 159;
Richard, 117–8;
Thomas, 131;
Buckland Common – Samuel, 172

Basset, Ralf, 77

Bate, William, 94

Beaker people, 19, 20

Belgae, 32, 46, 48

Bellingdon: Link with Hawridge, 76;
Baldwin and Batchelor families in, 83;
attendance at St. Leonards Chapel, 89;
land owned by Wrights of Botchmore
Farm, 156

Bentonpotts: see Porter's.

Berkhamsted: B. gap, 7, 12; Castle, 27;
link with Hawridge, 76;
Andrew Batchelor's lands in, 85;
quoits matches, 225

Birch, Edmund, 132

Bishop, Daniel, 200;
Joseph, Buckland Common, 204, 215–
216

Black Mere (Blackemere), 68, 71–2, 97

Black Prince, Lord of Hawridge and
Marsworth, 77

Blackwell, Elidad, 125

Botchmore Farm, 110, 127, 156, 162

Bottom Farm, 76, 110, 127, 137, 140–1,
156

Brackley family, 138, 172;
Thomas the Potter, 139;
at Folly Farm, 162;
Job, Lydia, Buckland Common, 204;
Teddy John, flint-knapper, 214;
Joshua, of Chivery, coal merchant,
George, 215; William, Hawridge, 219
Harris Hawridge, 220

Brass bands, St. Leonard's, 224–5

Braziers' End, 140; build up of estate, 157 ff, 200, 219
Brichtric, 77
Brickmaking, 136, 173, 214
Brigginshaw, Bringginsham, William, 94–95
Bronze Age:
  Agriculture, 31 ff, 42;
  burials, 43;
  craftsmen, 35–6;
  domestic animals, 33 ff;
  dress, 37 ff, 41–2;
  finds, 20;
  farmhouses, 37, 39–40;
  fort, 27 ff;
  jewellery, 25, 38–9;
  pottery, 36;
  world events in, 15, 17, 19 ff
Brown, Alfred, 214;
  Job, 204
Browne's Farm, 95, 97
Brun's Farm, 95, 97
Brythons (Britains), 46
Buckland, 67–8; enclosures in, 161
Buckland Common, 67–8; 80, 160;
  use of St Leonards' Chapel, 89;
  potteries, 138–9;
  farms, 162;
  inns and alehouses, 172;
  attendance at Cholesbury Church, 197;
  enclosure of *1842*, 204 ff
Buckland Grange (see Chapel Farm)
Burket, Joseph, 157–8

Carpenter, Matthew, 203
Cassivellaunus, 48, 52
Catechism, hearing of, 149
Catuvellauni, 52
Celts, 46
Chair bodgers, 137
Chalk digging, 178; pits, 214–5
Chapel Farm, (now called Buckland Grange) 85, 90–6, 162
Chesham, reaction to Ship Money, 127; defence of, *1643*, 130
Cheyney, Cheyne, 92, 115;
  Thomas, 117
Chivery, 73, 82, 91, 97;
  the Plough Inn, 172;
  field survey of *1582*, 92–5

Cholesbury, also appears as Chelwoldesbur, Chelewoldesbyr, Chelewoldesbyrie, Chelwerderbir, Chilwaldesburye, Chollsbury:
Etymology, 64; Bronze Age origin and inhabitants 19 ff; excavation in, 20–2, 26 n.;
general plan of, 31;
Iron age, 45 ff; finds, 48–9;
link with Drayton Beauchamp, 67;
medieval development, 73–6;
life in 16th–17th centuries, 112–23, 130–44;
ship money assessment, 128;
Neale Lectureship and 18th century life, 146–54;
Braziers End estate, 157–9,
Curates of, 171,
straw plaiting school, 174,
bankruptcy of, 186–93,
recovery and 19th century, 194–201, 207–10,
20th century, 212 ff
Church, 63, 65, 73–4:
  Edwardian inventory, 113–5;
  services, changes in, 131, 133;
  no maintenance for, 132;
  attendance at, 148;
  state of, in early 18th century, 148–9,
  Sunday school, 195;
  organ and choir 196–7;
  restoration of, in *1872*, 208;
Common:
  Enclosures in, 120;
  encroachments, 131–2, 182–3;
  management of, in 19th century, 198–9;
  use of, 220
Common Fields, 75;
  enclosure of, 118
Court Rolls, 75, 117 ff, 122 n., 131–132, 157–8
Fort, 20, 23–6, 27 ff, 48, 53 ff, 61
Manor, first reference to, 74
Manor House, 27, 116, 159
Cider-making, 173, 213
Cilternsaetan, 65
Cindery Bottom, 50, 97
Civil War, 129–30
Clay with flints soil, 10, 214
Clothing and fuel clubs, Cholesbury, 195;

St.Leonards, 222
Cobbett, William, interest in straw-
    plaiting, 174
Cokefield, William, (should be Tokefield),
    126
Collier, William, 200;
    Thomas, 214;
    John the Carter, 215
Collins, James, Hill Farm, 202
Common fields, enclosure of: Hawridge,
    100, 110–11;
    Cholesbury, 118
Cottage Industries, 174
Court Rolls: Cholesbury, 75, 116 ff,
    122 n., 131–2, 157–8;
    Hawridge, 110, 116 ff, 161 ff
Cox, David, transported convict, 201
Cricket Club, 225
Cublington: endowment in for Neale
    Lectureship 146;
    Trust Farm, 160;
    enclosure of 161;
    help to Cholesbury rates, 194
Culverhouse, William, butcher, 215

Darvell, John, 131
Dayrell, Edward and Robert, lords of the
    Manors of Cholesbury and Hawridge,
    156–7
de Crokesley, Henry, 71
de Clinton, Jordan, 69;
    William, 69, 71
Deering, Elizabeth (nee Plaistowe), 166 ff
del Broc family, 72, 78
Dell, Nicholas, will, 107
Dettingen, Battle of, 163–5
Domesday Survey, 60, 67–9, 73
Dorrien, and Dorriens Farm, 162, 194,
    204
d'Ouilly, Robert, 77
Drayton Beauchamp:
    link with Cholesbury, 67–8;
    assessment for Ship Money, 128;
    help to Cholesbury, 192
Dundridge Manor, 49, 57, 70 ff, 80, 82,
    95–9, 162;
    dinner to workmen, 159–60;
    Missenden Abbey, lands in, 71–2
Dwight, Stephen, 182

Eayre, Eayres, Eyres, John, 140, 157;
    Martha, 140;
    John (Dorrien's Farm), 204
Edinburgh Journal, article on Cholesbury,
    192–3
Edmunds, Richard, 120, 137
Edwardian inventory of Church property,
    Cholesbury 114; Hawridge, 234
Emigration to America, 131
Enclosure: of Common Fields, Hawridge,
    107, Cholesbury, 118;
    of Common land or waste, 120;
    of Open Fields in Vale of Aylesbury,
    161;
    of St.Leonards Common, 178–9;
    of Buckland Common, 203–6
Encroachments:
    Cholesbury, 120–1, 131–2, 182–3;
    Hawridge, 182, 220
Episcopal Visitations:
    Hawridge *1516*, and *1519*, 100–1,
    1584, 109, 114–5 *1662*, 134–5;
    Missenden Abbey *1531*, 112
    Cholesbury *1720*, 148, *1662*, 134–5
Escheat Rolls of *1330*, 75
Excavations: lack of, 20;
    in Cholesbury fort, 20, 26 n., 48–9

Fairs, fêtes, and festivals, 224, 226
Faithful, the Shepherd, 206
Fellowes, Richard Albion, 159, 200
Ferry, The Rev., 219
Field names: Dundridge, 72
    St.Leonards, 82, 91–2, 94, 97;
    Hawridge, 79, 85, 101, 104–5;
    Hawridge, Parsonage lands, 109;
    Cholesbury, 75, 112, 117–8
Field systems, 32, 54 ff.;
    St.Leonards, 72; Cholesbury, 75;
    Hawridge, 79
Fincher, Frederick, 219
Finds: see Archaeological
Flints: origin of, 12;
    use of, 16, 136–7, 178
Flint-knapper, 214
Folly Farm (now Kiln Cottage), 138,
    162, 204
Francis, Early Christopher,
    John Dunkin (stewards of the Manor)
    219

Franklin, George, 182;
    Thomas, 183
Free, George, 220

Galliner, Gulliner, Thos., Petty
    Constable, 126
Games, local; 'fidguts', quoits, bowls,
    cricket, 225
Geary, Gerueys: Rogeri, 73;
    John, Old Richard, Jasper, 103;
    Richard, 117;
    John, 124, 126–7, 137, 140–1;
    Daniel, 156
Geary's Wood, 22, 101.
Geological background, 7 ff
Ginger, John, 83
Gipsies, 179
Glebe Farm, 109, 110, 127
Goidals (or Gaels), 46
Gomm, Albert, 219
Gore, Charles Orlando, Lord of the
    Manor of Tring *1781,* 157
Grimes' graves, 16
Grim's Ditch or Dyke, 20, 47, 64, 68
Gurney, Joseph, at Parrotts Farm, *1781,*
    157

Hallcye, Thomas, 126–7
Hampden, John, 1, 124, 129–30
Hassell, George, Magistrate, of Brazier's
    End, 158
Hastoe, 223
Hawkes, Professor C., 20, 48
Hawkes, Thomas, the *Maidenhead,* 187
Hawridge, Harridge: Bronze Age sword,
    22,
    communications layout and fields,
    76–80;
    development 16th century, 100–111;
    Ship money assessment 126–7;
    Protestation return, 130;
    17th century life, 136 ff;
    18th century, 155–7, 161–2;
    population and poor relief 19th century,
    181–6;
    decline of small farmers, 201–3;
    school, 208;
    20th century, 212 ff

Church, 78;
    state of repair, 133–4; visitation,
    135;
    restoration *1855,* 203;
    Common, use of, 220;
    Court, 110, 127, 156, 219;
    Court Rolls and Book, 110–1, 161,
    182–3;
    Fort, 24, 31, 47–8, 61;
    Manor, 76;
    Parsonage Lands, 79; in Marsworth,
    101, 109
Heath End, 76, 79, 107, 110
Helgot, 73
'Hermit of the Woods' (St.Leonards), 69 ff
Highways: state of, 142–3, 212,
    repair of, 142–3, 214;
    in Cholesbury, 19th century, 199–200;
    in Hawridge, 203
Hill Farm, 76, 110, 140, 156, 202
Hill, Peter, curate of Cholesbury, 147 ff
Home Farm Cottage, 157, 187
Horwood, John, of Wigginton, 161;
    Thomas, blacksmith, 171;
    Thomas, wheelwright, 171;
    William, 182
Houses: dates of, 70, 95, 105–7, 116–7;
    use of local materials, 136
Household goods, 16th century, 105, 107;
    17th century, 137
Humphrey, Frederick, chalk digger, 215

Icknield Way, 4, 10, 16, 17, 20, 24–5,
    29, 45, 61–3, 65, 68
Inns and Alehouses, 172;
    unlicensed and disorderly, 144;
    St.Leonards–White Lion, 172;
    Chivery–Plough, 172, 213;
    Buckland Common–Boot and
    Slipper, Britannia, Rose and Crown,
    172;
    Cholesbury–Blue Ball (or Nine Pin
    Bowl), 172
    Castle, 172;
    Maidenhead (later Bricklayers Arms)
    172, 200;
    Queen's Head, 172, 200
    Hawridge–Half Moon (later Full
    Moon), 172, 182, 219;
    Mermaid, 172, 182; Rose and Crown,
    76, 172, 182

Chesham Vale, Black Horse; Swan
  Bottom–Swan; Tring–Slip Inn, 172
Iron Age, 29, 45 ff;
    agriculture, 54 ff;
    coins, 50, 52;
    dress, 58;
    farm houses, 56 ff;
    finds, 50;
    houses, 54;
    medicine, 58
Ivinghoe Beacon, 14, 24, 50 ff;
    excavations, 63

Jeffries, the Rev. John, 156
Jeston, the Rev. Henry, 191 ff
Joiner, John or 'Bottom', 156, 185
Jubilee Treat, Cholesbury, *1887,* 209–10

Kiln Cottage (see Folly Farm)
King, the Rev. Isaac, chaplain of St.
    Leonard's, 169–71, 206

La Tène period, 47, 54
Le Breton, Magno, 68, 73;
    Hugh, Will, 74
Library, Cholesbury, 195
'Limes' The, 127, 156, 200
Lincoln, Diocese of, 65;
    Atwater, Bishop of, 100;
    Longland, Bishop of, 112, 153
Location of villages; reasons for, 23
Lovett, Thomas, Brazier's End, 159

Mably, John, poor relief, 185;
    Susan, poor relief, 184
Mandelyns, Manor of, 78
    (see also Marlin Chapel Farm)
Manor house, Cholesbury, 27, 116, 159
Maple, John, 182
Marlin Chapel Farm, 24, 48, 78
Marsworth: link with Hawridge, 67, 69;
    lands belonging to Rector of Hawridge,
    101;
    enclosures in, 161;
    assistance to Cholesbury, 194
Mault Mill, 140

Mayo, Daniel, encroachment, 182
Medical care: 19th century, 185;
    20th century, 223
Megalithic people, 19
Mildmay Cottage, 110
Miller, Martin, the *Mermaid,* 171
Missenden Abbey, 70, 86, 112–13
Mortain, Count of, 77
Muster Roll, *1522,* 83

Neale, Joseph, 146 ff
Neale Lectureship, 146 ff;
    trust deed, 146–7;
    distribution of books to poor, 150–1;
    duty at Wigginton, burden of, 207–8
Nethercott, Mrs, baker, 216
Neolithic Age, 17
Norris, Daniel, of Hone's Farm, 187

Occupation: village craftsmen, 121;
    18th century, 171–4;
    20th century, 215;
    opportunities provided by Rothschilds,
    221–2
Orchard Cottage, 215
Osborn, Ezekial, 200
Owen, The Rev. Edward, 206

Packington, Dame Dorothy, 108–9
Pallett, coal merchant, 215
Palmer, Roger, 112–13
Parish boundaries, 67, 77
Parish offices, 141 ff
Parkinson, James Benners, Braziers End,
    159
Parslow, George, 220
Parrott's Farm, 30–1, 75, 118, 130, 157,
    187, 200
Parrott's Wood, 131
Parsonage houses, 110, 136, 201
Parsonage Lands, (see Glebe Farm)
Perot, Thomas, 75
Pheasant breeding, 182, 213
Philby, Henry, 203
Pipe rolls, *1196,* 69
Pitkin, George 202;
    Joseph, 203
Pitstone, 24, 63

Plaistowe, Playstowe, Plastow, Plested:
    Thomas, 82–3, 89, 162;
    Robert, 94–5;
    John, deputy steward of Hawridge,
    William of the Lee,
    Richard, Rector of Hawridge, 162;
    Richard and Battle of Dettingen, 163–
    165
Plaistowe Trust, 85, 166 ff
Poaching, 213
Ponds, 218
Poor Relief; 18th century, 143–4;
    19th century, 181 ff
Population; Cholesbury, 115, 121, 133,
    171, 207;
    Hawridge, 100, 171, 181, 207;
    St. Leonards, 82 ff., 170–1, 207
Porter's (now Bentonpotts), 105 ff., 127,
    156
Pottery; local, Bronze Age, 21;
    Buckland Common, 138–40
Potteries, The, 173, 204
Priest's Grove Wood, 201
Princes Risborough, 127
Protestation returns: Cholesbury, 130;
    Hawridge, 127, 130, 141
Puddephatt, Matthew, 200
Putnam, Puttenham: Origin of family
    name, 103;
    John, 103 ff;
    William, Richard, Edward, John,
    Thomas in Hawridge, 104;
    Henry, Thomas, William sen. in
    Cholesbury, 117–8;
    Thomas (d.*1644*) 124, 126–7, 130–1;
    Thomas (s. of above) 130–1, 140;
    Thomas the Emigrant, 132, 132 n.;
    Henry, 137;
    James, John, 140
Putnam's Farm, 110, 127
Pygmy cups, 20, 43

Quakers, 133, 148;
    William Dyer, 133

Ramsay, The Rev. John, curate of
    Cholesbury, 171
Ray's Common, 31
Redding, George, 219

'Richard', curate of Hawridge, 100–1
Roads (see also Icknield Way and High-
    ways): Roman, Watling St., Akeman
    St., 61; Ancient tracks, names of, 67–
    68
    Hog Lane, 76, 105;
    Arrewig Lane, Brode Street, 97;
    Berkhamsted Lane, Parsonage Lane,
    77
Roderick, The Rev. David, curate of
    Cholesbury, 171, 187
Romans, 60 ff
Rossway, 206, 219
Rothschilds: property of, 221;
    influence of, 221–3.

St Leonards: Bronze Age finds, 21–2;
    Iron Age finds, 49–50,
    Link with Aston Clinton, 67;
    medieval development, 69 ff;
    16th century, 82–99;
    agreement with Aston Clinton on
    rates, 142–3;
    lawsuit, 166–9;
    a pluralist Chaplain, 169–70.
    Strawplaiting school, 174;
    enclosure of common, 178–9;
    the Shepherd's Grave, 206–7;
    School, 208
    20th century 212 ff
    Chapel, first reference to, 71–2;
        enquiry, 87 ff
        decay of, 98, 131;
        repair and new endowments, 135;
        a local Gretna Green, 166
    Chapel Trust, formation of, 82 ff;
        lawsuit in 18th century, 166 ff;
        sale of woods by, 169;
        provision of wood to chaplain,
        169
St Leonard's Hospital, Aylesbury, 70
Salisbury, Countess of, 82, 86, 91
Saxons, 29, 62
Scott, Richard, 126–7
Schools; Cholesbury, 18th century, 149–
    50;
    National School House, St Leonards;
    School for Cholesbury and Hawridge,
    208
Seere, Seare, John, 126–7, 130, 156

Shepherd's Grave, 206–7
Ship Money, 124 ff;
    extracts from Writ, 125;
    queries from Sheriff, 126;
    assessment for Hawridge, 126;
    pleas for exemption, 127 ff;
    disposal of distresses, 128
Shops, 215–6
Silk Mill, Tring, employment of poor in,
    190–1
Sills, George, 200
Smith, The Rev. Joseph, chaplain of St.
    Leonard's, 169–70
Smith, Sarah, 161
Stanniford, shopkeeper, 215
Stewards of Manors, Cholesbury and
    Hawridge, 162
Stocken, William 117–8
Stonehills, William, 94
Straw-plaiting, 174 ff;
    plaiting schools, 174 ff;
    effect on health, 177;
    earnings from, 177
'Sunday dinner', typical, about *1910*,
    217–8
Sutton, Robert, 202, 206
Style, John, steward, 117
Swearers, presentments of, 144

'Tall Chimneys', Cholesbury, 'the house
    wherein Edward Avis formerly dwelt'
    76, 120, 141–2, 234–7
Tasburgh, Thomas, 108–9
Tax assessors, appointment of, 203
Temple, Sir Peter, 126
Terriers; Hawridge *c. 1620*, 109, *1707*,
    136, 148;
    Cholesbury *1709* 136
The Lee, 162, 172
'Thomas', chantry priest at St Leonard's,
    71
Thorpe, Mary, 161
Tomlin brothers, wheelwrights and under-
    takers, 215
Transport, 20th century, 226
Tring; religious principles in, 153,
    attempted encroachment in Hawridge,
    183; communications with 212;
    agricultural show, 222; fair, 224
Trinovantes, 52

Tudor Cottage, Hawridge, 76, 80, 110
Turner, H. J., Lord of the Manor, 219 ff
Turney, Richard, 220

Vestry; membership of, 187; functions of,
    198 ff

Walker, Fowler, 158
Water supply, 24, 144, 218, 222
Weedon, Thomas, 184
Wendover, 87, 151, 172, 223
Wigginton, 76–7, 212;
    Neale Trust, 146, 207–8;
    straw-plaiting school, 174–6;
    quoits matches, 225
Women, protection of interests, 161–2
Wood, Cornelius, John, 135
Wooster, Moses, 182
Wright: John senior, of Braziers End, 117–
    118;
    Rebecca, 161;
    William of Botchmore Farm 156, 161–
    162, 182–3, 203;
    Robert, the Butcher, 187

Yeoman Farmers, 83–4, 103;
    decline of, 155, 160, 202